A Catalog of Wind Repertoire before the Twentieth Century for One to Five Players

Books by David Whitwell

Philosophic Foundations of Education
Foundations of Music Education
Music Education of the Future
The Sousa Oral History Project
The Art of Musical Conducting
The Longy Club: 1900–1917
A Concise History of the Wind Band
Wagner on Bands
Berlioz on Bands
Chopin: A Self-Portrait
Schumann: A Self-Portrait In His Own Words
Mendelssohn: A Self-Portrait In His Own Words
La Téléphonie and the Universal Musical Language
Extraordinary Women
Aesthetics of Music in Ancient Civilizations
Aesthetics of Music in the Middle Ages
Aesthetics of Music in the Early Renaissance

The History and Literature of the Wind Band and Wind Ensemble Series

Volume 1 The Wind Band and Wind Ensemble Before 1500
Volume 2 The Renaissance Wind Band and Wind Ensemble
Volume 3 The Baroque Wind Band and Wind Ensemble
Volume 4 The Wind Band and Wind Ensemble of the Classical Period (1750–1800)
Volume 5 The Nineteenth-Century Wind Band and Wind Ensemble
Volume 6 A Catalog of Multi-Part Repertoire for Wind Instruments or for Undesignated Instrumentation before 1600
Volume 7 Baroque Wind Band and Wind Ensemble Repertoire
Volume 8 Classical Period Wind Band and Wind Ensemble Repertoire
Volume 9 Nineteenth-Century Wind Band and Wind Ensemble Repertoire
Volume 10 A Supplementary Catalog of Wind Band and Wind Ensemble Repertoire
Volume 11 A Catalog of Wind Repertoire before the Twentieth Century for One to Five Players
Volume 12 A Second Supplementary Catalog of Early Wind Band and Wind Ensemble Repertoire
Volume 13 Name Index, Volumes 1–12, The History and Literature of the Wind Band and Wind Ensemble

www.whitwellbooks.com

David Whitwell

A Catalog of Wind Repertoire before the Twentieth Century for One to Five Players

THE HISTORY AND LITERATURE OF THE WIND
BAND AND WIND ENSEMBLE, VOLUME II

EDITED BY CRAIG DABELSTEIN

WHITWELL PUBLISHING • AUSTIN, TEXAS, USA

Whitwell Publishing, Austin 78701
www.whitwellbooks.com

Printed in the United States of America

PAPERBACK
ISBN-13: 978-1-936512-52-2
ISBN-10: 1936512521

Composed in Bembo Book

Contents

Part 4 Music With Four Wind Instruments

Part 5 Music With Five Wind Instruments

Foreword

IN ASSEMBLING MATERIALS for the volumes of *The History and Literature of the Wind Band and Wind Ensemble* the focus of my work was in music for ensembles of six wind instruments or larger. In the course of looking through many European libraries for such material, I was, of course, aware of an even more enormous repertoire of music for single winds or for small ensembles. Even though such repertoire was not central to my own research, it was always clear to me that this repertoire was part of the history of wind ensembles. The music for smaller ensembles, for example, give us a record of the kind of music played in smaller palace rooms or for more private audiences. It was for these same circumstances that composers provided the repertoire given here for solo wind instruments. Among these the flute was a special problem for the intonation problems of the early form of the instrument caused it to be generally excluded from the larger indoor *Hautboisten* and *Harmoniemusik* ensembles. While the flute is therefore rarely mentioned in contemporary reviews of wind ensemble performances, we trust that the extensive list of solo flute repertoire included here will shed some light on their activities.

It was clear to me from the beginning that one lifetime would not be enough to write down information on everything I was seeing in European libraries, hence the limitation mentioned above, I did, from time to time, write down titles and call-numbers of some works for smaller ensembles which interested me for one reason or another. The purpose of this volume is to make these works and their sources available to whomever is interested.

As a matter of record, and for the purpose of helping establish the known repertoire for solo and smaller ensembles of winds before 1900, I have included, in addition to the music which I found in European libraries, references to similar music found in the following three works:

1. [1] A *Catalog* published at the end of the eighteenth century in Vienna by Johann Traeg. Traeg was one of two music dealers in Vienna who maintained a business of

supplying on demand manuscript copies of music which he had on hand. His extensive collection gives us an important insight into works which existed at that time, but which were never published.

2. *The Dictionary of Musicians* (London, 1825) by John S. Sainsbury is one of the earliest encyclopedias of composers and their music. While his information is often incomplete, many composers even lacking first names, on the other hand, Sainsbury provides valuable and interesting first-hand personal information about many composers who are today virtually unknown to today's performers.

3. *Die Musik in Geschichte und Gegenwart* (Basel: Barenreiter, 1958). I have included all the references for solo and small ensemble music from this great modern encyclopedia, which I give following the abbreviation MGG. For the most part, inclusion of repertoire in this encyclopedia can be taken to mean that the music probably actually still exists today. Often the articles in MGG do not give the library sources for each composition, but do preface their information by indicating the libraries where most of the composer's music can be found. Therefore the reader should consult MGG for this information relative to the music he is interested in.

In the case of the composers and names of instruments and compositions for the music which I found in libraries, I have given here the spellings as they occur in the original sources.

David Whitwell
Austin, Texas

Instrumentation Code

As an abbreviation for wind instrumentation I use a code of 0000-0000, representing:
flute, oboe, clarinet, bassoon - trumpet, horn, trombone, tuba.

Thus:

3000-	means a work for three flutes
-204	means a work for two trumpets and four trombones
1-1; 2 cornetts	means bassoon, trumpet, and two cornetts.

Text Abbreviations

MS	Manuscript
EP	Early Print
MP	Modern Print (after 1900)
cb	bass-continuo
bass	bass-continuo

Library Abbreviations for this Catalog

Where the location of a manuscript or early print is known, the library is given in abbreviation following the code of the international RISM system. Shelf-marks, or call-numbers, when known, are given immediately after the library abbreviations.

AUSTRIA

A:Llm	Linz, Oberosterreichisches Landesmuseum
A:Sca	Salzburg, Museum Carolino Augusteum
A:TU	Tulln, Katholisches Pfarramt
A:Wgm	Vienna, Gesellschaft der Musikfreunde
A:Wn	Vienna, Österreichische Nationalbibliothek

BELGIUM

B:Bc	Brussels, Conservatoire Royal de Musique
B:Lc	Liège, Conservatoire Royal de Musique

SWITZERLAND

CH:Bu	Basel, Öffentliche Bibliothek der Universität Basel
CH:EN	Engelberg, Benediktinerstift
CH:Zz	Zürich, Zentralbibliothek

CZECHOSLOVAKIA

CS:KRa	Kromeríz, Státní zamek a zahrady
CS:Pnm	Prague, Národni muzeum

GERMANY

D:B	Berlin, Staatsbibliothek der Stiftung Preussischer Kulturbesitz
D:BAs	Bamberg, Staatsbibliothek
D:Dlb	Dresden, Sächsische Landesbibliothek
D:DS	Darmstadt, Hessische Landes- und Hochschulbibliothek
D:Es	Eichstätt, Staats- und Seminarbibliothek

D:F	Frankfurt, Stadt- und Universitätsbibliothek
D:HR	Harburg, Fürstlich Oettingen-Wallerstein'sche Bibliothek
D:KA	Karlsruhe, Badische Landesbibliothek
D:Lr	Lüneburg, Ratsbücherei
D:LEm	Leipzig, Musikbibliothek der Stadt Leipzig
D:Mbs	Munich, Bayerische Staatsbibliothek
D:Nst	Nürnberg, Stadtbibliothek
D:NL	Nördlingen, Stadtarchiv
D:ROu	Rostock, Universitätsbibliothek
D:Rtt	Regensburg, Fürstlich Thurn und Taxissche Hofbibliothek
D:SWl	Schwerin, Mecklenburgische Landesbibliothek
D:TEG	Tegernsee, Pfarrkirche Bibliothek
D:W	Wolfenbüttel, Hertzog August Bibliothek

FRANCE

F:Pn	Paris, Bibliothèque Nationale
F:V	Versailles, Bibliothèque Municipale

GREAT BRITIAN

GB:Eu	Edinburgh, Edinburgh University Library
GB:Lbm	London, British Museum
GB:Lcm	London, Royal College of Music
GB:Lgc	London, Guildhall Library
GB:Och	Oxford, Christ Church Library

HUNGARY

H:Bn	Budapest, Orszagos Szecheny Konyvtar

ITALY

I:Ac	Assisi, Biblioteca Comunale
I:Bc	Bologna, Civico Museo Bibliografico Musicale
I:Bsf	Bologna, San Francesco (Convento Biblioteca)
I:Bsp	Bologna, San Petronio Basilica Archivio
I:Gl	Genova, Conservatorio di Musica N. Paganini
I:Ls	Lucca, Seminario Arcivescovile Biblioteca
I:Mc	Milan, Conservatorio di Musica G. Verdi
I:MAc	Mantova, Biblioteca Comunale

I:MOe	Modena, Biblioteca Estense
I:OS	Ostiglia, Biblioteca Musicale Greggiati
I:PAc	Parma, Biblioteca Palatina
I:Tf	Torino, Accademia Filarmonica
I:UDricardi	Udine, Biblioteca privata Federico Ricardi
I:Vcr	Venice, Casa di Ricovero
I:Vmc	Venice, Museo Correr
I:Vsmc	Venice, Santa Maria della Consolazione alla Fava

POLAND

P:GD	Danzig, Stadtbibliothek
P:GDj	Danzig, Kirchenbibliothek St. Johann

SWEDEN

S:L	Lund, Universitetsbiblioteket
S:Skma	Stockholm, Kunglia Biblioteket
S:Uu	Uppsala, Universitetsbiblioteket

UNITED STATES

US:Wc	Washington, Library of Congress

Acknowledgments

The reader is indebted for the second edition of this book
to Mr. Craig Dabelstein of Brisbane, Australia. Without his
contribution to design and all things involved as an editor this
book would never again have been available.

David Whitwell
Austin, 2012

PART I

Music With One
Wind Instrument

MUSIC WITH SOLO FLUTE

Abel, Carl F. (1732–1787)

(Six) *Sonate a Solo per il Flauto Traversa e Basso*, Op. 6
EP   (London: Bremner, ca. 1770)
    GB:Lbm H.32.3.g.(1)
    GB:Lbm G.280.c.(1.) [another copy]
    MGG attributes to Abel sonatas for flute and cembalo, Op. 2, 3, 4, and 9.

Abeltshauser, J. G. (German composer fl. ca. 1812–1830)

(Twelve) *Quartets* (c. 1822) for flute and strings [Sainsbury]

Aber, Johann (Italian composer, 1765–1783)

Sonata in D Major, for flute and [three] strings
MS I:Gl SS.B.1.13

Adam, I. J.

(Six) *Quartets* for flute and strings
MS (Wien: Traeg's *Catalog,* 1799)

Adler, F. B.

(Twenty-two) *Neue Walzer* ('Prag') for solo flute
MS A:Wgm XV 4251

Albrechtsberger, Johann (1736–1809)

(Two) *Quartets* for flute and strings
MS (Wien: Traeg's Catalog, 1799)

André, Johann Anton (1775–1842)

Concerto, Op. 3, in G Major, for flute
MS (Wien: Traeg's *Catalog,* 1799)
    MGG also attributes to Andre a *Concerto*, Op. 10, for flute and orchestra.

Andreozzi, Gaetano (1763–1826)

MGG attributes to Andreozzi (Three) *Quintets* (1793) for flute and strings.

Anfossi, Pasquale (1727–1787)

(Two) *Quintets* for flute and strings
MS   I:MOe Mus.D.4–8

Anonymous

The Bird Fancyer's Delight ('or Choice Observations and Directions concerning the Teaching of all sorts of Singing Birds after the Flagelet and Flute … with Lessons properly Compos'd within the Compass of each.')
EP   (London: Welsh, ca. 1730)
       GB:Lbm K.4.a.1

(Twelve) *Caprices* for solo flute
MS (Wien: Traeg's *Catalog*, 1799)

Compleat Tutor for the German Flute
EP   (London: Thompson, ca. 1755)
       GB:Lbm D.47.c.

Compleat Tutor for the German Flute
EP   (London: Simpson, ca. 1746)
       GB:Lbm D.47.f.(3.)

Compleat Tutor for the German Flute
EP   (London: Cahusac, ca. 1780)
       GB:Lbm B.170.b.(1.)
       GB:Lbm B.160.g.(3.) [a later edition, ca. 1798]

Compleat Tutor for the German Flute
EP   (London: Thompson, ca. 1765)
       GB:Lbm D.47.(2.)

Compleat Instructions for the Common Flute
EP   (London: Longman & Broderip, ca. 1780)
       GB:Lbm B.170.c.

Concerto for flute and orchestra
MS I: Ac Mss.N.564/6

French Dances, a collection for flute
EP   (London: Walsh, Randall, and Hare, 1710)
       GB:Lbm A.26.i.(2.)

Minuetti e Arietta da Balelo, for flute
MS I:Vmc Busta 59-72-N.64

Modern Musick-Master (includes, 'Directions for playing on the Flute ... Newest Method
  for German flute ... Instructions upon the Hautboy')
EP   (London: Bow Church Yard, 1731)
    GB:Lbm D.40

New Instructions for the German Flute, a method
EP   (London: Longman, Lukey, & Co., ca. 1775)
    GB:Lbm B.170.b.(2.)

Pieces for solo flute
MS (Wien: Traeg's *Catalog,* 1799)

Preludes, for flute ('Contriv'd for ye Improvement of ye Hand')
EP   (London: Walsh, Randall, and Hare, 1708)
    GB:Lbm H.250.g

(Three) *Quartets* for flute and strings
MS (Wien: Traeg's *Catalog*, 1799)

(Three) *Sinfonien*, for flute and continuo
MS A:Wn Sm 22778

(Six) *Solos*, for flute and bc
EP   (London: Oswald, ca. 1755)
    GB:Lbm E.1290.c.(1.)
    GB:Lbm E.1290.c.(3.) [another edition]

(A Second Set of Six) *Solos*, for flute and bc
EP   (London: Oswald, ca. 1755)
    GB:Lbm E.1290.c.(2.)

(Six) *Solos*, for flute and bc
EP   (London: Randall, ca. 1770)
    GB:Lbm E.1290.c.(4.)

(Six) *Sonatas*, for flute and bc ('Collected and Fitted by a Very Great Performer of
  yt Instrument')
EP   (London: Cooke, ca. 1780)
    GB:Lbm G.225.b.(6.)

Sonata, for flute and continuo
MS A:Wn E.M.66

(Thirty-three) *Sonatas* for flute and bass
MS (Wien: Traeg's *Catalog*, 1799)

Trio, for flute, violin and bass
MS I:MOe Mus.F.1626

Trio, for flute, violin, and cello
MS CH:Bu kr.IV 381, Nr. 1

(Twenty-four) *Valses*, for solo flute
MS A:Wn Sm 22789

Ansiaux, Hubert, Belgium (1781–1826)

Recueil d'airs for flute and guitare
MS B:Lc 289–2.L-VI

Armon, ? (nineteenth century)

Sainsbury attributes to Armon a *Sextet* (Offenbach: André, before 1822) for flute and strings.

Arnold, Samuel (English, 1740–1802)

Dr. Arnold's New Instructions for the German-Flute
EP (London: Harrison & Co., 1787)
    GB:Lbm B.23.(1.)

(Twelve) *Minuets*, for flute and harpsichord
EP (London: Welcker, ca. 1775)
    GB:Lbm B.57.b.(1.)

Asioli, Luigi

Sonata (1740) for flute and keyboard
MS I:MOe Mus.F.

Assuni, Ghillini (eighteenth century)

Sainsbury attributes to Assuni music for the flute published in 1795.

Babell, Wm. (d. 1722)

(Twelve) *Solos*, for violin, Hoboy or German Flute
EP (London: Hare, ca. 1725)
    GB:Lbm G.1090.(4.)

Bach, Johann Christian (1735–1782)

(Six) *Quartets*, Op. 8, for flute and strings
EP (London: Welcker, ca. 1775)
    GB:Lbm G.411.a.(5.)
    GB:Lbm G.417.a.(1.) [a later edition]

(Six) *Sonatas*, Op. 2, for flute and clavecin
EP   (London: the composer, 1763)
       GB:Lbm G.450

(Six) *Sonatas*, Op. 16, for flute with harpsicord or piano
EP   (London: Dale, ca. 1783)
       GB:Lbm E.5.f.(3.)

(Four) *Sonatas* and (Two) *Duetts*, Op. 18, for flute and harpsichord
EP   (London: Welcker, ca. 1775)
       GB:Lbm I.40.(1.)

(Six) *Sonatas*, Op. 19, for flute and piano
EP   (London: Freeman, ca. 1785)
       GB:Lbm G.450.a.(2.)

God Save the King, with variations, for flute and piano
EP   (London, ca. 1790)
       GB:Lbm G.807.(34.)

Bach, J. C. and Abel, Giardini

(Six) *Quartets* for flute and strings
EP   (London: Napier, 1777)
       GB:Lbm G.435.(2.)

Bach, Johann Sebastian (1685–1750)

Trio for flute and strings
MS (Wien: Traeg's *Catalog*, 1799)

Bach, K. P. E. (1714–1788)

(Two) *Concerti* for flute and strings
MS B:Bc Wotquenne 5515

(Two) *Concerti* for flute and strings
MS B:Bc Wotquenne 5516

Duo, for flute and violin
MS B:Bc Wotquenne 6366

Solo, for flute and bass
MS B:Bc Wotquenne 5518

(Ten) *Sonatas* for flute and bass
MS B:Bc Wotquenne 5517
MS A:Wn Sm 5506–5515 [copies of the B:Bc Mss]

Sonata (W.85) for flute
MS A:Wgm XI 36262
    This copy formerly owned by Brahms.

Sonata for flute
MS A:Wgm XI 37391

(Eleven) *Trios*, for flute, violin, and cello
MS B:Bc Wotquenne 6360

Trio for flute and strings
MS (Wien: Traeg's *Catalog,* 1799)

Ballicourt, ? (late Baroque)

Sainsbury identifies Ballicourt as, 'a celebrated flutist and composer for his instrument in
    London, about the year 1744.'

Baron, Ernest (German, 1696–1760)

Sonata (1730) for flute
MS D:LEm III.II.6a [according to MGG]

Barsanti, Francesco (Italian, 1690–1772)

Sonate, for flute and bc
EP (London, 1724)
    GB:Lbm G.261.a

Battino, ? (eighteenth century)

Duets, for 2 flutes
EP (London: Johnson, ca. 1760)
    GB:Lbm G.218.d.(1.)

Baulduino, Domenico (Italian, 1711–1779)

Concerto in D Major, for flute and orchestra
MS I:Gl M.3b.42.10

Baumgarten, Carl F. (eighteenth century)

Concerto, for oboe, flute or clarinet and orchestra
EP (London: Longman and Broderip, ca. 1790)
    GB:Lbm H.102.(3.)

(Six) *Quartets*, Op. 2, for oboe or flute and strings
EP   (London: Forster, ca. 1785)
        GB:Lbm G.437

Beecke, Notger (German, 1733–1803)

(Six) *Quartets* for flute and strings
EP   (1791) [cited in MGG]

Bellermann, Konstantin (French, 1696–1758)

MGG attributes to Bellermann three *Concerti* and six *Sonatas* for flute.

Bellinzini, Paolo Benedetto (1690–1757)

Sonate for flute and cembalo
EP   (Venezia: San Lorenzo, 1728)
        I:Bc

Benda, Frederic (German, 1752–1792)

(Three) *Concerti*, Op. 4, for flute and orchestra
EP   (Berlin: Hummel)
        I:Bc

Benda, Hans George (d. 1757)

MGG attributes to Benda the following works:
        (Three) *Sonatas*, Op.3, for clavecin with flute or violin
        (Three) *Sonatas* for Clavecin and flute
        (Three) Sonatas for flute and cembalo

Benda, Georg (1722–1795)

MGG attributes to Benda three *Sonatas* with violin or flute (Leipzig, 1779).

Benedikt, Walter (Austrian, twentieth century)

Sonata (1913) for flute
MS A:Wn Sm 23360

Sonata (1913) for flute
MS A:Wn Sm 23361

Benegger, Antonio (German, eighteenth century)

(Six) *Trios*, for flute and strings
EP (London: Johnson, ca. 1760)
  GB:Lbm H.5.b.(1.)

Benelli, Antonio (d. 1830)

Equando alla cascina, Arietta with flute and harp
EP (London: Monzani, 1800)
  GB:Lbm G.811.a.(6.)

Benoit, Petrus (Belgium, 1834–1901)

Concerto for flute and orchestra
MS B:Bc Wotquenne 5524

Benser, J. D. (German, eighteenth century)

Duet, for piano and violin or flute
EP (London: the composer, ca. 1790)
  GB:Lbm G.83

Berbiguier, Tranquillo (French, 1782–1838)

Concerto spirituoso, for flute and orchestra
MS A:Wn Sm 3445
  Sainsbury knew Berbiguier as a good flutist, student of Berton at the Paris Conservatory and author of 'an excellent method and some useful exercises for the flute. Berbiguier's compositions are excellent, full of beautiful passages, conducted with fine taste, knowledge … and always written both for the performer and the effect, according to the genius of the instrument.'

Bernardi, Franz (Austrian, b. 1767)

Sainsbury identifies Bernardi as, 'a flutist and composer for his instrument in Austria.'

Bernasconi, Andrea (Italian, 1706–1784)

MGG attributes to Bernasconi a *Concerto* for flute and strings.

Bertoni, Ferdinando (Italian, 1725–1813)

Quartet for flute and strings
MS (Wien: Traeg's *Catalog*, 1799)

Besozzi, Alessandro (1702–1775)

(Six) *Solos*, for flute, oboe, or violin and bc
EP (London: Chapman, ca. 1758)
    GB:Lbm G.221.(6.)
    GB:Lbm G.422.b.(3.) [another copy]

(Six) *Solos*, Op. 2, for flute or violin and bc
EP (London: Walsh, ca. 1764)
    GB:Lbm G.422.b.(4.)

Sonata for flute and bass
MS I:Ac Mss.N.140/10

(Three) *Sonatas* for flute and bass
MS I:Gl SS.A.1.16.(G.8)

(Six) *Sonatas*, for flute, violin and bc
EP (London: Walsh, ca. 1760)
    GB:Lbm G.241.(2.)

Sonata, Op. 3, Nr. 7, for flute, violin and bass
MS S:Uu Ms. 24

Betts, Arthur (English, 1776–1847)

(Six) *Waltzes*, for piano, flute, tambourine, triangle
EP (London: the composer, ca. 1798)
    GB:Lbm G.231.(2.)

Bewlay, Henry (English, d. 1797)

(Three) *Sonatas*, for piano with violin or flute ad lib
EP (London: the composer, ca. 1794)
    GB:Lbm G.186.(1.)

Binder, Christlieb (1723–1789)

MGG attributes to Binder eight *Trios* and four *Divertimenti* with flute, keyboard and bass.

Bingham, ?

Sainsbury identifies Bingham as a flute player and composer for flute in Amsterdam at the beginning of the eighteenth century.

Biscogli, Antonio

Concerto in G (1759) for flute and orchestra
MS S:Uu Ms. 29

Bitti, Martino

Solos, for flute and bc
EP (London: Walsh and Hare, ca. 1712)
    GB:Lbm D.161.a.(4.)

Bittoni, Mario (eighteenth century)

Concerto for flute and orchestra
MS I:Ac Mss.N.145/11

Blanc, ?

Sainsbury identifies Blanc as a composer for the flute before 1825.

Blavet, Michel (1700–1768)

Concerto for flute and strings
MS D:KA

(Six) *Sonatas*, Op. 2, for flute and bass
EP (Paris, 1731)

Sonatas, Op. 3, for flute and bass
EP (Paris, 1740), according to MGG

Boccherini, Luigi (1743–1805)

(Six) *Quintets*, Op. 21, for flute and strings
EP (Venezia)
    I:Bc

MGG attributes to Boccherini eighteen *Quintets* for flute and strings, and a *Concerto*, Op. 27
    (Paris: Frere).

(Six) *Sextets*, Op. 15, for flute and strings
EP (Paris: Le Duc Successeur, Mr. Chevardiere, 1773)
    I:Bc

Bochsa, Karl (d. 1821)

Sainsbury identifies Bochsa as the principal performer on the oboe at the Theatre at Lyons and composer of some music for the flute.

Boehm, Theobald (1794–1881)

MGG attributes to Boehm Concerti, Fantasies, Variations, and Salonstücke for flute and orchestra and Caprices and Etudes for solo flute.

Boismortier, Joseph Bodin de (1691–1755)

MGG attributes to Boismortier the following works:
  Sonatas, Op. 3 (1724), for flute and bass
  Sonatas, Op. 9 (1725), for flute and bass
  Sonatas, Op. 19 (1827), for flute
  Pieces, Op. 22 (1728)
  Sonatas, Op. 35 and Op. 44, for flute

Bononcini, Marc Antonio (Italian, 1675–1726)

Cantata for voice and flute
MS F:Pn D.1350 (6)

Bordet, ? (French, eighteenth century)

Variations for flute and bass
MS (Wien: Traeg's Catalog, 1799)

Sainsbury identifies Bordet as a flutist and composer for flute, including a method published in Paris in 1755.

Brandi, Gaetano

Sainsbury identifies Brandi as a composer of flute music in England before 1795.

Briscoli, Domenico

Sainsbury identifies Briscoli as a composer for the flute before 1825.

Brunetti-Pisano, August (Austrian, 1870–1943)

Elegie, for flute and klavier
MS A:Sca Hs. 1190

Burrowes, John Freckleton (b. 1787)

Sainsbury identifies Burrowes as the composer of a *Sonata*, Op. 4, for piano and flute and Twelve *Select Melodies* for flute and piano.

Cahusac, Thomas

Chausac's Pocket Companion for the German Flute
EP (London, ca. 1795, in 4 volumes)
    GB:Lbm A.15

Cambini, Giovanni (1746–1825)

Concerto, in G Major, for flute
MS (Wien: Traeg's Catalog, 1799)

(Six) *Duets*, Op. 20, for flute and violin
EP (Paris: Chez Le Duc, ca. 1775)
    GB:Lbm G.280.h.(1.)

(Six) Duets, Op. 20, for flute and violin
EP (London: J. Bland, ca. 1790)
    GB:Lbm G.421.p.(3.)
    Although this work has the same title as the above, this edition contains different music

(Eighteen) *Duets* for flute and violin
MS (Wien: Traeg's Catalog, 1799)

(Six) *Duets* for flute and viola
MS (Wien: Traeg's Catalog, 1799)

(Six) *Quartets*, Op. 10, for flute and strings
EP (Offenbach: J. André, ca. 1775)
    GB:Lbm G.396.a

(Six) *Quartets* for flute and strings
EP (Paris: Sieber)
    I:Bc

(Six) *Quartets*, for flute and strings
MS I:MOe Mus.F.133

(Twenty-four) *Quartets* for flute and strings
MS (Wien: Traeg's Catalog, 1799)

(Three) *Quintets* (in Eb, F, and A Major) for flute and strings
MS (Wien: Traeg's Catalog, 1799)

(Three) *Quintets* (in G, C, and B♭ Major) for flute and strings
MS (Wien: Traeg's Catalog, 1799)

(Three) *Solos,* for flute and bc
EP   (London: G. Florio, ca. 1785)
    GB:Lbm G.280.i.(3.)
EP   (London: Preston & Son, ca. 1790)
    GB:Lbm H.2140.d.(2.) [another edition]

(Six) *Sonatas,* for flute and bc
EP   (Paris: Chez Mussard, ca. 1775)
    GB:Lbm G.396.d.(1.)

(Six) *Trios* for flute and strings
MS (Wien: Traeg's Catalog, 1799)

Campagnoli, Bartolomeo (1751–1827)

(Six) *Duets* for flute and viola
MS (Wien: Traeg's Catalog, 1799)
MGG attributes to Campagnole in addition three *Concerti* and a *Concertante* for flute.

Campini, Giuseppe (1746–1825)

(Six) *Quartets*, Op. 1, for flute and strings
EP   (Berlin: J. J. Hummel, ca. 1775)
    GB:Lbm G.438

Canal, Guiseppe

(Three) *Sonatas* for flute and bass
MS I:Gl N.1.6.6.(sc.17)

Cannabich, Christian (1731–1798)

(Six) *Duettos,* for flute and viola
EP   (London: J. Fentum, ca. 1775)
    GB:Lbm G.280.j.(2.)

MGG attributes to Cannabich the following additional works:
    (Six) *Duetts*, Op. 4, for flute and violin (Mannheim: Gotz)
    (Six) *Quartets*, Nr. 1, for flute or violin and strings (Paris: Jolivet)
    (Six) *Quartets* for flute and strings (Amsterdam: Hummel)
    Concerto in D for flute and orchestra (MS, in D:KA)
    (Three) *Concerti* for flute and orchestra (MS, in D:Mbs)

Canobbio, Carlo (1741–1822)

(Six) *Duets* for flute and viola.
MS (Wien: Traeg's Catalog, 1799)

Card, W.

Sainsbury identifies Card as an English professor of flute, living in 1825, and composer of music for flute and piano.

Carr, Robert

The Delightful Companion, lessons for one, two and three flutes
EP   (London: J. Playford, 1686)
        GB:Lbm K.4.b.16

Cartelieri, Antonio (1772–1807)

Concerto, in D Major, for flute
MS (Wien: Traeg's Catalog, 1799)

Caselli, Giuseppe

Sonata in A Major, for flute and bass
MS I:Gl SS.B.1.14

Castelbarco, conte Cesare (nineteenth century)

Quintet, Op. 42, for flute, piano, and strings
EP   (Milan: Scotti)
        I:Bc

Cavalari, Francesco

(Six) *Solos*, for flute and bc
EP   (London: I. Walsh, ca. 1750)
        GB:Lbm G.270.1.(2.)
EP   (London: Harison & Co., ca. 1785)
        GB:Lbm B.480 [a later edition]

Cecere, Carlo

Concerto on G Major (1760) for flute and orchestra
MS S:Uu Ms. 59

Cervetto, Giacobbe (the Elder)

(Eight) *Solos*, Op. 3, for flute, harpsichord and bc
EP   (London: J. Johnson, ca. 1750)
   GB:Lbm E.202

(Six) *Solos*, for flute, harpsichord and bc
EP   (London: Harison & Co., ca. 1785)
   GB:Lbm B.170.a.(2.)

Checci, Rene

Sainsbury identifies Checci as the composer of some flute music published in Augsburg
   in 1798.

Chedeville, Esprit Philippe (1696–1762)

MGG attributes to Chedeville six *Sonatas* for flute and bass.

Chedeville, Nicholas

(Six) *Sonatas*, for flute, oboe, and bc
EP   (Paris: the composer, ca. 1740)
   GB:Lbm K.7.f.15.(5.)

Cheron, ?

Sainsbury identifies Cheron as a composer of flute music ca. 1720

Chiaparelli, ?

Sainsbury identifies Chiaparelli as a composer of flute music published in Paris in 1782.

Cimarosa, Domenico (1749–1801)

(Three) *Sonatas da camera* for flute and bass
MS   I:Gl N.1.6.7.(sc.40)

Cirri, Giovanni Battista

(Six) *Quartets*, Op. 10, for flute and strings
EP   (London, 1772)
   I:Bc

Ciurache, Giovanni (eighteenth century)

Concerto in G Major for flute and orchestra
MS   S:Uu Ms. 74

Clementi, Muzio (1752–1832)

Trio in C Major for flute and strings
MS   (Wien: Traeg's Catalog, 1799)

MGG attributes to Clementi three *Sonatas* for flute and clavecin, in editions in Paris and
    Offenbach (1788).

Sainsbury attributes to Clementi the following works:
    (Six) *Sonatas*, Op. 2, [for piano] with flute, or violin
    (Six) *Sonatas,* Op. 4, [for piano] with flute, or violin
    (Three) *Sonatas*, Op. 21, for flute, or cello and violin
    (Three) *Sonatas*, Op. 22, for flute, or cello and violin
    Grand Sonata, Op. 31 [for piano] with flute
    (Three) *Sonatas*, Op. 32, [for piano] with flute and cello
    (Three) *Sonatas*, Op. 33, [for piano] with flute and violin
    (Twelve) *Waltzes*, Op. 38, [for piano] with flute

Corelli, Arcangelo (1653–1713)

Sonata, for flute and bass
MS   I:PAc

Corrette, Michel (1709–1795)

MGG attributes to Corrette the following works:
    Sonatas for flute and bass, Op. 14
    Sonatilles, Op, 19, for flute and bass (before 1733)
    Menuets for flute and bass
    Method for flute a bec and another for flute traversiere, the latter in editions of 1773,
    1778, and 1781.

Cramer, Johann (1771–1858)

(Three) *Sonatas*, for piano with flute ad lib
EP   (London: L. Lavenu, ca. 1800)
        GB:Lbm G.142.(1.)

Sonatas, Op. 9, for piano with flute ad lib
EP   (London: Longman & Broderip, ca. 1795)
        GB:Lbm G.192.(2.)

Croft, William (1678–1727) and Seignr. Pepusch (1667–1752)

(Six) *Sonatas* contains a work for solo flute (by Pepusch)
EP   (London: Walsh and Hare, ca. 1705)
    GB:Lbm C.105.a.(1.)
EP   (London: I. Walsh, ca. 1710)
    GB:Lbm D.150.(3.)

MGG also attributes to Croft three *Sonatas*, ca. 1700, in GB:Lcm.

Czapek, Leopold, Bohemian (1792–1840)

Divertimento, Op. 12, for flute and piano
MS A:Wn Sm 18327

Danzi, Francois (1763–1826)

(Four) *Variations* for flute and piano
MS A:Wgm VIII 30510

MGG also attributes to Danzi, three *Petits Duos* for flute and cello and four concerti
    for flute.

Davis, Thomas

(Six) *Solos*, for flute and harpsichord
EP   (London: H. Waylet, ca. 1750)
    GB:Lbm G.418.c.(1.)
EP   (London: Longman, Lukey & Broderip, ca. 1778)
    GB:Lbm H.2140.(6.)

De Caix d'Hervelois, Louis (1680–1760)

MGG attributes to this man *Pieces* for flute and bass (Paris, 1726) and a second volume of
    the same (Paris, 1736).

DeMicco, Domenico

Concerto in G Major, for flute and orchestra
MS I:Gl T.C.3.3.(Sc.26)

(Three) *Sonatas* for flute and strings
MS I:Gl M.3.22.18/20

(Two) Sonatas for flute and strings
MS I:Gl M.4.28.3/4

Demoiver, ?

Sainsbury identifies Demoiver as a flutist and composer of flute music published in London at the end of the eighteenth century.

Desmarets, Henri (1662–1741)

MGG attributes to Desmarets, *Sonates* for flute and continuo (Paris: Bolvin).

Devienne, Francois (1759–1803)

Concerto in D Major for flute and orchestra
MS A:Wgm VIII 6600

(Two) *Concerti*, in G Major, and (Four) *Concerti* in D Major, for flute
MS (Wien: Traeg's *Catalog*, 1799)

MGG attributes to Devienne some ten *Concerti* for flute.

Collection of solos and duets, for flutes
EP (London: C. Wheatstone, ca. 1800)
    GB:Lbm G.239.b.(1.)

(Three) *Duos*, for flute and violin
EP (Paris: Imbault, ca. 1800)
    GB:Lbm G.421.p.(10.)

(Six) *Duetts*, Op. 5, for flute and viola.
EP (London: Longman & Broderip, ca. 1790)
    GB:Lbm G.421.p.(11.)

(Six) *Duets* for flute and violin
MS (Wien: Traeg's *Catalog*, 1799)

(Six) *Duets* for flute and viola
MS (Wien: Traeg's *Catalog*, 1799)

Nouvelle Methode Theorique et Pratique pour la Flute
EP (Paris: Naderman, ca. 1800)
    GB:Lbm G.239.a.

(Three) *Quartets* for flute and strings
MS I:Mc [according to MGG]

(Six) *Quartets*, Op. 2, for flute and strings
EP (Amsterdam: J. Schmitt, ca. 1785)
    GB:Lbm G.411.a.(3.)
EP (London: Wheatstone, ca. 1800)
    GB:Lbm G.417.c.(2.)

(Eighteen) *Quartets* for flute and strings
MS (Wien: Traeg's *Catalog*, 1799)

(Three) *Quartets*, Op. 62, for flute and strings
MS (Wien: Traeg's *Catalog*, 1799)

(Three) *Quartets,* Op. 64, for flute and strings
MS (Wien: Traeg's *Catalog*, 1799)

MGG also attributes to Devienne an additional thirty Quartets for flute and strings in editions Op. 1, 11, 16, Liv. 3, 66, and 73.

(Six) *Solos*, for flute and bc
EP (London: Longman & Broderip, ca. 1795)
    GB:Lbm G.280.k.(1.)

(Three) *Sonatas*, Op. 58, for flute and bc
EP (Offenbach: J. Andre, ca. 1800)
    GB:Lbm G.70.(8.)

(Six) *Sonatas*, Op. 73, for flute
EP (Offenbach: Andre)
    I:Bc

(Six) *Sonatas* for flute and bass
MS (Wien: Traeg's *Catalog*, 1799)

MGG also cites *Sonatas*, Op. 50, 59, and 68 for flute.

(Six) Solos with Preludes, for flute
EP (London: Goulding, ca. 1799)
    GB:Lbm G.280.k.(2.)

(Six) *Trios*, Op. 19, for flutes and bc
EP (London: Longman & Broderip, ca. 1790)
    GB:Lbm G.222.(1.)

(Six) *Trios*, Op. 61, Liv. 1, 2, for flute and strings
MS (Wien: Traeg's *Catalog*, 1799)

(Six) *Trios* for flute and strings
MS (Wien: Traeg's *Catalog*, 1799)

MGG attributes to Devienne six *Trios* for flute, piano, and bass and a *Trio* for clavecin, flute and bass, as well as several keyboard works with flute ad lib and a number of theoretical works for flute.

Sainsbury identifies Devienne as, 'a celebrated French flutist and professor of his instrument at the conservatory at Paris … At length the intensity [of his composition] affected his mental faculties, and he died insane at the Lunatic asylum at Charenton in 1803 at the early age of 43.'

F:Pn has a great number of solo works for flute by Devienne.

Dibdin, Charles (English, 1745–1814)

MGG attributes to Dibdin a *Sonata* of 1791 for keyboard with flute or violin.

Dieupart, Charles (d. 1740)

MGG attributes to Dieupart (Six) *Suites* for flute, violin and bass in both Amsterdam and London editions.

Dioter, ?

Concerto, in D Major, for flute
MS (Wien: Traeg's *Catalog*, 1799)

Distler, Johann Georg (1760–1799)

Concerto for flute
MS A:Wgm, according to MGG

Domenichini, Antonio (eighteenth century)

Concerto in G Major, for flute and strings
MS I:Gl SS.B.1.4

Domenichini, Carlo

(Six) *Duetti* for flute and cello
MS A:Wn Sm 22896

Donelli, ? (eighteenth century)

Concerto for flute and orchestra
MS I:MOe Mus.F.355

Doppler, Franz (1821–1883)

Fantasia pastorale ungheresse, Op. 26
EP   (Mainz: Schott)
    I:Bc

Doremieulx, H. I. L.

Sainsbury identifies Doremieulx as a flutist in Paris and composer of *Etudes pour la Flute* (Paris, 1802).

Dornel, Antoine (1685–1765)

MGG attributes to Dornel, *Sonates*, Op. 2 (Paris, 1711) for flute and bass.

Döthel, Nicolas (German, 1721–1810)

Concerto for flute and orchestra
MS I:Gl SS.A.2.5.(G.8)

Concerto for flute and orchestra
MS I:Gl T.C.3.4.(Sc.15)

Concerto for flute and orchestra
MS A:Wn Sm 22891

(Six) *Divertimenti,* Op. 2, for flute, cello, and harpsichord
EP (London: J. Oswald, ca. 1755)
     GB:Lbm G.227.b.

(Six) *Duetts*, for flutes
EP (London: Chapman, ca. 1760)
     GB:Lbm G.227.

(Six) *Sonatas*, for flute, violin, and harpsichord
EP (London: Walsh, ca. 1765)
     GB:Lbm G.242.(8.)

(Six) *Sonatas and trio* for flute, violin, and cello
MS A:Wn Sm 18626

(Two) *Trios* for flute, violin, and continuo
MS I:Gl SS.A.2.5.(G.8)

Dotzauer, Justus (German, 1783–1860)

MGG attributes to Dotzauer a *Concerto* and a *Quartet* for solo flute and strings.

Dourlen, Victor (French, 1780–1864)

MGG attributes to Dourlen a *Sonata*, Op. 9, for keyboard and flute.

Drobisch, Johannes Friedrich

MGG attributes to Drobisch, (Six) *Duos* (Berlin, 1786) for flute and violin.

Drouet, Louis (1792–1873)

MGG attributes to Drouet the following works:
 (Six sets of) *Variations* for solo flute
 Air Ecossais (Paris: Pleyel) for flute and piano
 Air Italien, Op. 25 (Paris: Richault) for flute and piano
 (Six) *Airs favoris varies*, Op. 26 (Paris: Richault)
 (Three) *Airs favoris varies*, Op. 30 (Paris: Richault)
 Ballade (Paris: Farrenc) for singer, flute and string quartet
 Barcarolle d'Aline variée (Paris: Duhan) for flute solo
 (Ten) *Concerti* for flute
 Cent etudes, Op. 120
 Cent etudes, Op. 31
 (Six) *Fantaisies* for flute and harp or piano
 Adagio et Rondo brillant, Op. 197 (Paris: Farrenc) for flute and string quartet
 Methode pour la flute
 Rondo provencale (Paris: Duhan)
 Sonate, Op. 40 (Paris: Richault) for flute and piano
 Variations (Paris: Farrenc) for flute and piano or string quartet
 Vive Henri IV, Op. 13 (Paris: Pleyel) for flute and orchestra]

Sainsbury identifies Drouet as, 'a celebrated flutist, born in Holland about 1792, who came to London in 1817, where his talents as a performer deservedly received the most brilliant applause ... Drouet had amazing facility in performing rapid passages, but it is said he was deficient in taste in adagio movements.'

Ducreux, ?

Sainsbury identifies Ducreux as a French composer for the flute at the end of the 18th century.

Dulon, Freidrich Ludwig (1769–1826)

MGG attributes to Dulon the following works for solo flute:
 (Three) *Duos* for flute and violin, Op. 1 (Leipzig, 1800)
 (Twelve) *Variations* for flute and violin, Op. 2 (Leipzig, 1800)
 (Three) *Duos* for flute and violin, Op. 3 (Leipzig, 1801)
 (Three) *Duos* for flute and violin, Op. 6 (Leipzig)
 Premier Concerto in G Major for flute

Dumonchau, Charles-François (1775–1820)

MGG attributes to Dumonchau (Twenty-four) *Sonatas* for keyboard and flute or violin
(Op. 4, 13, 15, 20, 23, 24).

Duncan, Giacomo

Minuetti, for flute and bass
MS I:PAc

Dussek, Jan

(Six) *Sonatines*, Op. 19, for flute and piano
EP (London: Longman & Broderip, ca. 1792)
      GB:Lbm G.161.e.(3.)

Sainsbury identifies Dussek as born in Czaslau in Bohemia in 1762, and composer of
(Three) *Sonatas*, Op. 35, for violin or flute and violin.

Dussek, Oliva (1797–1847)

MGG attributes to Dussek the following works:
      (Twenty-three) Piano *Trios*, with flute
      (Sixty) *Sonatas* for flute or violin and keyboard
      (Three) *Sonatas* for flute and cello

Eberwein, Christian (1750–1810)

MGG attributes to Eberwein a set of *Variations*, Op. 2 (Leipzig, 1807), for flute
and orchestra.

Ehrenfried, ?

Sainsbury identifies Ehrenfried as a flutist at Mainz and composer of flute music between
the years 1794 and 1798.

Eichner, Ernest (German, 1740–1777)

(Six) *Quartets*, Op. 4, for flute and strings
EP (London: Bremner, ca. 1770)
      GB:Lbm G.413.(7.)
EP (London: Preston & Son, ca. 1790)
      GB:Lbm G.439.(1.)

(Six) *Quartets* for flute and strings
MS A:Wn Sm 11790–11795

(Six) *Quartets* for flute and strings
MS (Wien: Traeg's *Catalog,* 1799)

MGG also attributes to Eichner the following works:
(Two) *Quintets* for flute and strings
Sextet for flute and strings
(Six) *Sonatas* for flute and bass

Eiffert, Philip

(Six) *Solos,* Op. 2, for flute and bc
EP   (London: Welcker, ca. 1770)
GB:Lbm G.280.c.(3.)

Eler, André-Frédéric (Austrian, 1764–1821)

(Three) *Quartets* for flute and strings
MS A:Wn Sm 2920

(Three) *Quartets* for flute and strings
MS (Wien: Traeg's *Catalog,* 1799)

Ellis, Samuel (b. 1776)

Sainsbury identifies Ellis as an organist and flute professor, whose compositions for flute remained in manuscript in 1825.

Esch, Louis von

Russian Divertimento, for piano and flute
EP   (London: Broderip & Wilkinson, ca. 1800)
GB:Lbm G.186.(10.)

Essex, Dr.

Sainsbury identifies Essex as composer of *The Guaracha,* 'a Rondo in imitation of the Spanish Style,' for piano and flute.

Eybler, Josef (Austria, 1765–1846)

Quintet for flute and strings
MS A:Wgm XI 23321

Farrenc, Jacques Hyppolite (French, 1794–1865)

MGG attributes to Farrenc a *Trio*, Op. 45, for piano, flute, and cello.

Fasch, Johann Friedrich (1688–1758)

MGG attributes to Fasch two *Sonatas* in G Major and a *Trio* in D Major for flute, violin, and cembalo.

Faure, Gabriel-Urbain (1845–1924)

MGG attributes to Faure a *Fantaisie*, Op. 79 (1898) for flute and piano.

Ferrandini, Giovanni (Italian, 1710–1791)

MGG attributes to Ferrandini flute *Sonatas* published in Amsterdam ca. 1730.

Sainsbury identifies Ferrandini as a flutist and composer of flute music published in Amsterdam in 1799.

Ferrari, Carlo (Italian, 1710–1789)

MGG attributes to Ferrari a *Sonata* for flute and bass (MS, D:KA).

Fesca, Friedrich Ernst (German, 1789–1826)

MGG attributes to Fesca a *Quintet*, Op. 22, for flute and strings.

Fesch, Willem de (Dutch, 1687–1757)

MGG attributes to Fesch the following works:
    (Twenty-seven) English *Songs* with flute
    (Six) Sonatas for flute or violin and bass (Amsterdam, ca. 1732)
    Concerto for flute (London, 1741)

Fétis, Francois Joseph (Belgium, 1784–1871)

Concerto (1869) for flute and orchestra
MS B:Bc Wotquenne 5540

Field, John (1782–1837)

Sainsbury identifies Field as the celebrated pianist and student of Clementi. Among his compositions Sainsbury mentions a *Quintet* for piano, flute, and strings.

Filtz, Anton [Fils, Antonio] (German, 1730–1760)

Concerto for flute and orchestra
MS B:Bc Wotquenne 5541

Divertimento for flute, violin, and cello
MS A:Wgm XI 3327

Trio for flute, cello, and keyboard
MS A:Wgm XI 2181

Trio for flute, cello, and keyboard
MS A:Wgm XI 10771

(Three) *Trios,* for flute, cello, and bass
MS B:Bc Wotquenne 6571

(Six) *Trios,* for flute and bc
EP (London: Welcker, ca. 1770)
     GB:Lbm H.2852.a.(14.)

Finger, Gottfried (ca. 1660–1723)

MGG attributes to Finger the following:
     (Three) *Sonatas* for flute (London, ca. 1690)
     Sonatas for violins and flutes (London, 1691)
     (Ten) *Sonatas* for flute and continuo, Op. 3
     (Six) *Sonatas* for flute and continuo (London: Walsh)

Fiorillo, Federigo (Italian, 1755–1823)

(Six) *Quartets* for flute and strings
MS (Wien: Traeg's *Catalog,* 1799)

(Three) *Trios* for flute and strings
MS (Wien: Traeg's *Catalog,* 1799)

MGG also attributes to Fiorillo the following:
     (Six) *Quartets,* Op. 4, for flute and strings (Paris)
     (Six) *Quartets,* Op. 6, Liv. 2, for flute and strings (Paris: Sieber)
     (Six) *Quartets,* Op. 7, for flute and strings (Amsterdam: Hummel, 1798)
     (Three) *Trios concertantes,* Op. 31, for flute, violin, viola (London: Kelly, 1810)
     Ninth *Divertimento,* Op. 58, for piano or harp and flute (London: Birchall, 1814)
     A Fourth *Grand Duett Concertante* for piano, harp and flute (London: Birchall, 1815)
     Rondo, for flute and piano (Paris: Erard)

Fischer, Johann (German, 1733–1800)

(Three) *Quartets,* for flute and strings
EP   (London: the composer, ca. 1795)
   GB:Lbm H.110.(7.)

(Ten) *Sonatas,* for flute and harpsichord
EP   (London: Longman & Broderip, ca. 1780)
   GB:Lbm G.72

Flath, P.

Sainsbury identifies Flath as a flutist in Paris who has composed much flute music
   since 1790.

Florio, Pietro Grassi (d. 1795)

(Six) *Quartets,* for flute and strings
EP   (London: Linley, ca. 1796)
   GB:Lbm H.2830.(2.)

(Six) *Trios,* for flute and strings
EP   (London: the composer, ca. 1780)
   GB:Lbm G.222.(2.)

Fodor, ?

(Six) *Quartets* for flute and strings
MS (Wien: Traeg's *Catalog,* 1799)

Forkel, Johann Nikolaus (German, 1749–1818)

MGG attributes to Forkel a *Sonata* (1770) for flute and harp in D:B.

Förster, ?

Concerto for flute and strings
MS   B:Bc Wotquenne 5543

Förster, Emanuel (Austrian, 1748–1823)

MGG attributes to Forster, three *Duette,* Op. 5, for piano and flute.

Franz, Étienne

Variations for flute
MS   A:Wgm VIII 1102

Friedrich II, 'the Great' (1712–1786)

MGG attributes to Friedrich 121 *Sonatas* for flute and cembalo and four *Concerti* for flute and orchestra.

Fritz, Kasper (Swiss, 1716–1783)

MGG attributes to Fritz (Six) Sonatas, Op. 2 (before 1750), for flute or violin and bass.

Frühling, Carl (Austrian, 1868–1937)

MGG attributes to Fruhling a *Fantasie*, Op. 55, for flute and orchestra and a *Rondo*, Op. 66, for flute and piano.

Fuchs, ?

(Three) *Duets*, Op. 19, for flute and violin
MS (Wien: Traeg's *Catalog*, 1799)

Fürstenau, Anton Bernard (German, 1792–1852)

Concerto for flute and orchestra
MS A:Wgm VIII 6125

Fuss, Johann Evangelist (Hungarian, 1777–1819)

MGG attributes to Fuss a *Quartet*, Op. 5, for flute and strings.

Gabrielsky, W. (nineteenth century)

Sainsbury identifies Gabrielsky as having, 'the reputation of being one of the best flautists in Europe; he is also reported as a good composer. He resides in Vienna.' Among his compositions, Sainsbury lists:
  Adagio and Rondo for flute and orchestra
  Adagio and Polonoise for flute and orchestra
  (Two) *Concerti*
  (Nine sets) of *Trios* for flute and strings
  (Nineteen sets) of *Variations* for flute

Gaelle, Meingosus (German, 1752–1816)

MGG attributes to Gaelle two *Sonatas* for piano flute (or violin) and viola.

Gagnebin, Henri (b. 1886)

MGG attributes to Gagnebin 23 *pieces recreatives* (Paris: Leduc) for flute alone and a *Marche des gais hurons*, for flute and piano.

Galliard, Johann (German, b. 1687)

(Six) *Sonatas*, Op. 1, for flute and bc
EP   (London: Cross, ca. 1710)
      GB:Lbm E.700
EP   (Amsterdam: Roger, ca. 1710)
      GB:Lbm G.280.b.(3.) [another edition of one of these sonatas]

Gänsbacher, Johann Baptist (Austrian, 1778–1844)

MGG attributes to Gansbacher the folowing works:
    Sonata in G Major (Wien: Chem. Druckerei, 1808) for flute and piano
    Sonata in C Major, Op. 11 (Innsbruck, 1812)
    Serenade, Op. 14, for flute (or violin) and guitar (Prag, 1812)

Garaudé, Alexis (1779–1852)

MGG attributes to Garaude (Three) *Quartets*, Op. 33 (Paris: Imbault, 1810) for flute and strings.

Garnier, 'le jeune'

Sainsbury identifies Garnier as a professor of flute and performer of the Paris Opera in 1799 with published flute music.

Garzaroli, ?

(Six) *Sonatas* for flute
MS A:Wn E.M. 32

Gasparini, Giovanni (Italian, 1661–1727)

A Collection of Overtures ('to which is added that incomperable Sonata for a flute and Bass')
EP   (London?, ca. 1710)
      GB:Lbm H.17.(5.)

Gassmann, Florian (Bohemian, 1729–1774)

Divertimento, for flute and two strings
MS A:Wn Sm 16942

Divertimento, for flute and two strings
MS A:Wn Sm 16943

Divertimento, for flute and two strings
MS A:Wn Sm 16944

Divertimento, for flute and two strings
MS A:Wn Sm 16945

Divertimento, for flute and two strings
MS A:Wn Sm 16946

Divertimento, for flute and two strings
MS A:Wn Sm 16947

Quintet, for flute and strings ('Viaggiatore Ridicolo, 1792)'
MS A:Wn Sm 11561
    I:MOe Mus.D.104

Quintet, for flute and strings
MS I:MOe Mus.D.102

(Three) *Quintets,* for flute and strings
MS I:MOe Mus.D.103

(Three) *Quintets,* for flute and strings
MS I:MOe Mus.D.103

Sextet, for flute, oboe, and strings
MS I:MOe Mus.D.100

Trio for flute, violin and bass
MS CH:Bu kr.IV, 106
MP (Lippstadt: Kistner & Siegel)

Trio for flute, violin and bass
MS CH:Bu kr.IV, 107
MP (Lippstadt: Kistner & Siegel)

Trio for flute, violin and bass
MS CH:Bu kr.IV, 108
MP (Lippstadt: Kistner & Siegel)

Trio for flute, violin and bass
MS CH:Bu kr.IV, 109
MP (Lippstadt: Kistner & Siegel)

Trio for flute, violin and bass
MS CH:Bu kr.IV, 110

Trio for flute, violin and bass
MS CH:Bu kr.IV, 111
MP (Lippstadt: Kistner & Siegel)

Gatayes, Guillaume Pierre (1774–1846)

MGG attributes to Gatayes four *Duets* for flute and guitar.

Gautier, Pierre (1643–1697)

MGG attributes to Gautier 41 works in (Four) *Duet-Suites* and (Five) *Trio-Suites* for flute and violin.

Gayer, Johann Nepomuk (Bohemian, 1746–1811)

MGG attributes to Gayer a *Concerto* for flute.

Gebauer, François (1773–1844)

(Three) *Duos concertants*, Op. 12, for flute and violin
EP (Paris: Magasin de Musique a l'usage de fetes Nationales)
    I:Bc

Gebauer, Josef (French, 1763–1812)

Polonaise for flute and guitar
MS A:Wgm XI 1524

Gelinek, Joseph (Czech, 1758–1825)

MGG attributes to Gelinek an *Introduction, Chanson, and Variations*, Op, 88 (Paris: Richault, Janet and Cotelle) for flute, violin, and piano.

Geminiani, Francesco (1679–1762)

MGG attributes to Geminiani (Twelve) *Sonatas* for flute, or violin, or oboe and bass.

Gernsheim, Friedrich (German, 1839–1916)

MGG attributes to Gernsheim a *Divertimento*, Op. 53 (Luckhardt, 1888), for flute and strings.

Gianella, Luigi

(Six) *Quartets*, Op. 1, for flute and strngs
EP (Venice: Bertoia)
   I:Bc

Sainsbury identifies Gianella as 'a celebrated flutist at Paris, [who] has published duets, trios, and concerti for flute since 1803.'

Giannotti Pietro (Italian, d. 1765)

MGG attributes to Giannotti *Sonates,* Op. 5 (Paris: Leclerc) for flute and bass.

Giardini, Felice (1716–1796)

MGG attributes to Giardini the following works:
   (Six) *Sonate* di cembalo con violino o flauto (Paris and London, ca. 1755)
   Quartet for flute and strings (MS, GB:Lbm Add. 14337)
   Sonata for flute and bass (MS, D:KA Ms. 166)
   (Two) *Trios* for flute and strings (Leipzig)
   (Six) *Trios* for flute and strings (MS, I:Mc)

Giordani, Tommaso (1730–1806)

(Six) *Quartets* for flute and strings
MS I:Gl N.1.5.9.(Sc.27)

(Six) *Chamber Concerti*, Op. 3, for flute and strings
EP (London: Johnston, Longman, Lukey, ca. 1775)
   GB:Lbm G.666.b.(1.)

(Six) *Concerti*, Op. 9, for flute and strings
EP (London: Longman & Broderip, ca. 1780)
   GB:Lbm G.666.b.(2.)

(Six) *Concerti* for flute
MS (Wien: Traeg's *Catalog,* 1799)

(Six) *Quartets*, two of which are for flute and strings
EP (London: Johnston, ca. 1775)
   GB:Lbm G.413.(8.)

(Six) *Easy Solos*, Op. 9, for flute
EP (London: Johnston, Longman, Lukey, ca. 1775)
   GB:Lbm E.340.(1.)

(Six) *Trios*, for flute and strings
EP (London: Napier, ca. 1780)
    GB:Lbm G.415.(2.)

(Six) *Trios* for flute and strings
MS (Wien: Traeg's *Catalog*, 1799)

Gitter, Joseph

Sainsbury identifies Gitter as the composer of three *Quartets* (Mannheim and Mainz, 1784) for flute and strings.

Giuliani, Giovanni

Quintet, Op. 13, for flute and strings
EP (Firenze: Pagni)
    I:Bc

Gleissner, Franz (German, 1759–1818)

MGG attributes to Gleissner a *Quartet*, Op. 38 (Leipzig: Baumgärtner) for flute and strings.

Gluck, Christoph Willibald (German, 1714–1787)

MGG attributes to Gluck a *Concerto* in G Major.

Godard, Benjamin Louis (French, 1849–1895)

MGG attributes to Godard a *Suite de 13 morceaux* (Paris: Durand) for flute and piano.

Goetzel, Francois Joseph

Sainsbury identifies Goetzel as flutist of the Elector of Saxony in Dresden in 1756 and 'celebrated for his talent and composition for his instrument.'

Gorlier, Simon (French, fl. ca. 1550–1584)

MGG attributes to Gorlier a published *Livre de tablature de flute d'alemand*, of 1558.

Götz, Francois (nineteenth century)

Fantaisies amusantes for flute, viola, and piano
MS A:Wgm XI 11303

Graf, Christian Ernst (1726–1804)

(Six) *Quartets*, Op. 12, for flute and strings
EP   (London: Welcker, ca. 1775)
    GB:Lbm G.417.i.(1.)

(Six) *Quartets*, for flute and strings
EP   (Amsterdam et Berlin: J. J. Humel, ca. 1775)
    GB:Lbm G.411.a.(6.)

Graf, Friedrich Harmann (German flautist, 1727–1795)

(Four) *Quartets* for flute and strings
MS   A:Wgm XI 23522

(Twelve) *Sonatas* for flute and bass
MS (Wien: Traeg's Catalog, 1799)

(Two) *Trios* for flute and strings
MS (Wien: Traeg's *Catalog*, 1799)

(Twenty-four) *Concerti* for flute
MS (Wien: Traeg's *Catalog*, 1799)

Concerto for flute and violin and orchestra
MS (Wien: Traeg's *Catalog*, 1799)

Concerto, in G Major, for flute d'amore
MS (Wien: Traeg's *Catalog*, 1799)

MGG attrbutes to Graf the following early prints:
    Concerto for flute (London: Preston)
    (Three) *Concerti* for flute (Berlin: Hummel)
    (Six) *Quartets* (Amsterdam & Berlin: Hummel) for flute and strings
    (Two) *Quartets* (city of publication unknown) for flute and strings
    (Six) *Quartets* (Hamburg, 1766) for flute and strings
    Trio, Nr. 1 (London: Preston) for flute and strings

Graff, ?

(Twelve) *Quartets* for flute and strings
MS (Wien: Traeg's *Catalog*, 1799)

Graff, Johann (1711–1787)

(Six) *Duetts*, for flute and strings
EP   (London: Bland, ca. 1780)
    GB:Lbm G.421.g.(2.)

(Six) *Solos*, Op. 5, for flute and bc
EP (London: Birchall, ca. 1795)
     GB:Lbm H.2140.a.(2.)

Granman, ?

Concerto a tre, for flute, violin, and bass
MS I:Gl SS.B.1.8.

Grano, Giovanni

Solos, for flute or oboe and harpsichord
EP (London: Walsh and Hare, ca. 1730)
     GB:Lbm G.422.j.(4.)

Granom, Lewis

Plain and Easy Instructions for Playing on the German-Flute
EP (London: Bennett, 1766)
     GB:Lbm E.201

(Twelve) *Solos*, Op. 1, for flute and harpsichord
EP (London: Simpson, ca. 1750)
     GB:Lbm G.280.i.(4.)

(Six) *Solos or Sonatas*, Op. 7, for flute and harpsichord
EP (London: Bremner, ca. 1762)
     GB:Lbm E.201.a.(4.)

(Six) *Solos or Sonatas*, Op. 8, for flute and harpsichord
EP (London: Bremner, ca. 1765)
     GB:Lbm E.201.a.(5.)

New Songs, Op. 4, ('with their Symphonies for flute')
EP (London: Bennett, 1752)
     GB:Lbm E.600.m.(3.)

Graun, ?

(Six) *Sonatas* for flute, violin and bass
MS P:GD Ms.4053

Graun, August Friedrich (1698–1765)

MGG attributes to Graun the following works:
> *Concerti grossi* with flute and oboe (or flute) as concertino
> *Concerto a tre*, with flute, violin (or flute) and oboe as concertino
> *Concerto* for flute and strings (MS, 'Grauen' in D:KA)
> *Concerto* for flute and strings (MS, 'Grauen' in D:B)

Graun, Carl Heinrich (1703–1759)

(Two) *Concerti* for flute and orchestra
MS B:Bc Wotquenne 5545

(Four) *Sonatas* for flute and bass
MS B:Bc Wotquenne 5546

(Three) *Trios,* for flute, violin, and cello
MS B:Bc Wotquenne 6613

MGG also attributes to Graun:
> *Diana allentonata*, for Soprano, flute and continuo
> *Concerto grosso* for flute and strings
> (Six) *Concerti* for flute and strings
> *Quintet* in D Major for flute and strings

Graupner, Christoph (1683–1760)

MGG attributes to Graupner (Three) *Sonatas* (MS, D:KA) for flute and cembalo.

Greber, Jakob (early eighteenth century)

MGG attributes to Greber a solo *Cantata* for Soprano, flute and continuo.

Greeting, Thomas (d. 1682)

MGG attributes to Greeting *The Pleasant Companion or New Lessons and Instructions for the Flaglet* (London: Playford, 1667, with following editions in 1672, 1673, 1680, 1682, 1683, and 1688).

Gregora, Franz (Czech, 1819–1887)

MGG attributes to Gregora a set of variations for flute.

Grenser, Johann Friedrich (1758–1794)

Sainsbury identifies Grenser as a professor of oboe to the King of Sweden in 1783 and the composer of (Six) *Trios* (Berlin, 1779) for flute and strings.

Grenser, Karl Augustin (1794–1864)

MGG attributes to Grenser (Three) *Grands Duos*, Op. 7 (Leipzig: Probst) for 2 flutes.

Griesbach, William (English, nineteenth century)

(Three) *Quartets*, Op. 1, for flute or oboe and strings
EP   (London: Birchall, ca. 1800)
   GB:Lbm H.111.(20.)

Gruber, Georg Wilhelm (1729–1796)

MGG attributes to Gruber three *Sonatas* with flute and cembalo printed in Nürnberg.

Grund, Eduard (German, 1802–1871)

MGG attributes to Grund a *Grand divertissement*, Op. 23, for piano and flute.

Guillemant, Benoit

MGG attributes to Guillemant (Six) *Sonatas,* Op. 4 (Paris, 1746) for violin, flute (or oboe) and bass and a *Concerto* (1754) which is lost.

Guilmant, Felix-Alexandre (1837–1911)

MGG attributes to Guilmant a *Berceuse*, Op. 78, (Mainz: Schott) for flute and piano.

Gunn, John (1765–1824)

The Art of Playing the German Flute
EP   (London: the author, 1793)
   GB:Lbm H.2098.(1.)

The School of the German Flute
EP   (London: the author, ca. 1795)
   GB:Lbm H.2098.(2.)

Gyrowetz, Adalbert (1763–1850)

(Three) *Quartets* for flute and strings
MS   A:Wgm XI 4706

(Three) *Quartets* for flute and strings
MS (Wien: Traeg's Catalog, 1799)

(Three) *Quartets*, Op. 20 for flute and strings
MS (Wien: Traeg's *Catalog*, 1799)

(Three) *Sonatas*, Op. 20, for piano with a violin or flute
EP (London: Linley, 1796)
　　GB:Lbm G.161.g.(2.)

(Three) *Trios*, Op. 2, for flute and strings
MS (Wien: Traeg's *Catalog*, 1799)

(Three) *Trios*, Op. 4, for flute and strings
EP (London: Hamilton, ca. 1800)
　　GB:Lbm G.274.b.(1.)

(Six) *Trios*, Op. 6, Liv. 1, 2, for flute and strings
MS (Wien: Traeg's *Catalog*, 1799)

MGG attributes to Gyrowetz (Twelve) *Notturni* for flute and piano, dating from 1793.

Gyrowetz, Naturna

(Three) *Quartets*, Op. 32, for flute and strings
MS (Wien: Traeg's *Catalog*, 1799)

Hahocker, Johann

[Untitled work] for flute and piano
MS A:Wgm XI 38900

Haigh, T.

Sainsbury identifies Haigh as a pianist, student of Haydn and composer of *Variations* for piano and flute as well as popular songs accompanied by piano and flute, such as 'Far from this throbbing bosom.'

Haindl, Franz Sebastian (1727–1812)

MGG attributes to Haindl a *Concerto* in G Major for flute.

Handel, Georg F.

Concerto for flute and strings.
MS (Wien: Traeg's *Catalog*, 1799)

Solos, Op. 1, for flute or oboe and harpsicord
EP (London: Walsh, ca. 1733)
     GB:Lbm G.74.c.(2.)
     GB:Lbm G.74.h. [another edition]

Hanot, Francois (French, 1697–1770)

MGG attributes to Hanot (Six) *Sonatas*, Op. 1, (Rotterdam, 1740) and (Six) *Sonatas* (1745)
     for flute and continuo.

Hänsel, Peter (German, 1770–1831)

MGG attributes to Hansel the following:
     Theme varie (Wien: Cappi and Offenbach: Andre, 1802) for flute and strings
     Grand Quatuor, Op. 21 (Wien: Imprimerie chimique, 1809) for flute and strings
     Quatuor, Op. 25 (Wien, 1811) for flute and strings

Hanssens, Charles-Louis (Belgium, 1802–1871)

Concerto (1866) for flute and orchestra
MS B:Bc Wotquenne 5550
MS B:Bc Wotquenne 5551 [version with piano]

Harbordt, Gottfried (German, 1768–1837)

MGG attributes to Harbordt (Three) *Concerti* for flute and small orchestra.
Sainsbury identifies Harbordt as a German composer who, since 1796, has published music
     for piano and flute at Brunswick.

Hartmann, C.

Collection of *Preludes* for solo flute
MS (Wien: Traeg's *Catalog*, 1799)

(120) *Cadences* for solo flute
MS (Wien: Traeg's *Catalog*, 1799)

Concerto, Op. 2, in G Major, for flute
MS (Wien: Traeg's *Catalog*, 1799)

Sainsbury identifies Hartmann as a German composer for the Russian court and later a
     member of the Royal Academy of Music in Paris and, 'much celebrated as a flautist.'
     To the above, Sainsbury adds his *Six Airs, Francais et Russe*, a set of Variations for flute
     accompanied by violin and cello, which was published in Paris.

Hasse, ?

(Two) *Concerti* for flute and strings
MS B:Bc Wotquenne 5556

Concerto for flute and orchestra
MS B:Bc Wotquenne 5557

Sonata for flute and bass
MS B:Bc Wotquenne 5558

Hasse, Johann Adolf (1699–1783)

(Twelve) *Concerti,* Op. 3, for flute
EP   (London: Walsh, ca. 1760)
        GB:Lbm G.979.a.(1.)

(Six) *Concerti*, Op. 6, for flute
EP   (London: Walsh, ca. 1760)
        GB:Lbm G.979.a.(2.)

(Three) *Concerti* for flute and orchestra
MS A:Wn Sm 3701

(Two) *Concerti* in G Major, for flute and orchestra
MS I:Gl SS.B.1.4.(H.8)

Concerto in D Major, for flute and orchestra
MS I:Gl SS.B.1.4.(H.8)

(Six) *Sonatas* [Trios], for flute and strings
EP   (London: Tyther, ca. 1750)
        GB:Lbm H.5.b.(2.)

(Four) *Sonatas* for flute and bass
MS I:Gl SS.B.1.4.(H.8)

MGG attributes to Hasse the following:
        (Six) *Sonatas*, Op. 2 (London: Walsh) for flute and bass
        (Six) *Solos*, Op. 5 (London: Walsh) for flute and harpsichord
        (Twelve) *Sonatas*, Op. 1 (Paris: Le Clerc) for flute and bass

Hauptmann, Moritz (1792–1868)

MGG attributes to Hauptmann *Aure amiche* for singer, violin or flute, and piano.

Haydn, Franz Joseph (1732–1809)

Divertimento for flute and two strings
MS (Wien: Traeg's *Catalog*, 1799)

(Six) *Quartets*, Op. 5, for flute and strings
EP (London: Bremner, ca. 1772)
   GB:Lbm G.413.(11.)

(Six) *Quartets* for flute and strings
MS (Wien: Traeg's *Catalog*, 1799, as well as another eighteen quartet arrangements of Haydn's music)

(Six) *Sonatas* for flute and [three] strings
MS I:Gl HA.4.1/6

Sonata, for flute, violin, and cello
MS B:Bc Wotquenne 6666

Trio, Op. 59, for flute, cello, and piano
EP (Londres: Bland, c. 1788)
   GB:Lbm G.192.(5.)

(Nine) *Trios* for flute and strings
MS (Wien: Traeg's *Catalog*, 1799)

Heberle, Antonio

Concertino for flute and orchestra
MS A:Wgm VIII 17349

Variations for flute and orchestra
MS A:Wgm VIII 17350

Variationi Grandi for flute and orchestra
MS A:Wgm VIII 17348

Heine, Samuel Friedrich (1764–1821)

MGG attributes to Heine two *Concerti*, in D and G Major for flute.

Henkel, Michael (b. 1780)

Sainsbury identifies Henkel as organist at Fulda and composer of some published music for flute and guitar.

Hennig, J. C. (German)

(Three) *Quartets,* Op. 2, for flute and strings
MS (Wien: Traeg's *Catalog,* 1799)

Sainsbury identifies Hennig as a flutist and composer of nineteen flute works published in Offenbach, Berlin, and Paris.

Hertel, Johann Wilhelm (1727–1789)

(Two) *Concerti* for flute and orchestra
MS B:Bc Wotquenne 5560

Concerto for flute and orchestra
MS B:Bc Wotquenne 5561

Trio for flute, violin, and cello
MS B:Bc Wotquenne 6694

Hesse, Ernst Christian (1676–1762)

Sonata for flute and bass
MS D:ROu, according to MGG

Heyse, A. G.

Sainsbury identifies Heyse as a harpist at Halle who had published several works for the flute after 1792.

Hillemacher, Paul Joseph (French, 1852–1933)

MGG attributes to Hillemacher a *Serenade* (Paris: Leduc, 1898) for flute and piano.

Himmel, Frederick Heinrich (1765–1814)

Sainsbury identifies Himmel as 'Chapel-master to the King of Prussia' and composer of the following works published in Leipzig:
    Chanson de Rousseau, with flute guitar, piano, and cello
    (Six) *Deutsche Lieder,* with flute, cello, and piano
    Sonate for piano and flute
    Quartet (Berlin, 1803) for piano, flute, violin, and cello

Hoeberechts, John Lewis (1760–1820)

MGG attributes to Hoeberechts the following works:
    A Fifth Overture (London: Longman and Broderip, 1790) for flute and harpsichord

(Three) *Sonatas*, Op. 10 (London: Goulding, 1797), for piano and flute or violin
Air with Variations (London: Wilkinson, 1810) for piano, harp, organ and flute
Air with Variations, Nr. 3 (London: Monzani and Hill, 1810) for piano and flute
Thema with Variations, Nr. 5 (London: Monzani and Hill, 1819) for flute and piano

Hoffman, Leopold (Austrian, 1738–1793)

(Three) *Divertimenti* (ca. 1766) for flute and three strings
MS A:Wn Sm 11946–11948

(Nine) *Trios* for flute and two strings
MS A:Wn Sm 12622–12630

MGG also attributes to Hofmann a *Quartet* (London: Betz, 1785) for flute and strings and a
   Divertimento (MS, CS:KRa) for cembalo and flute.

Hoffmann, Philipp Carl (1769–1842)

MGG attributes to Hoffmann a *Sonata*, Op. 12 (Mainz: Zulehner) for flute and piano.

Hoffmeister, Franz Anton (1754–1812)

Concerto for flute and orchestra
MS A:Wgm VIII 1397

Concerto for flute and orchestra
MS I:Bc

(Five) *Concerti* for flute
MS (Wien: Traeg's *Catalog*, 1799)

Concerto for flute and violin and orchestra
MS (Wien: Traeg's *Catalog*, 1799)

(Three) *Duets* for flute and viola
MS (Wien: Traeg's *Catalog*, 1799)

Etude, Op. 35, for solo flute
MS (Wien: Traeg's *Catalog*, 1799)

(Fifty) *Ferma* for flute
MS A:Wgm VIII 30699

(Two) *Quartets* for flute and strings
MS I:Gl SS.A.1.11.(G.7)

(Six) *Quartets* for flute and strings
MS A:Wgm XI 1176

Quartet for flute and strings
MS A:Wgm XI 10723

Quartet for flute and strings
MS A:Wgm XI 10724

(Twelve) *Sonatas* for flute and bass
MS (Wien: Traeg's *Catalog*, 1799)

(Twelve) *Variations* for flute and strings
MS (Wien: Traeg's *Catalog*, 1799)

(Three) *Quartets*, Op. 33, for flute and strings
MS (Wien: Traeg's *Catalog*, 1799)

(Twenty-four) *Quartets* for flute and strings
MS (Wien: Traeg's *Catalog*, 1799)

(Two) *Quintets*, in D and G Major, for flute and strings
MS (Wien: Traeg's *Catalog*, 1799)

Quintet in E♭ Major for flute and strings
MS (Wien: Traeg's *Catalog*, 1799)

Quintet in E Major for flute and strings
MS (Wien: Traeg's *Catalog*, 1799)

(Six) *Solos*, Op. 21, for flute and bass
EP (Wien: the composer, ca. 1790)
      GB:Lbm G.221.(8.)

(Twelve) *Trios* for flute and strings
MS (Wien: Traeg's *Catalog*, 1799)

Hoffmeister, J. F.

A Study for the Flute in all keys
EP (London: Goulding, ca. 1800)
      GB:Lbm G.280.e.(1.)

Hofmeister, Henrich

Neu verbessertes Fundament (A method for an instrument with '1 or 2 1/2 keys')
EP (Not known) A:Llm I/39

Holzbauer, Ignaz Jakob (1711–1783)

MGG attributes to Holzbauer a *Concerto* for flute and strings in D:KA.

Holmes, Augusta Mary-Anne (1847–1903)

MGG attributes to Holmes *Trois petites pieces* (Paris: Durand, 1897) for flute and piano.

Hook, James (1746–1827)

(Six) *Sonatas*, Op. 92, for piano and flute
EP   (London: Preston, ca. 1800)
    GB:Lbm G.144.a.(3.)

MGG also attributes to Hook:
    *A Military Divertiment*o with piano and flute ad lib (ca. 1821)
    (Six) *Solos* for flute and bass (London: Thompson, 1770)
    (Six) *Familiar Son*atas (Harrison: 1797) for flute and bass

Horn, Karl Friedrich (1762–1830)

MGG attributes to Horn (Three) *Sonatas*, Op. 2 (London: Clementi, 1800) for piano and violin or flute.

Sainsbury attributes to Horn *Twelve Themes, with Variations* for piano and flute, or violin.

Horsley, Charles (1822–1876)

MGG attributes to Horsley a *Sonata*, Op. 9 (London: Wessil, 1846) for flute and piano.

Hotteterre, Jacques (d. 1761)

Principes de la Flute Traversiere
EP   (Amsterdam: d'Estienne Roger, c. 1710)
    GB:Lbm 7899.c.11
EP   (Paris: Ballard, 1722)
    GB:Lbm 7899.h.12

Sainsbury adds Hotteterre's *L'Art de preluder* (Paris, 1722) and writes that he was 'called the Roman, from being born in that city, was chamber-musician to the King of France in 1710 and considered the best flutist of his time.'

Hranailovich, F. X.

Introduction and Variations Brillantes, for flute and orchestra
MS H:Bn Ms.Mus.1467

Hugot, Antoine (d. 1803)

Le Celebre Pollonoise, for flute
EP   (Londres: Walker, ca. 1800)
   GB:Lbm G.280.f.(14.)

Concerto in D Major ('dedicated to 'Monsieur de La Chenaye') for flute and orchestra
MS   I:Gl N.1.6.6.(Sc.17)

(Three) *Solos,* for flute
EP   (Paris: Pleyel, ca. 1800)
   GB:Lbm G.280.f.(13.)

Sainsbury identifies Hugot as flutist at the Opera Comique in Paris and professor of flute at the conservatory and 'an excellent performer. In an excess of brain fever, in 1803, he wounded himself several times with a knife, and threw himself out of a window of the fourth story of a house into the street. He was 42 years old.' Among his works are:
   Methode de Flute, 'written with Wunderlick and used at the Conservatory'
   (Six) *Airs varies* for flute and bass
   (Six) *Sonatas*, Op. 8, for flute and bass
   (Four) *Concerti* (1797–1802)

Hugot, F. G.

(Three) *Concertante Duetts*, Op. 1, for flutes
EP   (London: Fentus, ca. 1800)
   GB:Lbm G.71.e.(5.)

Hummel, Johann Nepomuk (1778–1837)

Sonata for flute and piano
MS   A:Wn Sm 27418

MGG also attributes to Hummel the following:
   (Two) *Sonatas*, Op. 2 (Offenbach, Andre, 1792), for flute or violin and piano
   Variations, Op. 14 (Wien: Artaria) for flute or violin
   Sonata in G Major, Op. 28 (Wien: Cappi) for flute or violin
   Sonata in D Major, Op. 50 (Wien: Artaria)
   Grand Sonata, Op. 64 (Wien: Artaria) for flute or violin and viola

Sainsbury also attributes to Hummel the following:
   (Three) *Sonatas*, Op. 5, for piano and flute
   Adagio, Variations, and Rondo on a Russian Theme, Op. 78, for piano, flute, and cello
   Sonata in A Major, Op. 64, for piano and violin or flute

Hummel, Ferdinand (1855–1928)

MGG attributes to Hummel (Three) *Fantasiestücke*, Op. 14 (Leipzig: Siegel, 1884), for flute and piano.

Hummell, Charles

(Three) *Trios*, for flute and strings
EP   (London: the composer, ca. 1790)
   GB:Lbm G.222.(4.)

Hunt, Richard (d. 1683)

MGG attributes to Hunt *The Circle or Conversations on Love and Gallantry ...* (London: Neel, 1676) and the *Genteel Companion* (1683) for recorder.

Hünten, Franz (1793–1878)

MGG attributes to Hunten the following works:
   Nocturne, Op. 5 (Berlin, 1821)
   Divertissement sur un motif de l'opera Robert Devereus de Donizetti, Op. 121 (Leipzig: Hofmeister, 1842)
   Variations on a Valse by the Duke of Reichstadt, ca. 1842, for flute.

Hupfeld, Bernerd (1717–1796)

MGG attributes to Hupfeld a *Concerto* for flute and orchestra.

Iansen, Giovanni

Grand Sonata for flute and piano
MS I:Bc

Ivanschiz, Amandus (eighteenth century)

MGG attributes to Ivanschiz the following manuscripts in D:KA:
   (Three) *Sonatas* in G, G, and D Major for flute and strings
   (Two) *Sonatas* in C Major for flute and strings
   (Two) *Sonatas* in C and F Major for flute and strings
   Trio in F Major for flute and strings
   Trio in G Major for flute and strings

Jadassohn, Salomon (1831–1902)

MGG attributes to Jadassohn the following:
Serenade in D Major, Op. 80, for flute and strings
Notturno in G Major, Op. 133 (1897), for flute and piano
Capriccio in D Minor, Op. 137 (1898), for flute and piano

Jadin, Hyacinthe (1769–1802)

Trio, for flute, harp, and piano
EP   (Paris: Naderman, ca. 1800)
    GB:Lbm H.173.b.(7.)

MGG also attributes to Jadin three *Quartets* for flute and strings.

Jadin, Louis Emmanuel (1768–1853)

MGG attributes to Jadin the following works:
Nocturne (Paris: Erard) for flute or violin and piano
(Three) *Sonatas*, Op. 10, (Paris: Imbault) for clavecin and flute
(Three) *Sonatas*, Op. 13 (Paris: Imbault) for flute and piano
Fantasie avec variations (Paris: Duhan) for piano and flute
Grand Nocturne Concertante (Paris: Sieber) for piano and violin or flute
(Three) *Nocturnes* for flute
Sonata in G Major for flute and piano
Symphonie concertante for piano and flute

Janitsch, Johann Gosslich

(Nine) *Quartets* (ca. 1794) for flute and strings
MS A:Wn Sm 12027–12035

(Five) *Quartets* for flute and strings
MS (Wien: Traeg's *Catalog*, 1799)

Jansa, Leopold (1795–1875)

MGG attributes to Jansa the following works:
Variations, Op. 4 (Paris: Costallat) for flute and strings
Variations sur une Cavatine de Carafa, Op. 6, for flute and strings
Polonaise Brilliante, Op. 31 (Leipzig: Cranz) for flute and piano

Jenson, Niels Peter (1802–1846)

MGG attributes to Jenson the following works:
> (Twelve) *Etudes*, Op. 25 (Kopenhagen: Milde) for flute
> (Three) *Fantasies or Caprices*, Op. 14 (Kopenhagen: Milde) for flute
> (Six) *Solos*, Op. 17 (Kopenhagen: Milde) for flute
> *Themes Varies* (Hamburg: Cranz) for flute
> *Sonata* for flute and piano
> *Concerto* for flute and orchestra

Jusdorff, ?

Sainsbury identifies Jusdorff as a flutist at Göttingen and composer of several volumes of flute music published in Offenbach after 1799.

Kaiser, Johann

> *Fantasie* for flute
> MS A:Wgm VIII 9158

Kalick, ?

Sainsbury identifies Kalick as a German composer of flute music in Vienna before 1799.

Kalkbrenner, Friedrich Wilhelm (German, 1785–1849)

MGG attributes to Kalkbrenner the following:
> *Sonata*, Op. 39 (Simrock) for piano and flute, with ad lib cello
> *Duo*, Op. 47 (Leipzig: Breitkopf & Härtel), for piano and violin, or flute
> *Notturno* in G Major, Op. 86 (Kistner) for piano and flute

Sainsbury attributes to Kalkbrenner a *Grand Waltz*, Op. 63, for piano and flute.

Kalliwoda, Johann Wenzel (German, 1801–1866)

> *Grand Divertissement* in G Major, Op. 52 for flute and orchestra
> MS D:KA, according to MGG

Kammel, A. (Czech composer)

> (Eight) *Quartets* for flute and strings
> MS (Wien: Traeg's *Catalog*, 1799)

Kauer, Ferdinand (Moravian, 1751–1831)

MGG attributes to Kauer a *Symphonie concertante* for flute and orchestra and (Three) *Sonatas* for flute and piano.

Keiser, Reinhard (German, 1674–1739)

MGG attributes to Keiser two *Sonatas* (1720) for flute and strings.

Keith, Robert William

Sainsbury attributes to Keith instruction books for flute.

Keller, C.

Sainsbury identifies Keller as a German composer of flute music living in Vienna in 1825. Among his compositions, Sainsbury includes:
Variations for flute and piano
Fantaisie, Op. 6, for flute and piano
Pot-pourri, Op. 4, for flute and strings
Grand Polonoise, Op. 13, in D Major for flute and orchestra

Khayll, Aloys (German, 1791–1868)

MGG attributes to Khayll a *Variations brilliant*, Op. 1 (Wien, 1829) for flute and piano.

Kirnberger, J. Philippe (German, 1721–1783)

Solo for flute and bass
MS B:Bc Wotquenne 5570

Kleinknecht, Jakob Friedrich (1722–1794)

MGG attributes to Kleinknecht (Six) Sonatas da Camera (Nurnberg: Haffner, 1748) and a *Sonata* in D Major (MS, D:Mbs) for flute and bass.

Klingenbrunner, G.

Sainsbury identifies Klingenbrunner as the composer of (Fifteen) *Variations on a Theme d'Alcina*, Op. 1 (Leipzig, 1802), for flute.

Kloffler, Johann Friedrich (d. 1792)

Sainsbury identifies Kloffler as the composer of many published works for flute.

Klose, F. J.

Sainsbury identifies Klose as the composer of a *Fourth Divertimento* for piano and flute, or horn.

Knorr, Iwan Otto (German, 1853–1916)

MGG attributes to Knorr a *Trio* for flute, violin and viola.

Koczwara, Franz

MGG attributes to Koczwara (Six) *Easy Duetts*, Op. 8 (1780), for violin and flute.

Kohault, Josef (Czech composer)

Concerto in G Major for flute and strings
MS I:Gl M.4.27.8

König, Johann Mattheus

Sonata in A Major for flute and violin discordato and bass
MS D:B Mus.Ms. 11825 [cited in MGG]

Konink, Servaas de (Dutch, d. 1717)

(Twelve) *Sonatas* for flute and bass
MS D:W [cited in MGG]

Körner, Gotthilf Wilhelm

(Thirteen) *Variations on a theme of Mozart*
MS A:Wgm VIII 1520

(Thirteen) *Variations*, Op. 1, for flute and bass
MS (Wien: Traeg's *Catalog*, 1799)

(Eleven) Variations, Op. 2, for flute and bass
MS (Wien: Traeg's *Catalog*, 1799)

Körner, Johann

Variations for flute and bass
MS I:Gl M.4.27.7

Sainsbury identifies a J. Wilhelm Korner as a flutist at Cassel and composer of flute works published in Offenbach in 1798.

Kospoth, Otto Karl (German, 1753–1817)

MGG attributes to Kospoth (Six) *Quartets*, Op. 5 (Offenbach: André) for flute and strings.

Krasinsky and Vogel, Louis

(Six) *Duetts*, for flute and violin
EP   (London: Walker, ca. 1800)
  GB:Lbm G.421.p.(1.)

Kraus, Joseph Martin (German, 1756–1792)

Quartet for flute and strings
MS   A:Wgm XI 23523

Quintet in D Major for flute and strings
MS   (Wien: Traeg's *Catalog*, 1799)

MGG also attributes to Kraus a *Quintet* in D Major, Op. 7 (Paris: Pleyel, 1799) for flute and strings.

Krebs, Johann Tobias (German, 1690–1762)

MGG attributes to Krebs three *Sonatas* (MS, D:B) for flute and bass.

Krebs, Johann Lewis (d. 1780)

Sainsbury identifies this composer as the court organist to the Duke of Saxe-Weimar and the pupil of Bach. He was the composer of eight *Sonatas* for harpsichord and flute.

Kreith, Carl (Austrian, 1746–1809)

Divertimento for flute solo
MS   A:Wgm VIII 6278

Divertimento for solo flute
MS   (Wien: Traeg's *Catalog*, 1799)

(Six) *Variations* for flute solo
MS   A:Wgm VIII 1151

(Twelve) *Variations* for flute
MS   A:Wgm VIII 8889
  A:Wgm has numerous EP's of Kreith's music.

(Six) *Variations*, Op. 55, for flute solo
EP   (Bronsvico: Magazino di Musica, ca. 1800)
  GB:Lbm G.71.(4.)

(Eighteen) *Variations* for solo flute
MS (Wien: Traeg's *Catalog*, 1799)

(Three) Trios for flute and strings
MS (Wien: Traeg's *Catalog*, 1799)

Sainsbury identifies Kreith as a flutist in Vienna.

Krenn, Franz (Austrian, 1839–1890)

Offertorium, for Bass, flute solo, organ, and orchestra
MS A:Wn Sm 0595, ch XIX 7 fol.

Kress, Johann Jakob (German, d. 1730)

MGG attributes to Kress the following works:
    (Seven) *Sonatas* for flute and bass
    Solo for flute and bass
    Concerto for violin or flute and bass

Kretschmer, Edmund (1830–1908)

MGG attributes to Kretschmer a *Sextet*, Op. 40 (Berlin: Luckhardt) for flute and strings.

Kreusser, Georg Anton (German, 1743–1810)

(Six) *Quartets*, Op. 8, for flute and strings
EP   (Amsterdam: Hummel, ca. 1780)
        GB:Lbm G.425.

(Six) *Quartets* for flute and strings
MS (Wien: Traeg's *Catalog*, 1799)

(Six) *Quintets* [Op. 10] for flute and strings
MS (Wien: Traeg's *Catalog*, 1799)

Krommer, Franz (Bohemian, 1759–1831)

Concerto in F Major, for flute and orchestra
MS A:Sca Hs. 1825

Concerto in G Major, for flute and orchestra
MS A:Sca Hs. 1826

Concerto in F Major, for flute and orchestra
EP   (1802)
        A:Sca 43575

Concerto in G Major, Op. 30, for flute and orchestra
EP (Paris: Duhan)
  F:Pn Vm.24.161

Polonaise for flute and 3 strings
MS A:Wgm XI 10725

Quartet for flute and strings
MS A:Wn Sm 16170

Quartet, Op. 13, for flute and strings
MS (Wien: Traeg's *Catalog*, 1799)

Quintet ('Alla Pollacca') for flute and strings
MS A:Wgm XI 1496

Variations for flute and 3 strings
MS A:Wgm XXI 1097

Kugler, Lorenz (German composer)

Concert Fantasie, for flute and orchestra
MS H:Bn Ms.Mus.92

Kuhlau, Friedrich (German/Danish, 1786–1832)

(Two) *Stücke,* Op. 112, for flute and piano
MS A:Wn Sm 22793

Kunze, Carl H.

Sainsbury identifies Kunze as a professor of music at Heilbronn and composer of music for the flageolet, 1793–1800.

Kunzen, Adolph Carl (1720–1781)

MGG attributes to Kunzen eight *Concerti* for flute.

La Barre, Michel de (1675–1743)

Premier Livre de Pieces pour la Flute
EP (Paris: the composer, 1710)
  GB:Lbm C.64.

MGG also attributes to La Barre *Pieces*, Op. 4 (Paris: Ballard, 1703) and *Deuxieme livre* (Paris, 1710) for flute.

Lacy, Raphino (1797–1867)

Sainsbury identifies Lacy as a Spanish violinist and composer of works for piano and flute and a *Quintet* for flute, piano and strings.

Lambert, Johann Henry

Sainsbury identifies Lambert as the author of *Observations sur les Tons des Flutes*, which Sainsbury calls, 'a very interesting subject, and well treated in the *Memoires de l'Academie de Berlin, 1775.*'

Lang, Johann Georg (Bohemian/German, 1724–1800)

(Six) *Sonatas* for cembalo, flute, and strings
MS D:B Mus.Ms. 12 511/1/6 [cited by MGG]

Latilla, Gaetano (Italian, 1711–1788)

Trio, for flute and strings
MS I:Gl M.3b.24.34

Latour, T. (1766–1837)

MGG attributes to Latour two *Sonatas*, Op. 2 (London: Bland & Weller, 1796) for piano and flute.

Lebrun, Ludwig (1752–1790)

MGG attributes to Lebrun (Two) *Concerti* (Paris: Sieber) and a *Concerto* in C Major (Breitkopf & Härtel, 1782–1784) for flute.

Le Chevalier, Amedée (French, 1654–1720)

Solo for flute and bass
MS D:KA Ms. 80

Concerto for flute and strings
MS D:KA Ms. 81 [cited in MGG]

Leffloth (or Loffelloth), Johann Matthaus (b. 1705)

MGG attributes to Leffloth (Six) *Sonatas* (Nürnberg, 1729) for flute (or violin) and bass and a *Concerto* in D Major (Nürnberg, 1730) for flute and cembalo.

Leidesdorf, Maximilian (1787–1840)

MGG attributes to Leidesdorf five editions of works for flute and piano.

Leister, Franz (German composer)

Fantaisie, Op. 7, for flute
EP   (Wien: Artaria, ca. 1800)
    GB:Lbm G.71.(10.)

Lemoyne, Jean Baptist (d. 1796)

MGG attributes to Lemoyne a *Sonata*, Op. 22 (Paris: the composer) for flute and piano.

Lessel, François (Polish, 1780–1835)

Quartet for flute and strings
MS A:Wgm XI 1103
EP   (Wien: Artaria, 1806)

MGG attributes to Lessel a *Variations* for flute and orchestra.

Leuis, ?

Concerto for flute and orchestra
MS A:Wgm VIII 1403

Lichtenthal, Peter (1780–1853)

MGG attributes to Lichtenthal a *Concertino* (1823) or flute and orchestra and a *Variations* (1820) for flute and piano.

Lickl, F. Georg (Austrian, 1769–1843)

Sainsbury identifies Lickl as the composer of (Three) *Quartets*, Op. 5 (Wien, 1798) for flute and strings.

Lidarti, Cristiano (Austrian, 1730–1793)

(Six) *Duets* for flute and clavicembalo
MS I:Gl SS.A.1.21.(G.8)

Lidel, ?

(Six) *Duets* for flute and bass
MS (Wien: Traeg's *Catalog*, 1799)

Liebeskind, Johann Henrick

Sainsbury identifies Liebeskind as the author of a study of the flute published in the Leipzig *Musikzeitung*, '*Bruchstucke aus einem noch ungedruckten philosophisch-praktischen Versuche uber die Natur und das Tonspiel der deutschen Flote.*'

Linley, Francis

(Three) *Solos*, for flute with cello ad lib
EP (London: Walker, ca. 1800)
   GB:Lbm G.280.g.(17.)

Locatelli, Pietro (Italian, 1695–1764)

(Twelve) *Sonatas*, Op. 2, for flute
EP (Amsterdam: the composer, 1732)
   GB:Lbm G.280.i.(5.)
EP (London: Walsh, ca. 1736)
   GB:Lbm G.294.b

Loeillet, Jean, of Ghent (d. 1728)

Sonatas, Op. 1, for flute and harpsichord
EP (London: Walsh and Hare, ca. 1710)
   GB:Lbm I.26.(1.)

(Twelve) *Sonatas*, Op. 2, for flute
EP (London: Walsh and Hare, ca. 1715)
   GB:Lbm I.26.(2.)

(Twelve) *Sonatas*, Op. 3, for flute
EP (London: Walsh and Hare, ca. 1715)
   GB:Lbm I.26.(3.)

(Six) *Sonatas*, Op. 5, for flute, oboe, or violin and bc
EP (Amsterdam: Roger, ca. 1725)
   GB:Lbm G.685.b.(2.) [Book 1]
   GB:Lbm G.685.b.(3.) [Book 2]

Sonata (Nr. 5) for flute and bass
MS B:Bc Wotquenne 5575 [bass part realized by F. A. Gavaert]

Sainsbury identifies this Loeillet as a 'famous master of the flute … who by his industry acquired a fortune of 16,000 Pounds.'

Loeillet, John (of London)

Sonatas, Op. 1, 'for a Comon flute or Hoboy, also for two flutes and bc'
EP (London: Walsh and Hare, ca. 1725)
   GB:Lbm G.685.b.(1.)
   GB:Lbm H.17.(6.) [another copy]

(Twelve) *Solos*, Op. 3, for flute
EP (London: Walsh and Hare, ca. 1725)
   GB:Lbm H.3845.
   GB:Lbm H.3845.a. [another edition by the same publisher]

Lorenzoni, Antonio

Saggio per ben sonare il Flatotraverso
EP (Venice: Francesco Modena, 1779)
   GB:Lbm 7897.h.3.

Mahault, Antoine (Dutch/German flautist)

(Four) *Concerti* for flute and orchestra
MS B:Bc Wotquenne 5577

Sainsbury identifies 'Mahout' as the author of a flute *Method*, which appeared in two editions, in addition to nine volumes of solos, duets, Concerti, etc. for flute. He adds that the composer, in 1760, 'fled from his creditors to a convent in France.'

Mainzer, ?

Sainsbury identifies Mainzer as a clarinetist at the court of the Margrave of Schwendt and the composer of some flute music published in Offenbach.

Malzat, Ignaz (Austrian, 1757–1804)

Quartet for flute and strings
MS (Wien: Traeg's *Catalog*, 1799)

(Two) *Quintets*, in D and G Major, for flute and strings
MS (Wien: Traeg's *Catalog*, 1799)

Mancinelli, Domenico (1775–1802)

(Six) *Notturni* for flute and violin
MS (Wien: Traeg's *Catalog*, 1799)

(Five) *Sonatas* for flute and bass
MS I:Gl SS.B.1.3.(H.8)

Sainsbury indicates Mancinelli published much flute music in Paris, London, and Berlin, ca. 1775

Mancini, Francesco (Italian, 1672–1737)

MGG attributes to Mancini twelve *Concerti* for flute and strings.

Marcello, Benedetto (Italian, 1686–1739)

Svonate a fluto
EP   (Venetia: Sala, 1712)
   I:Bc

Fourth Sonata for flute and piano
EP   (Bologna: Tedeschi)
   I:Bc

MGG attributes to Marcello (Twelve) *Suonate*, Op. 2 (Venedig, 1772 and later Amsterdam: Roger, 1732) for flute and bass.

Marchal, P. A.

Sainsbury identifies Marchal as a German musician in Paris who published in 1795 (Six) *Rondos,* Op. 10, for piano and flute, or violin.

Martinn, Jacques Joseph (1775–1836)

MGG attributes to Martinn *Trios*, Op. 25 (Paris: Leduc), for flute and strings and *Duos*, Op. 35 (Paris: Dufaut & Dubois), for flute and violin.

Matauschek, ?

Sainsbury identifies Matauschek as an abbe, resident in Vienna who published, ca. 1803, *Quatorze Variations*, Op. 5, for flute.

Mattei, Stanislao (1750–1825)

(Two) *Responsori* (1784), for TTB, flute, viola, and organ
MS I:Bsf M.Mattei II-10

Mattheson, Johann (1681–1764)

Der Brauchbare Virtuoso, for flute and claviere
EP   (Hamburg: Schiller- und Kissnerischen, 1720)
      GB:Lbm H.52.b.

MGG also attributes to Mattheson (Twelve) *Sonatas* (Hamburg: Schiller-Kissnerischen, 1720), for violin or flute and bass.

Mazzinghi, Felice (eighteenth century)

MGG attributes to Mazzinghi the following works:
      (Three) *Quartets*, Op. 3 (1789) for piano, flute, or violin, and viola
      The Siege of Bangalore, Op. 8 (1792) for piano and flute, or violin
      (Twenty-four) *Sonatas* for piano and violin, or flute (eight series of three each: Op. 9, 10, 14–16, 19, 28, and 29, 1793–1800)

McGibbon, William (Scottish, 1690–1756)

MGG attributes to McGibbon (six) *Sonatas* (Edinburgh: Cooper, 1740) for flute or violin.

Mederitsch, Johann (1752–1835)

MGG attributes to Mederitsch a *Concerto* for flute and two *Quintets* (Wien: Hoffmeister, 1796) for piano, flute, and strings.

Mele, Giovanni Battista (b. 1701)

MGG attributes to Mele a *Concerto* (1725) for flute and strings.

Menesini, Bartolomeo

Sonata in G, for flute and bass
MS   S:Uu Ms. 198

Mercy, Louis (French, d. 1751)

(Six) *Solos*, for flute and bc
EP   (London: Walsh and Hare, ca. 1725)
      GB:Lbm G.524.

Mereaux, Jean-Nicolas (1767–1838)

MGG attributes to Mereaux *Sonates* (Paris: Pacini) and *Nocturne* (Paris: Richaut) for flute and piano.

Metzger, Georg (d. 1794)

Sainsbury identifies Metzger as a flutist in the Bavarian court and composer of the following, all 1782–1789:

(Six) *Concerti*, Op. 1, Nr. 1–6, for flute
(Six) *Trios*, Op. 2, for flute and strings
(Six) *Quartets*, Op. 5, for flute and strings
(Six) *Sonatas*, Op. 6, for flute and bass
(Three) *Trios Concerti*, Op. 7, Nr. 7–9, for flute

Metzger, K.

Trio for flute, violin, and keyboard
MS   A:Wgm XI 10930

Mica, Jan Adam, Moravian, 1746–1811

MGG attributes to Mica (Six) *Quartets or Quintets* for flute and strings.

Miller, Edward (1735–1807)

MGG attributes to Miller (Six) *Solos*, Op. 1 (London: Johnson, 1763) for flute and *The New Flute Instructor* (London, 1800).

Miller, F. J.

Sainsbury identifies Miller as the composer of (Three) *Quintets* (Mannheim, 1797) for cembalo, flute and strings.

Minguet e Irol, Pablo (d. 1801)

MGG attributes to Minguet the *Reglas y advertencias generales para taner la flauta ...* (1754).

Mizler von Kolof, Lorenz (1711–1778)

MGG attributes to Mizler four *Sonatinas* for flute (Leipzig, 1754).

Molique, Wilhelm Bernhard (1802–1869)

MGG attributes to Molique a *Quintet*, Op. 35, for flute and strings.

Molter, Johann Melchior (1695–1765)

MGG attributes to Molter nine *Concerti* for flute and one *Concerto* for flute d'amore (MS, D:KA).

Mondrik, ?

Sainsbury identifies Mondrik as the composer of an *Air varié* (Paris, 1792) for flute.

Monn, Georg Matthias (1717–1750)

(Three) *Parthias* for flute and strings
MS (Wien: Traeg's *Catalog*, 1799)

(Three) *Trios* for flute and strings
MS (Wien: Traeg's *Catalog*, 1799)

Montéclair, Michel Pinolet (1667–1737)

MGG attributes to Monteclair *Concerts* (Paris: Boivin) for flute alone.

Monzani, Tebaldo (1762–1839)

MGG attributes to Monzani the *Instructions for the German Flute* (1804) and *A Word or Two on the Flute* (1826).

Moralt, Adam (1741–1811)

MGG attributes to Moralt two *Quartets* (München: Falter) for flute and strings.

Moscheles, Ignaz (1794–1870)

MGG attributes to Moscheles a *Grand Sonata concertante*, Op. 44 (Wien: Artaria, 1819) for flute and piano and a *Divertissements a la Savoyarde*, Op. 78 (Leipzig: Hofmeister, 1829) for piano and flute.

Mosel, Giovanni Felice

Serenata for flute and three strings
MS (Wien: Traeg's *Catalog*, 1799)

Sainsbury identifies Mosel as the first violinist in the orchestra at Florence in 1788.

Mosonyi, Mihaly (Hungarian, 1815–1870)

MGG attributes to Mosonyi a *Septet* for flute and strings.

Mozart, Wolfgang A. (1756–1791)

(Two) *Duets* for flute and bass
MS (Wien: Traeg's *Catalog*, 1799)

Grand Trio for flute and strings
MS (Wien: Traeg's *Catalog*, 1799)

Mühling, Heinrich (1786–1847)

MGG attributes to Muhling a *Quintet*, Op. 27 (Leipzig) for flute and strings.

Müller, ?

(Six) *Duets* for flute and violin
MS (Wien: Traeg's *Catalog*, 1799)

(Six) *Quartets* for flute and strings
MS (Wien: Traeg's *Catalog*, 1799)

Muller, Adolph, Jr.

Liebesgruss (1856), for singer, flute, and piano
MS A:Wn Sm 23694

Müller, August Eberhard (1767–1817)

(Two) *Concerti* for flute
MS (Wien: Traeg's *Catalog,* 1799)

(Six) *Duets* for flute and violin
MS A:Wn Sm 2962

Fantasia for flute and orchestra
MS A:Wn Sm 15735

MGG also attributes to Müller the following:
    (Eight) *Concerti* for flute and orchestra
    Variations and Polonaise, Op. 23
    Fantasia, Op. 40
    Grosse Sonata, Op. 38 for piano and flute
    Various educational materials

Sainsbury mentions that Müller's *Grand Sonate*, Op. 26, for piano, 'has the peculiar fate
    of being in many places copied with Mozart's name, and is still considered by many as
    belonging to that composer.' The flute works he attributes to Müller are:
    (Two) *Concerti,* Op. 6, 7 (Berlin, 1795) for flute
    Concertino, Op. 10 (Offenbach) for flute
    Grand Concerto, Op. 16, in D Major (Leipzig, 1798)
    Journal pour la Flute … Pieces d'une difficulte progress (Hamburg, 1799, Cah. 1–4)

Concerto, Op. 19 (Leipzig) in E Minor
Concerto, Op. 20 (Leipzig) in D Major
An unpublished *Concerto*, 'in a strong style'
Theme varie (on Mozart) for flute and flute with violin (Leipzig)
Grand concerto, Op. 27 (Leipzig) in C Major
Grand Concerto, Op. 30 (Leipzig) in G Major]

Müller, F.

Sainsbury identifies Muller with (Three) *Quartets*, Op. 1 (Hamburg, 1799), for flute and strings.

Müthel, Johann Gottfried (1728–1788)

MGG attributes to Muthel a *Sonata* (MS, *D:B*) for flute and bass.

Nageli, Hans Georg (1773–1836)

MGG attributes to Nageli ten unnamed works for flute and piano.

Nardini, Pietro (1722–1793)

Concerto in G Major for flute and orchestra
MS I:Gl M.23.38

Concerto in D Major for flute and orchestra
MS I:Gl M.3.23.37

Sonata in D Major for flute and bass
MS I:Gl M.3b.23.32

Sonata in G Major for flute and bass
MS I:Gl M.3b.23.33

(Two) *Sonatas* for flute, violin and bass
MS I:Gl M.3.23.36 e 39

(Three) *Sonatas* for flute, violin and bass
MS I:Gl M.3.23.19/21

Sainsbury identifies Nardini also as the composer of (Six) *Trios* (London) for flute and strings.

Naudot, ?

Sainsbury identifies Naudot as a flautist in Paris and composer of flute music published there between 1720–1726.

Neubauer, Franz (Bohemian, 1760–1795)

Concerto, Op. 13, in G Major, for flute
MS (Wien: Traeg's *Catalog*, 1799)

(Three) *Trios*, Op. 14, for flute and strings
EP   (Offenbach: Andre, ca. 1800)
      GB:Lbm G.694.
MS (Wien: Traeg's *Catalog*, 1799)

Sainsbury identifies Neubauer as the concert-master to the Princess of Schaumburg at
    Buckeburg, adding, 'On Bach's death, Neubauer got in full possession of his place.
    His *Harmony for Wind Instruments only, accompanied by a violin and a Bass*, in which all the
    intricacies of wind instruments, calculated for the utmost effect, are intended to be
    concentrated in one piece.' Sainsbury gives the following additional works for flute
    by Neubauer:
      (Three) *Trios*, Op 3 (Augsburg), for flute and strings
      (Six) *Sonatas*, Op. 21 (Brunswick, 1798), for flute and bass
      (Three) *Quartets* (Vienna) for flute and strings

Neubauer, Johann (German composer)

(Six) *Quartets*, for flute and strings
EP   (Wien: Hoffmeister, ca. 1800)
      GB:Lbm G.467.

Neumann, G. (Dutch composer)

Sainsbury identifies Neumann as a German composer of (Three) *Pieces* for piano with flute,
    or violin.

Neusser

Concerto, in D Major, for flute
MS (Wien: Traeg's *Catalog*, 1799)

Nicholson, Charles (1795–1837)

Sainsbury identifies Nicholson as an 'eminent flutist' and lists his following works for flute:
      Preceptive Lessons for the Flute
      A Volume of Studies … in the form of Preludes … and Exercises
      Twelve Select Melodies, with Variations, with piano
      Four Volumes of Flute Beauties (48 works)
      Twelve Select Airs, with Variations, with piano

Le Bouquet, or Flowers of Melody
Potpourri, with piano
(Six) *Fantasias*
Mayseder's Polonaise, with piano
Introduction and Variations on 'The Fall of Paris,' with piano

Nicolai, Johann Gottlieb (German composer)

(Six) *Sonatas* for flute and continuo
MS   A:Wn Sm 2963

(Six) *Sonatas* for flute and bass
MS   (Wien: Traeg's *Catalog*, 1799)

Oestreich, Carl (Frankfurt composer, nineteenth century)

Quintet for flute and strings
MS   BRD:F Mus.Hs. 751 [incomplete]

Sonata for flute and klavier
MS   BRD:F Mus.Hs. 801

[Untitled work] ('1833') for singer, chorus, flute, and piano
MS   BRD:F Mus.Hs. 769

Variations (1824) for flute
MS   BRD:F Mus.Hs. 757

Oswald, James (1711–1768)

(Six) *Solos*, for flute and harpsichord
EP   (London: Randall, ca. 1775)
       GB:Lbm E.1290.c.(5.)

MGG attributes to Oswald (Six) *Divertimenti*, Op. 2 (1747), for flute and bass.

Pacini, Giovanni (1796–1867)

(Three) *Domine*, for Tenor, flute, and orchestra
MS   I:Ls B.65

Parcham, Andreas (d. 1730)

Sainsbury identifies Parcham as the composer of (Twelve) *Sonatas* (Amsterdam) for flute and bass.

Parke, William

(A Second Set of Three) *Solos*, Op. 8, for flute
EP   (London: Fentum, ca. 1800)
    GB:Lbm G.70.b.(12.)

Parry, John (b. 1776)

Sainsbury identifies Parry as the author of a great many works for winds, especially for the 'double and single flageolet,' and flute.

Pepusch, Johann (1667–1752)

(Six) *Cantatas*, four with flute and two with trumpet and voice
EP   (London?)
    GB:Lbm G.222.(2.)

Solos, for flute and bassoon with harpsicord
EP   (London: Walsh, Randall, and Hare, ca. 1710)
    GB:Lbm H.250.c.(2.)

Pesch, ?

Quartet, for flute and strings
MS B:Bc Wotquenne 6891

Petersen, P.

Sainsbury identifies Petersen as a flutist at Hamburg toward the end of the eighteenth century, 'second only to Dulon on his instrument.' He apparently composed much flute music in addition to mechanical improvements for the instruments, several of which Sainsbury describes.

Pez, Johann Christoph (Italian, 1664–1716)

Sonata da camera for 1 or 2 flutes
MS   D:Dlb [according to MGG]

Pezold, Christian (German, 1677–1733)

MGG attributes to Pezold a *Trio* in D Major for violin, flute and bass.

Pfeiffer, A.

Air varie for flute and guitar
MS A:Wgm XI 49852

Introduction and Variations for flute and piano
MS A:Wgm VIII 30639

Variations for flute and guitar
MS *A:Wgm* VIII 30641

Variations for flute and guitar
MS A:Wgm XI 49853

A:Wgm has numerous EPs by this composer.

Pfeiffer, Johann (German, 1697–1761)

MGG attributes to Pfeiffer two *Concerti* and a *Sonata* for flute.

Philbert, Philippe (1650–1712)

Menuet for flute
MS F:Pn Vm.7.3555, p. 112 [according to MGG]

Philidor, Michel Danican (1683–1722)

MGG attributes to Philidor two sets of *Pieces pour la flute* (Paris, 1716, 1718).

Piazza, Gaetano

Concerto for flute and orchestra
MS CH:Bu kr.IV.205

Pichl, Wenzel (Czech, 1741–1805)

Divertimento, Nr. 2, for flute, violin, and keyboard
MS A:Wgm XI 10918

Divertimento, Nr. 6, for flute, violin, and keyboard
MS A:Wgm XI 10919

(Six) *Divertimenti* for flute and strings
MS (Wien: Traeg's *Catalog*, 1799)

(Three) *Quartets*, Op. 12, for flute and strings
EP (Paris: Sieber, ca. 1790)
    GB:Lbm G.469.(2.)

(Three) *Quartets* for flute and strings
MS (Wien: Traeg's *Catalog*, 1799)

Sonata for flute, violin, and cello
MS B:Bc Wotquenne 6893

Sonata for flute and bass
MS (Wien: Traeg's *Catalog*, 1799)

(Two) *Trios* for flute, violin and bass
MS B:Bc Wotquenne 6894

Plach, Giovanni

(Three) *Quartets*, for flute and strings
MS I:Gl N.1.7.3.(Sc.39)

(Four) *Sonatas* for flute, violin and bass
MS I:Gl M.4.25.21/24

Sonata for flute, violin and bass
MS I:Gl SS.A.1.15.(G.7)

Platti, Giovanni (1700–1763)

(Six) *Sonatas* for flute and bass
MS (Wien: Traeg's *Catalog*, 1799)

Pleyel, Ignaz (Austrian, 1757–1831)

Concerto for flute
MS I:Bc

(Twelve) *Duos*, Liv. 1, 2, 4, and 5, for flute and violin
MS (Wien: Traeg's *Catalog*, 1799)

(Three) *Quartets*, Op. 17, for flute and strings
EP (London: Longman & Broderip, ca. 1790)
    GB:Lbm H.318.(6.)

(Three) *Quartets*, Op. 19, for flute and strings
EP (London: Longman & Broderip, ca. 1790)
    GB:Lbm H.318.(7.)

(Two) *Quartets*, for flute and strings
MS I:Vmc Busta 59–72-N.68, N. 61

(Six) *Quartets* for flute and strings
MS A:Wn Sm 12256–12261

Quartet, Nr. 2, for flute and strings
MS (Wien: Traeg's *Catalog*, 1799)

(Three) *Quartets,* Op. 28, for flute and strings
MS (Wien: Traeg's *Catalog*, 1799)

(Six) *Quartets,* Op. 4, Liv. 1 & 2, for flute and strings
MS (Wien: Traeg's *Catalog*, 1799)

(Three) *Quartets,* Op. 23, for flute and strings
MS (Wien: Traeg's *Catalog*, 1799, as well as forty-nine Quartets being arrangements under
    Pleyel's name)

Quintet, Op. 18, for flute and strings
MS (Wien: Traeg's *Catalog*, 1799)

MGG attributes to Pleyel (Six) *Quintets* for flute and strings.

(Three) *Solos* for flute and viola
MS (Wien: Traeg's *Catalog*, 1799)

(Four) *Sonatas* for flute and bass
MS (Wien: Traeg's *Catalog*, 1799)

Grand Trio for flute, cello, and piano
MS A:Wgm XI 968

Trio, for oboe or flute, violin, and cello
MS I:Vmc Busta 54–58-N.58

Trio, Op. 2, for flute and strings
MS (Wien: Traeg's *Catalog*, 1799)

(Three) *Trios* for flute and strings
MS (Wien: Traeg's *Catalog*, 1799)

Sainsbury adds the following works:
    (Six) *Sonates*, Op. 16 (Offenbach, 1790) for clavecin and flute
    (Three) Quartets, Op. 20 (1789) for flute and strings
    (Three) *Quartets*, Op. 25 (Offenbach) for flute and strings

Poessinger, Franz (1767–1827)

(Six) *Quartets* for flute and strings
MS (Wien: Traeg's *Catalog*, 1799)

MGG attributes to Poessinger the following works:
    Quintet, Op. 19 (Wien: Kunst u. Industrie ..., 1806)

(Three) *Quartets*, Op. 17 (Wien: Artaria, 1806)
(Three) *Themes variés*, Op. 29 (Wien: Artaria, 1808)
(Twelve) *Ländler*, Op. 26 (Wien: Artaria, 1808) for flute

Pohl, G.

(Three) *Quartets*, Op. 6, for flute and strings
MS (Wien: Traeg's *Catalog*, 1799)

Pollet, Jean

Sonata, for harp and flute
EP (Paris: the composer, ca. 1790)
      GB:Lbm H.173.b.(13.)

Ponzo, Giuseppe

Sonata a tre (1760), for flute, violin and bass
MS I:Gl SS.B.1.12.(H.8)

Popp, Guglielmo

Third Concerto, Op. 216, for flute and orchestra
EP (Amburgo: Cranz)
      I:Bc

Concertstuck for flute and orchestra
EP (Amburgo: Cranz)
      I:Bc

Porro, Pierre-Jean (1759–1831)

MGG attributes to Porro *Airs varies et prelude*s for '1 or 2 Flageolette.'

Praeger, Heinrich Aloys (1783–1854)

MGG attributes to Praeger a *Quartet*, Op. 20, for flute and strings.

Prati, Alessio (1750–1788)

MGG attributes to Prati a *Concerto* in G Major for flute.

Proto, Tommaso

Concerto in G Major for flute, 2 violins and bass
MS S:Uu Ms. 244

Concerto in G Major for flute and orchestra
MS S:Uu Ms. 245

Punto, Giovanni [pseud. for Stich, Johann] (1748–1803)

(Six) *Trios*, for flute and strings
EP (London: Napier, ca. 1790)
    GB:Lbm H.2852.a.(10.)

Trio for flute, violin and bass
MS B:Bc Wotquenne 6946

Purcell, Daniel (1664–1717, brother to Henry Purcell), and Finger, Gottfried (Moravian, 1656–1730)

(Six) *Sonatas*, for flute and bc
EP (London, ca. 1710)
    GB:Lbm H.17.(2.)

MGG attributes to Purcell nine *Sonatas* for flute and bass, 1698–1710.

Quanten, Chevalier de

Sainsbury identifies Quanten as the composer of (Six) *Solos*, Op. 1 (Amsterdam, 1780)
    for flute.

Quantz, Johann (1697–1773)

Andante (1752) for flute and piano
MS A:Wn Sm 24379

Arioso concertant, for flute, 2 violins, and viola
MS B:Bc Wotquenne 6947

(Thirty-four) *Caprices* for flute and bass
MS (Wien: Traeg's *Catalog*, 1799)

(Eight) *Caprices* for solo flute
MS (Wien: Traeg's *Catalog*, 1799)

Concerto for flute and orchestra
MS B:Bc Wotquenne 5583

Concerto in G Major for flute and strings
EP (Leipzig: Breitkopf & Härtel)
    I:Bc

Concerto, in C Major, for flute
MS (Wien: Traeg's *Catalog*, 1799)

(Fifteen) *Fantasien and Preludien* for solo flute
MS (Wien: Traeg's *Catalog*, 1799)

(42) *Pieces* for solo flute
MS (Wien: Traeg's *Catalog*, 1799)

(Eight) *Solos* for flute and bass
MS (Wien: Traeg's *Catalog*, 1799)

(Four) *Sonatas* for flute and bass
MS B:Bc Wotquenne 5584

Sonata in B♭ and *Sonata* in A minor, for 2 flutes and bc., and (Two) *Sonatas* in G, for flute,
    violin and bc
MS GB:Lbm R.M.21.b.7.

Concerto in G, for flute and strings
MS GB:Lbm Add. 31902.

Arioso, for flute and orchestra
MS GB:Lbm Add. 32147.

Concerto in D, for flute and orchestra
MS GB:Lbm Add. 32158.

Concerto in C, for flute and orchestra
MS GB:Lbm Add. 32593. [incomplete by Quantz; finished by Frederick the Great]

Concerto in C, for flute and orchestra
MS GB:Lbm Add. 33217.

(Two) *Concerti*, (1758), for flute and orchestra
MS GB:Lbm Add. 33295)

Solos, Op. 1, for flute or oboe with bc
EP (London: Walsh, ca. 1730)
    GB:Lbm G.281.

Solos, Op. 2, for flute or oboe, with bc
EP (London: Walsh, ca. 1730)
    GB:Lbm G.1090.(1.)

Trio for flute, violin and bass
MS B:Bc Wotquenne 6948

Trio for flute, violin and bass
MS B:Bc Wotquenne 6951

Versuch einer Anweisung die Flote
EP   (Breslau, Korn dem altern, 1789)
  GB:Lbm 7897.cc.1. [third edition]

Quattordici, Domenico (1710–1740)

Quartet for flute and strings
MS I:Gl M.4.28.18

Quentin, Bertin (d. 1770)

MGG attributes to Quentin *Sonates* (Paris: the composer, 1730) for flute and bass.

Queralt, Francisco (1740–1825)

MGG attributes to Queralt the *Aria*, 'Donzells triunfante,' for voice and flute.

Raimondi, Ignazio (1737–1813)

(Six) *Quartets*, Op. 10, for flute and strings
EP   (London: the composer, c. 1790)
  GB:Lbm G.470.b.(1.)

MGG also attributes to Raimondi (Three) *Trios concertants*, Op. 14 (London: Monzani, 1800), for flute and strings and (Two) *Quartuors concertants*, Op. 7 (Amsterdam: Hummel, 1780) for flute and strings.

Ranish, John

(Eight) *Sonatas*, Op. 1, for flute and bc
EP   (London: Simpson, ca. 1740)
  GB:Lbm F.15.

(Twelve) *Solos*, Op. 2, for flute and bc
EP   (London: Walsh, ca. 1740)
  GB:Lbm G.73.

Rault, Felix

A Grand Solo, for flute
EP   (London: Fentum, ca. 1790)
  GB:Lbm G.70.b.(13.)

(Three) *Trios* for flute and strings
MS (Wien: Traeg's *Catalog*, 1799)

Sainsbury identifies Rault as a 'celebrated French flautist,' and composer of (Two) *Concerti*, in D and G Major (Paris) for flute.

Rava, Gennaro (d. 1779)

Concerto in B Minor (dedicated to 'S.E., Duca di Reitano') for flute and strings
MS I:Gl M.4.28.5

Concerto in B Minor (dedicated to 'S.E., Duca di Reitano') for flute and strings
MS I:Gl M.4.28.6

Reichardt, G. F.

(Six) *Quartets* for flute and strings
MS (Wien: Traeg's *Catalog*, 1799)

Reichelt, F. G. (d. 1798)

Sainsbury identifies Reichelt as the composer of a *Divertimento* for piano, flute, and strings (1798) as well as a 'controversial' treatise.

Reid, John (1721–1807)

MGG attributes to Reid *A Collection of Airs and Marches* for 2 violins or 2 flutes (1756) and (Six) *Solos* (London: Oswald, 1756) for flute and bass.

Reinards, William

(Six) *Sonatas* for flute, violin and bc
EP (London: Welcker, ca. 1770)
    GB:Lbm G.409.g.(4.)

(Six) *Sonatas*, Op. 2, for flute and bc
EP (London: Fentum, ca. 1770)
    GB:Lbm G.70.c.(4.)

Sainsbury identifies Reinards as a flutist who published many works for flute in Amsterdam and Berlin between 1765–1797.

Reymann, Giovanni

Concerto, in G Major, for flute
MS (Wien: Traeg's *Catalog*, 1799)

Quartet for flute and strings
MS (Wien: Traeg's *Catalog*, 1799)

Rhein, Fr.

(Two) *Concerti* for flute
MS (Wien: Traeg's *Catalog*, 1799)

Cadenzen 'for all keys' for solo flute
MS (Wien: Traeg's *Catalog*, 1799)

Sainsbury identifies two flutists with this name: a 'celebrated' flutist and composer for flute
who died in Vienna before 1799; and a flutist engaged in 1800 in the Theater des Vari-
etes, Paris, who published there duets for flutes.

Richard, ?

(Four) *Quartets* for flute and strings
MS (Wien: Traeg's *Catalog*, 1799)

Richter, Franz Xavier (1709–1789)

Divertimento for flute, cello, and clavecin
MS B:Bc Wotquenne 6980

MGG attributes to Richter the following additional works:
    (Three) Concerti in G Major for flute (MS, D:Rtt)
    (Two *Concerti* in D Major for flute (MS, D:Rtt)
    Concerto in G Major for flute (MS, D:KA)
    Concerto in G Major for flute (EP, Catalog Dunwalt, 1770)

Riedt, Friedrich (1710–1783)

MGG attributes to two *Solos* for flute and a Quartet for flute and strings.

Riepel, Joseph (1709–1782)

Sainsbury identifies Riepel as Director of music for the Prince of Tour and Taxis in
Regensburg during the middle of the eighteenth century and composer of the following works:
    Sonata, Op. 48, for piano and flute
    Divertimento, Op. 62, for piano and flute
    (Two) *Sonatas*, Op. 76, for piano and flute

Rietz, Johann Christian (1767–1828)

MGG attributes to Rietz a *Sonata* in G Minor, Op. 42 (Leipzig: Breitkopf & Härtel) for flute and piano.

Ries, Ferdinand (1784–1838)

MGG attributes to Ries a *Quartet*, Op. 145 and a *Quintet*, Op. 107, for flute and strings.

Rigel, Anton (1745–1807)

Quintet for flute and strings
MS B:Bc Wotquenne 6982

MGG attributes to Rigel (Six) *Quartets*, Op. 1 (Paris: Le Menu et Boyer, 1776), for flute and strings and (Six) *Trii* for flute and strings (MS, D:KA).

Rimbault, Stephen Francis (English, 1773–1837)

Sainsbury identifies Rimbault as the composer of (Three) *Grand Sonatas* for piano and flute.

Rolla, Alessandro

(Two) *Quartets*, Op. 2, for flute and strings
EP (Wien: Cappi, ca. 1800)
    GB:Lbm H.2801.a.(2.)

(Six) *Quartets* for flute and strings
MS (Wien: Traeg's *Catalog*, 1799)

(Six) *Quartets* for flute and strings
MS I:Bc

Quintet for flute, 2 Mandolini, viola, and bass
MS I:Gl SS.B.1.1.(H.8)

Röllig, Johann Georg (1710–1790)

MGG attributes to Rollig four *Concerti* and (Six) *Trios* for flute and strings.

Romberg, Andreas (1767–1821)

Sainsbury identifies Romberg as the composer of (Three) *Quintets* for flute and strings.

Romberg, Bernhard Heinrich (1767–1841)

MGG attributes to Romberg a *Concerto* in D Major, Op. 30, for flute.

Roseingrave, Thomas (1690–1766)

MGG attributes to Roseingrave (Twelve) *Solos* (London: Cooke, 1730) for flute and bass.

Sainsbury relates of Roseingrave, a church organist, that, 'if any one coughed, sneezed, or blew his nose,' during his performance, 'would instantly stop playing and run out of the church, seemingly in the greatest pain and terror.'

Rosetti, Antonio (1746–1792)

Concerto, in G Major, for flute
MS (Wien: Traeg's *Catalog*, 1799)

(Three) *Quartets* for flute and strings
MS (Wien: Traeg's *Catalog*, 1799)

Sainsbury identifies Rosetti as the composer of three *Concerti* for flute published in Paris.

Roth, Philipp Jakob (1779–1850)

MGG attributes to Roth the following works:
 Trois themes varies (Wien: Artaria, 1807) for flute and strings
 Rondo for flute and orchestra
 Concerto in G Major for flute and orchestra
 Concerto in D Major (Leipzig: Breitkopf & Härtel, 1819) for flute and orchestra

Roussel, Albert (1869–1937)

Trio, Op. 40, for flute, viola, and cello
MP (Paris: Durand, 1930)
 A:Wgm

Ruge, Filippo

(Eighteen) *Capricci* for flute solo
MS I:Gl N.1.6.7.(Sc.40)

Concerto in A Major for flute and strings
MS I:Gl N.1.2.7.(Sc.40)

(Two) *Concerti* in G and D Major, for flute and strings
MS I:Gl SS.A.1.15.(G.7)

Ruppe, Christian Friedrich (1753–1826)

MGG attributes to Ruppe a *Sonata*, Op. 11 (1801) for flute, or violin, and bass.

Rust, ?

(Twenty-four) *Variations* for flute and bass
MS (Wien: Traeg's *Catalog*, 1799)

Rutherford, David

MGG attributes to Rutherford the following works:
 The Complete Tutor for ye Flute (1750)
 The Gentleman's Pociket Guide (c. 1765)
 The Compleat Tutor for the Fife (1750)

Ryba, Jakub Jan (Czech, 1765–1815)

MGG attributes to Ryba two *Quartets* for flute and strings.

Salieri, Antonio (1750–1825)

Concerto for flute and orchestra
MS A:Wn Sm 3722

Concerto for flute and orchestra
MS A:Wn Sm 3723

Sammartini, Giovanni Battista (1698–1775)

MGG attributes to Sammartini a large number of unnamed Duets, Trios, Quartets and
 Quintets for flute and strings and gives more information for the following:
 (Six) *Sonatas call'd Notturni*, Op. 9 (London: Walsh, 1762) for flute and strings
 (Six) *Solos*, Op. 8 (London: Walsh, 1759) for flute and violin
 (Six) *Easy Solos* (London: Bremner, 1765) for flute

Sammartini, Giuseppe (1693–1751)

MGG attributes to Sammartini the following works:
 (Twelve) *Sonatas*, Op. 2 (Amsterdam, 1736) for flute and bass
 (Six) *Solos*, Op. 13 (London: Johnson, 1760) for flute or 'Hautboy'
 (Six) *Sonatas* (London: Cox, 1762)

San Martini, Giovanni

(Six) *Easy Solos*, for flute and bc
EP (London: Bremner, ca. 1765)
 GB:Lbm G.280.b.(13.)

(Six) *Sonatas*, for flute and bc
EP   (London: Hummel, ca. 1765)
    GB:Lbm G.409.g.(5.)

San Martini, Giuseppe

(Six *Solos*), Op. 2, for flute and bc
EP   (London: Walsh, ca. 1740)
    GB:Lbm G.422.b.(6.)

(Twelve) *Sonatas*, Op. 2, for flute and bc
EP   (Amsterdam: Le Cene, ca. 1730)
    GB:Lbm G.86.f.

(Six) *Solos*, Op. 4, for flute and bc
EP   (London: Walsh, ca. 1740)
    GB:Lbm G.422.b.(7.)

(Six) *Solos*, Op. 8, for flute, violin, or oboe and bc
EP   (London: Johnson, ca. 1760)
    GB:Lbm G.422.b.(8.)

Sarri, Domenico Natale (1679–1744)

MGG attributes to Sarri a *Concerto* for flute.

Scarlatti, Pietro Alessandro (1660–1725)

MGG attributes to Scarlati the following works:
    Clori mia, (1699) for Soprano and flute
    Ardo, e ver, for Soprano and flute
    Fuori di sua capanna for Soprano, violin or flute and bass
    Sonata in F Major for flute and strings
    Sonata for D Major for flute and strings
    Suite in F Major (1699) for flute and bass
    Suite in G Major (1699) for flute and bass

Schafrath, Christoph (b. 1709)

Sainsbury identifies Schafrath as the composer of (Six) *Duetti*, Op. 1 (1752) for cembalo and
    violin or flute.

Schale, Christian Friedrich (1713–1800)

MGG attributes to Schale the following works:
    Three *Concerti* for flute
    Solo for flute and bass
    (Two) *Soli* for flute and bass in *Allerley v. Verschiedenen Tonkunstlern* (Berlin, 1760)

Scheibe, Johann Adolph (1708–1776)

Concerto for flute and strings
MS B:Bc Wotquenne 5588

Schetky, Johann (German, 1740–1820)

(Six) *Sonatas* for flute and strings
MS (Wien: Traeg's *Catalog*, 1799)

(Six) *Trios* for flute and strings
MS (Wien: Traeg's *Catalog*, 1799)

Schickhard, Johann

L'Alphabet de la Musique, (Twenty-four) *Sonatas*, Op. 30, for flute and bc
EP (Londres, ca. 1735)
    GB:Lbm E.203.

Solos, Op. 20, for flute or oboe with bc
EP (London: Walsh and Hare, ca. 1730)
    GB:Lbm H.3055.(2.)
    GB:Lbm G.1090.(3.) [another copy]

(Twelve) *Sonatas*, Op. 17, for flute and bc
EP (London: Walsh and Hare, ca. 1730)
    GB:Lbm H.250.c.(5.)

Schloeger, Mathaeus (Austrian, 1722–1766)

Concerto in G Major for flute and strings
MS I:Gl SS.A.1.15.(G.7)

Schmitt, Joseph, German, 1734–1791

(Six) *Quartets*, Op. 10, for flute and strings.
EP (Amsterdam: the composer, c. 1785)
    GB:Lbm G.427.(2.)

(Six) *Quartets* for flute and strings
MS (Wien: Traeg's *Catalog*, 1799)

(Six) *Trios*, Op. 8, for flute and strings
EP (Amsterdam: Diederichs, ca. 1790)
     GB:Lbm G.415.(9.)

MGG also attributes to Schmitt the following:
     (Six) *Quatuors*, Op. 3 (Hummel, 1768), for flute and strings
     (Three) *Quatuors*, Op. 9 (1778), for flute, cembalo and strings
     (Six) *Trios*, Op. 13 (Amsterdam: Diederichs, 1782), for flute and strings
     (Three) *Trios*, Op. 16 (Amsterdam, 1785), for flute and strings

Schmittbaur, Joseph (1718–1809)

(Three) *Quartets*, Op. 3, for flute and strings
EP (Wien: Artaria, ca. 1775)
     GB:Lbm G.389.

(Six) *Quartets* for flute and strings
MS (Wien: Traeg's *Catalog*, 1799)

MGG also attributes to Schmittbaur the following:
     (many) Concerti for flute
     (Six) *Quartets*, Op. 1 (Mannheim: Gotz; also Karlsruhe and Ofenbach) for flute
          and strings
     (Three) *Quartets*, Op. 3 (Offenbach: André) for flute and strings

Schmotzer, Jacob Edward

Fantasie for flute and orchestra
MS A:Wgm VIII 18948

Schmügel, Johann Christoph (1727–1798)

Divertimento for flute and strings
MS B:Bc Wotquenne 7041

Quartet for flute and strings
MS B:Bc Wotquenne 7040

Schneider, ?

Concerto, in D Major, for flute
MS (Wien: Traeg's *Catalog*, 1799)

Schnell, Johann Jakob (1687–1754)

MGG attributes to Schnell the following:
  (Six) *Parthiae Trisonae*, Op. 2 (Erlangen: Schmatz, 1731) for flute, violin and bass
  (Six) *Sonatae Trisonae*, Op. 4, for violin, flute and viola d'amour
  (Six) *Trios,* Op. 5, for violin, flute and bass
  (Six) *Trios*, Op. 7, for violin, flute, and bass

Schnepf, Josef (b. 1785)

MGG attributes to Schnepf (Three) *Lieder* (Prag, 1820) for 3 voices, flute, and piano.

Schonebeck, C. S. (1758–1800)

Concerto for flute and orchestra
MS B:Bc Wotquenne 5593

Schroeter, Johann Samuel (German, 1752–1788)

(Six) *Sonatas* for flute and cimbalo
MS I:Bsf M.S.I-14

Schubert, Joseph (1757–1837)

MGG attributes to Schubert a *Concerto*, Op. 1 (Berlin, 1789), for flute.

Schültz, Lebrecht (eighteenth century)

Concerto in G Major for flute and strings
MS D:KA Ms. 893

(Three) *Sonatas*, in E Minor, G and D Major, for flute and cello
MS D:KA Ms. 894–896

Sonata in D Major for flute, violin and cello, or bassoon
MS D:KA Ms. 898 [according to MGG]

Schültze, J. C.

Concerto for flute a bec and orchestra
MS B:Bc Wotquenne 5594

Concerto for flute traversiere and orchestra
MS B:Bc Wotquenne 5595

Schumann, Friedrich

(Three) *Sonatas*, Op. 3, for harpsichord and flute
EP (London: the composer, ca. 1760)
     GB:Lbm G.418.a.(5.)

(Six) *Sonatas*, Op. 8, of which three are for flute and strings
EP (London: Napier, ca. 1780)
     GB:Lbm H.2852.a.(13.)

Schuster, Joseph (1748–1812)

Concerto in D Major for flute and orchestra
MS I:Gl M.4.32.1/2

Schwindel, Friedrich (1737–1786)

Concerto in A Major for flute and strings
MS I:Gl SS.A.1.15.(G.7)

(Six) *Trios* for flute and strings.
MS (Wien: Traeg's *Catalog*, 1799)

Serini, Giovanni (b. 1710)

MGG attributes to Serini (Six) *Sonatas* for flute.

Seyeller, ?

Concerto, in F Major, for flute
MS (Wien: Traeg's *Catalog*, 1799)

Seydelmann, Franz (1748–1806)

MGG attributes to Seydelmann (Six) *Sonatas* (Dresden: Hilscher, 1785) for flute
    and cembalo.

Seyfert, Johann Gottfried (1731–1772)

MGG attributes to Seyfert (Six) *Trios* (Leipzig: Breitkopf, 1762) for flute and strings.

Shield, William (1748–1829)

(Six) *Quartets*, Op. 3, of which one is for flute and strings.
EP (London: Napier, ca. 1780)
     GB:Lbm G.417.i.(3.)

MGG also attributes to Shield *The Highland Reel* (London: Longman & Broderip, 1788) for flute.

Skotscoffsky, G. V.

Trio for flute and strings
MS (Wien: Traeg's *Catalog,* 1799)

Sola, Charles (b. 1786)

Sainsbury identifies Sola as the composer of two *Trios* for piano, flute, and a string instrument, and a great deal of popular arrangements for flute.

Somis, Giovanni Battista (1686–1763)

Sinfonia for flute and bass
MS I:PAc [according to MGG]

MGG also attributes to Somis three Concerti for flute.

Sorge, Georg Andreas (1703–1778)

MGG attributes to Sorge (Six) *Sonatas* for flute and bass and a *Trio* for flute and strings.

Sperger, Johann (d. 1812)

Sainsbury identifies Sperger as the composer of (Three) *Trios,* (1796) for flute and strings.

Spourni, Wenceslaus

(Six) *Sonatas,* for flute and bc
EP (London: Simpson, ca. 1745)
    GB:Lbm G.409.(10.)

Stabingher, Mathias (1750–1815)

Divertimenti, for flute, violin, and cello
MS I:Vmc Busta 21–30-N.27

Duet for flute and violin
MS I:Gl M.4.29.41

Quartet for flute and strings
MS A:Wgm XI 8580

(Two) *Sonatas* for flute, violin and bass
MS I:Gl SS.A.1.15.(G.7)

(Five) *Sonatas* for flute and bass
MS I:Gl M.4.29.32 e 34 e 35/37

(Two) *Sonatas* for flute, violin and bass
MS I:Gl M.4.29.33 e 39

MGG also attributes to Stabinger (Six) *Quatuors concertants*, Op. 4 (Venedig, 1792) for flute and strings and *Sextuors concertants*, Op. 5 (Venedig, 1792) for flute strings and 2 horns.

Stadler, Joseph Franz (1725–1765)

Concerto for flute and orchestra
MS CH:EN [according to MGG]

Stamitz, ?

Trio for flute, violin and bass
MS B:Bc Wotquenne 7070

Stamitz, Anton (1754–1809)

MGG attributes to Stamitz a *Concerto* for flute.

Stamitz, Carl

Concerto, in D Major, for flute
MS (Wien: Traeg's *Catalog*, 1799)

(Six) *Trios*, Op. 14, for flute and strings
EP (London: Welcker, ca. 1780)
    GB:Lbm G.415.(8.)

Stamitz, Johann Carl

Concerto, for flute and orchestra
EP (London: Welcker, ca. 1770)
    GB:Lbm G.474.a.(18.)

Stamitz, Johann Wenzel Anton (1717–1757)

MGG attributes to Stamitz the following works:
      (Three) *Concerti* for flute (MS, D:KA)
      (Three) *Concerti* for flute (MS, D:Rtt)
      Trio in C Major for flute and strings (MS, B:Bc)
      Trio in G Major for flute and strings (MS, D:DS)
      Trio in F Major for flute and strings (MS, D:KA)

Stanley, John (1713–1786)

(Eight) *Solos,* Op. 1, for flute and harpsichord
EP   (London: Johnson, ca. 1745)
      GB:Lbm E.17.(2.)

(Six) *Solos*, Op. 4, for flute
EP   (London: Johnson, ca. 1745)
      GB:Lbm E.17.(1.)

MGG also attributes to Stanley (Six) *Concerti*, Op. 2 (London: the composer, 1742) for flute
   and strings.

Steibelt, Daniel (1756–1823)

(Three) *Sonatas*, Op. 36, for piano and flute
EP   (London: Dale, ca. 1799)
      GB:Lbm H.301.(3.)

(Three) *Sonatas*, Op. 38, for piano and flute
EP   (London: Preston, ca. 1800)
      GB:Lbm H.301.(4.)

Steinfeld, Albert Jacob (1741–1815)

MGG attributes to Steinfeld (Six) *Solos*, Op. 1 (Berlin: Hummel, 1784) for flute and bass.

Stölzel, Gottfried Heinrich (1690–1749)

MGG attributes to Stolzel *Concerti* in E Minor and C Major for flute.

Stricker, Augustin Reinhard (1675–1720)

MGG attributes to Stricker the following works:
      Sonata for flute, violin, and bassoon (MS, D:ROu)
      Sonata for flute and cembalo (MS, D:ROu)
      Trio for violin, flute and bass (MS, D:Dlb)

Struck, Paul (1776–1820)

MGG attributes to Struck (Three) *Sonatas*, Op. 4, for piano, flute, and bass.

Strunz, Georg (1781–1852)

MGG attributes to Strunz a *Concerto* for flute.

Stuntz, Joseph Hartmann (1793–1859)

Concerto for Flute
MS D:Mbs Mus.Ms. 4029

Suppé, Franz von (1819–1895)

In primo amore for flute and piano
EP (Wien: Spinas)
    A:Wgm VIII 25949

Sutton, W. W. (b. 1793)

Sainsbury identifies Sutton as the composer of *Six Airs, with Variations* for the flute.

Tacet, Joseph

(Six) *Divertimenti*, Op. 4, for flute and bc
EP (London: the composer, 1770)
    GB:Lbm E.340.(4.)

(Thirty-six) *Preludes*, for flute, oboe, or violin
EP (London: Longman, Lukey, ca. 1775)
    GB:Lbm A.205.

(Six) *Solos*, Op. 1, for flute and bc
EP (London: the composer, ca. 1770)
    GB:Lbm E.18.

(Six) *Sonates*, Op. 1, for flute and bc
EP (Paris: Marchand, 1771)
    GB:Lbm E.201.b.(5.)

Tadolini, Giovanni (1793–1872)

Introduzione e rondo for flute and piano
MS I:Bc

Taffanel, Paul (1844–1908)

MGG attributes to Taffanel unnamed works for flute and piano, as well as various educational materials.

Taillard, l'aine

Sainsbury identifies Taillard as first flute at the Concert Spirituel in Paris in 1760 and composer of music for his instrument.

Tartini, Giuseppe (1692–1770)

(Four) *Concerti* for flute and orchestra
MS S:Uu Ms. 291–294

MGG attributes to Tartini two *Concerti* (MS, S:Skma and one in 'Neapel, Kons.,
   Ms.24.1.4') for flute.

Tauber, J. F. (d. 1803)

Sainsbury identifies Tauber as a flutist and composer for his instrument.

Telemann, Georg (1681–1767)

Concerto for flute and orchestra
MS B:Bc Wotquenne 5598

Concertino for flute and strings
MS (Wien: Traeg's *Catalog*, 1799)

(Six) *Quartets*, for flute and strings
EP (Paris: the composer, ca. 1740)
      GB:Lbm G.401.(2.)

Sonata for flute, violin and clavecin
MS B:Bc Wotquenne 7117

Terschak, Adolf (Czech, b. 1832)

Nachtschatten, Polka Mazurka for flute and piano
MS A:Wn Sm 5811

Plaisir du soire for flute and piano
MS A:Wn Sm 24685

Schuff ('*Lieder ohne Worte*') for flute and piano
MS A:Wn Sm 35686

Tessarini, Carlo (1690–1766)

(Twelve) *Solos*, Op. 2, for flute or oboe
EP (London: Walsh, 1736)
      GB:Lbm G.688.

Thornowets, ?

Sonate da Camera, for flute and bc
EP (Londres: Meares, ca. 1720)
    GB:Lbm G.689

Sonate da Camera, for flute and bc
EP (London: Walsh and Hare, ca. 1725)
    GB:Lbm G.280.b.(15.)

Tischler, Conrad

Flöten-Schule
MS A:Wn Sm 22917

Todt, Johann Christoph (1833–1900)

MGG attributes to Todt three *Concerti* for flute.

Toeschi, Carlo (1722–1788)

Concerto in C Major for flute and strings
MS I:Gl SS.A.2.11.(H.7)

Concerto in D Major for flute and strings
MS I:Gl T.C.1.1.(Sc.122)

(Six) *Quartets*, Op. 1, for flute and strings
EP (London: Welcker, ca. 1770)
    GB:Lbm G.413.(16.)

(Six) *Quartets*, for flute and strings
EP (Paris: Chevardiere, ca. 1775)
    GB:Lbm G.417.d.(1.)

Toeschi, Giovanni (1735–1800)

Duos for flute and cembalo
MS A:Wgm XI 988

Quartet for flute and strings
MS B:Bc Wotquenne 7131

Tollet, Thomas (seventeenth century?)

Sainsbury identifies Tollet as the author of a work on the 'directions to play on the French flageolet.'

Tolou, A.

(Six) *Sonates*, for solo flute
EP (Paris: the composer, 1741)
　　GB:Lbm K.7.f.16.(1.)

Topham, William

(Six) *Sonates*, for flute
EP (London: Walsh and Hare, ca. 1700)
　　GB:Lbm D.150.(5.)

(Six) *Sonatas*, Op. 2, for flute
EP (London: Walsh, Hare, and Randall, ca. 1710)
　　GB:Lbm C.105.a.(6.)

Torlez, C.

(Six) *Duetti* for flute and violin
MS A:Wn Sm 3001

MGG also attributes to Torlez (Six) *Duos*, Op. 1 (Paris: Boyer, 1783) for flute and violin and a *Concerto* (Paris, 1783) for flute and orchestra.

Traeg, A.

(Seven) *Fantasies* for solo flute
MS (Wien: Traeg's *Catalog*, 1799)

Trento, Vittorio (1761–1833)

Trio, for flute, violin, and bass
MS I:Vmc Busta 31–53–N.45

Triebensee, Joseph (1772–1846)

(Twenty-Four) *Variations* ('on a theme d'Augustin')
MS A:Wgm VIII 3535

Tromlitz, Johann

Uber die Flöten, (a method)
EP   (Leipzig: Böhme, 1800)
  GB:Lbm 7897.cc.16.

Unterricht die Flöte
EP   (Leipzig: Böhme, 1791)
  GB:Lbm 7896.de.1.

Tuch, Heinrich (1766–1821)

MGG attributes to Tuch a *Sinfonia pastorale*, Op. 25 (1810) for piano, flute, and strings.

Uber, Alexander (1783–1824)

MGG attributes to Uber an *Air varié*, Op. 1 and 2, for flute and orchestra and (Three) *Themes varié* for solo flute.

Uccelli, Giovanni

(Six) *Quartets* for flute and strings
MS   I:Gl SS.B.2.31/34

Umlauff, Ignaz (1746–1796)

(Six) *Quartets* for flute and strings
MS   A:Wn Sm 12547 [according to MGG]

Umstatt, Joseph (d. 1762)

MGG attributes to Umstatt the following works:
  (Two) *Quartets* for flute and strings (MS, D:B and D:KA)
  (Seven) *Concerti* for flute (six in D:KA; one in D:Dlb)
  Trio for flute and strings (MS, D:KA)

Valentine, Robert (English flautist, 1680–1735)

(Twelve) *Sonatas*, Op. 2, for flute and bc
EP   (London: Walsh and Hare, ca. 1710)
  GB:Lbm G.422.(1.)
  GB:Lbm H.11.a.(1.) [another copy]

(Twelve) *Sonatas*, Op. 3, for flute and bc
EP   (London: Walsh and Hare, ca. 1710)
        GB:Lbm H.11.a.(2.)
EP   (Amsterdam: Roger, ca. 1712)
        GB:Lbm E.22.

(Twelve) *Sonatas*, Op. 5, for flute and bc
EP   (London: Walsh and Hare, ca. 1715)
        GB:Lbm H.11.a.(3.)

Sonatas, Op. 11, for flute and bc
EP   (London: Walsh and Hare, ca. 1730)
        GB:Lbm H.11.a.(4.)

Sonata, Op. 12, for flute and bc
EP   (Roma: Cleton, 1730)
        GB:Lbm E.22.d.

Sonatas, Op. 13, for flute and bc
EP   (London: Walsh, 1735)
        GB:Lbm H.11.a.(5.)

(Twelve) *Sonatas* (c. 1780), for flute and bass
MS I:PAc

Sonata, for flute and bass.
MS I:Vmc Busta 124–149-N.124

Vanderhagen, Armand Jean (Dutch, 1753–1822)

MGG attributes to Vanderhagen a set of *Variations* for flute.

Vern, Auguste G.

MGG attributes to Vern a *Theme varié*, Op. 13 (Leipzig, 1830), for flute and piano.

Vogel, ?

(Six) *Duetti* for flute and violin
MS (Wien: Traeg's *Catalog*, 1799)

Vogl, ?

Concerto, in G Major, for flute
MS (Wien: Traeg's *Catalog*, 1799)

Sonata for flute and bass
MS   B:Bc Wotquenne 5603

Waelput, Hendrik (Flemish, 1845–1885)

MGG attributes to Waelput a *Concerto symphonique* (1866) for flute.

Wagenseil, Georg (1715–1777)

Quartet for flute and strings
MS   I:Gl T.C.1.1.(Sc.122)

MGG also attributes to Wagenseil four *Concerti* for flute and two *Sonatas* for flute
  and continuo.

Wagner, ?

(Three) *Trios* for flute and strings
MS   (Wien: Traeg's *Catalog*, 1799)

Wagner, B.

(Six) *Sonatas*, Op. 1, for flute
EP   (Paris: Berault, ca. 1780)
      GB:Lbm G.280.

Wagner, Karl Jakob (1772–1822)

MGG attributes to Wagner (Three) *Trios*, Op. 1 (Heilbrunn, 1795) for flute and strings.

Walter, Johann Ignaz (1755–1822)

MGG attributes to Walter 'various flute concerti.'

Wanhal, Jan (Bohemian, 1739–1813)

Divertimento for flute and piano
MS   A:Wn Sm 12559

Divertimento for flute and strings
MS   A:Wgm XI 10730

Quartet for flute and strings
MS   A:Wgm XI 10731

(Six) *Quartets* for flute and strings
MS   (Wien: Traeg's *Catalog*, 1799)

(Six) *Quartets*, Op. 7, for oboe or flute and strings
EP   (London: Welcker, ca. 1785
     GB:Lbm G.413.(19.)

(Six) *Sonatas*, Op. 10, for flute and bc
EP   (London: Bland, ca. 1780)
     GB:Lbm G.225.b.(8.)

(Two) *Sonatas*, Op. 10, for flute and bc
EP   (London: Campbell, ca. 1780)
     GB:Lbm G.280.c.(5.)

Variations for flute and bass
MS (Wien: Traeg's *Catalog*, 1799)

MGG attributes to Vanhal the following works:
  (Eight) *Concerti* for flute (with locations for three in manuscript)
  (Six) *Quartets*, Op. 7 (London, c. 1780), for flute and strings
  (Two) *Sonatas*, Op. 10 (London: Campbell, ca. 1780) for flute and cembalo
  (Six) *Sonatas*, Op. 10 (London, 1781)
  Quartet for flute and strings (MS, CS: Bm)
  Divertisement (Offenbach, 1790) for flute, piano, and strings
  Quadro (MS, CS:Pnm XLII E. 170) for solo flute, solo violn, viola, cello

Wassermann, Heinrich Joseph (1791–1838)

MGG attributes to Wassermann a *Quartet* in G Major, Op. 18 (München: Falter) for flute and strings.

Weideman, Charles (English, d. 1782)

(Twelve) *Sonatas* for flute and bc
EP   (London: Walsh, ca. 1745)
     GB:Lbm G.674.

Weigel, Christoph (1654–1725)

MGG attributes to Weigel (Eighteen) *Divertimenti* (MS, D:Nst) for flute and continuo.

Weiss, Franz (German, 1778–1830)

MGG attributes to Weiss a *Caprices et Variations*, Op. 3 (Wien: Kunst and Industrie, 1803), for flute and an *Introduction and Variations* (Wien: Diabelli) for flute, or violin, guitar and piano.

Weiss, G.

(Three) *Quartets*, Op. 5, for flute and strings
EP   (London: the composer)
GB:Lbm H.229.(9.)

Weiss, Karl I (1735–1795)

(Six) *Quartets*, Op. 4, for flute and strings
EP   (London: the composer, ca. 1782)
GB:Lbm G.411.a.(2.)

(Six) *Solos*, Op. 3, for flute
EP   (London: Welcker, ca. 1780)
GB:Lbm G.280.c.(6.)

(Six) *Trios,* for flute and strings
EP   (London: Welcker, ca. 1775)
GB:Lbm H.2852.a.(4.)

(Six) *Trios*, Op. 2, for flute and strings
EP   (London: Napier, ca. 1780)
GB:Lbm H.2852.a.(5.)

Sainsbury provides a description of the extraordinary life of this flautist and composer. Among his compositions for flute, Sainsbury lists numerous 'Fantasias' on various popular songs, educational works, and the following:
Concerto in D Major, Op. 1
200 *Studies* for flute, in Seven Books, Op. 3
Twelve Solos, Op. 68
Twelve Preludes, Op. 70

Weiss, Karl II (1777–1845)

MGG attributes to Weiss the following works:
Concerto, Op. 1, in D Major, for flute
Fantasias, Op. 12, 13, 14, 24, and 44 for flute
Airs variés for flute and piano
200 Studies, Op. 3, for flute
New Methodical Instructional Book, for flute

Wendling, Johann (German, 1720–1797)

Concerto, for flute or oboe
EP   (London: Preston, ca. 1785)
GB:Lbm H.3213.j.(16.)

(Six) *Sonatas*, Op. 5, for flute, violin and bc
EP   (London: Napier, c. 1775)
       GB:Lbm G.409.(12.)

(Six) *Sonatas*, Op. 7, for flute, violin and bc
EP   (London: Welcker, 1776)
       GB:Lbm H.2852.a.(1.)

Trio for flute, violin and bass
MS B:Bc Wotquenne 7183

Wenkel, Johann Friedrich (1734–1792)

MGG attributes to Wenkel a *Sonata* (Berlin: Birnstiel, 1761) for flute.

Westenholz, Friedrich (1756–1802)

MGG attributes to Westenholz a *Divertissement* Nr. 1 for flute and guitar.

Westerhoff, Heinrich (1760–1806)

MGG attributes to Westerhoff a *Concerto* (Braunschweig: Höhe, 1799) for flute.

Widerkehr, Jacob (1759–1823)

Sinphonie Concertante, for clarinet, flute, bassoon and orchestra
EP   (Paris: Erard, ca. 1800)
       GB:Lbm H.2136.b.

Concertainte, for flute, oboe, bassoon and orchestra
EP   (Paris: Erard, ca. 1800)
       GB:Lbm H.2136.a.

Wiedner, Johann Gottlieb (1714–1783)

MGG attributes to Wiedner a *Concerto* for flute and strings.

Willman, Samuel David (German, 1780–1813)

Sainsbury identifies Willman as the composer of (Three) *Quartets* (Berlin, 1789) for piano, flute and bass and (Three) *Solos* (Berlin, 1796) for flute and piano.

Wilms, Johann (1772–1847)

MGG attributes to Wilms a *Concerto* in D Major, Op. 24, and a *Concertino* in G Minor for flute.

Winter, Peter (German, 1754–1825)

MGG attributes to Winter a *Concerto* for flute.

Witt, Friedrich (1770–1836)

MGG attributes to Witt a *Concerto*, Op. 8 (Leipzig: Breitkopf & Härtel), for flute and orchestra.

Woelfl, Joseph

Sainsbury identifies Woelfl as the composer of the following:
    (Three) Sonatas, Op. 11 (Leipzig, 1800), for piano and flute
    Sonata, Op. 3 (1801), for piano and flute
    Grand Duet, Op. 46 for piano [four-hands] and flute

Wolf, Ernst Wilhelm (1735–1792)

MGG attributes to Wolf two *Quintets* (Dresden: Hilscher) for cembalo, flute and strings.

Wragg, J.

The Flute Preceptor, a method
EP (London: the author, 1790)
    GB:Lbm B.117.(1.)

Solo, Op. 4, for flute and piano
EP (London: the composer, ca. 1795)
    GB:Lbm G.221.(9.)

A Fifth Solo, for flute or oboe, with bassoon
EP (London: the composer, ca. 1800)
    GB:Lbm G.221.(10.)

Wranizky, P. (Moravian, 1756–1808)

(Six) *Quartets* for flute and strings
MS (Wien: Traeg's *Catalog*, 1799)

(Six) *Quartets* for flute or oboe and strings
MS (Wien: Traeg's *Catalog*, 1799)

Wunderlich, Johann Georg (1755–1819)

Flute method
MS A:Wn Sm 8998

MGG attributes to Wunderlich the following works:
> *Sonatas* for flute and continuo
> (Six) *Soli* for flute with 5 keys
> (Six) *Divertissement*
> (Nine) *Great Soli*
> A Volume of Studies

Sainsbury identifies Wunderlich as a flautist in the Paris Opera in 1800 and a professor in the Conservatory. Among his compositions is (Three) *Sonatas*, Op. 1 (Paris, 1802), for flute and bass.

Zach, Johann (1699–1773)

MGG attributes to Zach six *Concerti* for flute and a *Quartet* in D Major for flute and orchestra.

Zani, Andrea (Italian, 1696–1757)

MGG attributes to Zani three Concerti and a *Sonata* for flute (MS, D:KA).

Zannetti, Francesco (b. 1740)

(Six) *Solos*, for flute
EP   (London: Thorowgood, ca. 1772)
> GB:Lbm G.420.b.(8.)

(Six) *Solos*, for flute and bc
EP   (London: Thorowgood and Horne, ca. 1770)
> GB:Lbm G.71.f.(11.)

Sonata for flute and cello
MS   I:Ac Mss.N.349/5

Zarth, Georg (1708–1778)

MGG attributes to Zarth the following works:
> *Solo*, Op. 1, in G Major for flute and bass (MS, D:B)
> *Solo* in G Major for flute and bass (MS, DK:Kk)
> *Solo* in E Major for flute and bass (MS, DK:Kk)
> *Trio* in G Major for flute and strings (MS, B:Bc and D:SWl)

Zellbell, Anders (1680–1727)

MGG attributes to Zellbell a *Concerto* for flute.

Zielche, Johann Heinrich

Sainsbury identifies Zielche as a flutist to the King of Denmark and composer of flute music published in Berlin between 1775 and 1790.

Zimmermann, ?

(Twelve) *Quintets* for flute and strings
MS (Wien: Traeg's *Catalog*, 1799)

Zumsteeg, Johann Rudolf (1760–1802)

MGG attributes to Zumsteeg two *Concerti* for flute and orchestra and (Three) *Duos* for flute and cello.

MUSIC WITH SOLO OBOE

Anfossi, Pasquale (1727–1797)

(Three) *Quintets*, for oboe and strings
MS I:MOe Mus.D.4–8

Anguillar, Sante (Italian oboist, 1804–1860)

Concerto in D Major (1806) for oboe and orchestra
MS I:Bc

Anonymous

Concerto in F Major (18th c.) for oboe and orchestra
MS *D:Ds* Mus.Ms. 1239

Compleat Tutor for the Hautboy
EP   (London: Simpson, ca. 1746)
      GB:Lbm D.47.f.(2.)

Compleat Tutor for the Hautboy
EP   (London: Thompson, ca. 1790)
      GB:Lbm B.160.g.(4.)

Modern Musick-Master (includes, 'Directions for playing on the Flute … Newest Method for German flute … Instructions upon the Hautboy')
EP   (London: Bow Church Yard, 1731)
      GB:Lbm D.40

New and Complete Instructions for the Oboe or Hoboy
EP   (London: Longman & Broderip, ca. 1780)
     GB:Lbm B.160.h.

Rondeau ('as performed by Mr. Fischer') for oboe
EP
     GB:Lbm H.141.a.(18)

(Five) *Trios* for oboe and strings
MS (Wien: Traeg's *Catalog*, 1799)

Babell, Wm. (d. 1722)

(Twelve) *Solos*, for violin, Hoboy or German Flute
EP   (London: Hare, ca. 1725)
     GB:Lbm G.1090.(4.)

(Twelve) *Solos*, for violin, Hoboy or German Flute
EP   (London: Hare, ca. 1725)
     GB:Lbm G.1090.(5.)
     GB:Lbm G.908 [another edition]

Bach, Johann Christian (1735–1782)

Quartet for oboe and strings
MS I:Gl SS.A.1.11.(G.7)

Quartet for oboe and strings
MS I:Gl SS.A.2.7.(G.8)

Quartet for oboe and strings
MS I:Gl SS.A.2.12

Bach, K. P. E. (1714–1788)

Concerto for oboe and strings
MS B:Bc Wotquenne 5519

Concerto for oboe and strings
MS B:Bc Wotquenne 5520

Solo for oboe
MS B:Bc Wotquenne 5521

Barbandt, Carl (1716–1775)

(Six) *Sonatas* for 2 flutes, oboes, or violins
EP (London, ca. 1755)
   GB:Lbm F.14

Barth, Cristiano

Concerto, Op. 12, for oboe and orchestra
EP (Leipzig: Breitkopf & Härtel)
   I:Bc

Divertimento, Op. 8, for oboe and string quartet
EP (Leipzig: Breitkopf & Härtel)
   I:Bc

Rondo svizzero, Op. 10, for oboe and orchestra
EP (Leipzig: Breitkopf & Härtel)
   I:Bc

Baumgarten, Carl F.

Concerto, for oboe, flute or clarinet and orchestra
EP (London: Longman and Broderip, ca. 1790)
   GB:Lbm H.102.(3.)

(Six) *Quartets*, Op. 2, for oboe or flute and strings
EP (London: Forster, ca. 1785)
   GB:Lbm G.437

Besozzi, Alessandro (1702–1775)

Concerto in G Major ('for Johann Fischer, 1757') for oboe and strings
MS GB:Lbm Add.34717

(Six) *Solos*, for flute, oboe, or violin and bc
EP (London: Chapman, ca. 1758)
   GB:Lbm G.221.(6.)
   GB:Lbm G.422.b.(3.) [another copy]

Bitti, Martino (1656–1743)

Concertos ('dont il y en a un pour la Trompette ou le Haubois')
EP (Amsterdam: Roger, ca. 1715)
   GB:Lbm G.917

Bissoli, Mattio (1711–1780)

Sonata in G Minor, for oboe and bass
MS   I:Gl SS.B.1.10

Bochsa, Karl (d. 1821)

(Three) *Quartets* for oboe and strings
EP   (Paris: Imbault)
   F:Pn Vm.7.6664

(Three) *Quartets* for oboe and strings
EP   (Paris: Imbault)
   F:Pn Vm.7.10.404

Braun, Charles (English, b. 1868)

(Eighteen) *Caprices* for oboe
EP   (Leipzig: Breitkopf & Härtel)
   I:Bc

Sainsbury identifies Braun as 'a celebrated performer on the oboe in Berlin. He has lately
   published a curious paper on the character and treatment of the oboe, an extract from
   which may be seen in the *Harmonicon*, I, 163.']

Caffare, Giuseppe

Concerto in D Major, for oboe and orchestra
MS   I:Gl SS.B.1.15

Cardonne, Jean Baptiste (1730–1792)

MGG attributes to Cardonne a *Concerto* in G Major of 1778.

Danzi, Franz (1763–1826)

(Seven) *Quartets* for oboe and strings
MS   A:Sca Hs. 54

DeMicco, Domenico

Concerto in D Major, for oboe and orchestra
MS   I:Gl M.3b.24.2

DeSimoni, Pietro

Concerto in C Major, for oboe and orchestra
MS I:Gl SS.B.1.13

Devienne, François (1759–1803)

MGG attributes to Devienne (Six) *Sonatas* (Paris: Sieber) and (Six) *Sonatas* (Paris: Le Duc) for oboe and bass.

Dittersdorf, Karl (1739–1799)

MGG attributes to Dittersdorf (three) *Concerti* for oboe and a *Divertimento* in F Major for solo violin, solo oboe, 2 horns and strings.

Druschetzky, Georg (1745–1819)

Concerto for oboe, timpani and orchestra
MS H:Bn Ms.Mus. 1515

Quartet, for oboe and strings
MS H:Bn Ms.Mus.1558

Quartet, for oboe and strings
MS H:Bn Ms.Mus.1559

Quartet, for oboe and strings
MS H:Bn Ms.Mus.1560

Quartet, for oboe and strings
MS H:Bn Ms.Mus.1561

Quartet, for oboe and strings
MS H:Bn Ms.Mus.1562

Quartet, for oboe and strings
MS H:Bn Ms.Mus.1566

Quartet, for oboe and strings
MS H:Bn Ms.Mus.1568

Quartet, ('una cosa rara') for oboe and strings
MS H:Bn Ms.Mus.1577

(Three) *Quartets* for oboe and strings
MS H: Bn Ms.Mus 1577

Quintet, for oboe and strings
MS H:Bn Ms.Mus. 1571

Quintet, for oboe and strings
MS H:Bn Ms.Mus. 1572

Eberl, Anton Franz Josef (1765–1807)

MGG attributes to Eberl a *Quintet*, Op. 48 (1806), in C Major, for oboe and strings.

Fasch, Johann Friedrich (1688–1758)

(Fourteen) *Concerti* for one or two oboes
MS D:Ds Mus.Ms. 290/6 through 290/18; and 1229/4

Ferlendis, Giuseppe (1755–1802)

Concerto in C Major, for oboe and orchestra
MS I:Gl M.4.31.37

Concerto in C Major, for oboe and orchestra
MS I:Gl M.4.31.38

Sainsbury identifies Ferlendis as, 'a celebrated performer on the hautboy,' born in Venice and arriving in London in 1793. He composed much music for the oboe.

Fiala, Joseph (1754–1816)

Concerto (1802) for oboe and orchestra
MS A:Sca Hs. 81

Concerto (1804) for oboe and orchestra
MS A:Sca Hs. 1691

(Six) *Quintets* for violin, oboe, and strings
MS (Wien: Traeg's *Catalog*, 1799)

Fischer, Johann Christian (1733–1800)

Concerto, Nr. 1, for oboe and harpsichord
EP (London: Welcker, ca. 1770)
     GB:Lbm H.726.1.(4.)
     GB:Lbm G.474.a.(13.) [another edition]

Concerto, Nr. 7, for oboe and orchestra
EP (London: Longman & Broderip, ca. 1780)
     GB:Lbm H.241.(2.)

According to MGG these two English publishers issued in all nine concerti, three of which were also issued for piano accompaniment. MGG also cites two *Concerti* for flute and orchestra in GB:Lbm.

Sainsbury identifies Fischer as, 'a celebrated performer on the hautboy [who] resided for some years in London. In the Spring of 1800, while performing the solo part in his Concerto at the queen's house, after having executed his first movement in a style equal to the best performance during any part of his life, in the course of his adagio, he was suddenly seized with an apopletic fit, and fell down. Prince William of Gloucester, observing the accident, supported him out of the apartment, whence he was conveyed to his residence in Greek Street, Soho, where he expired in about an hour afterwards. The king was very much affected, and he had the first medical assistance called to his aid. In his last moments, Fischer desired that all his manuscript music might be presented to his majesty, George the Third.

Fish, W. (b. 1775)

Sainsbury identifies Fish as the composer of a *Concerto* for oboe.

Fisher, John Abraham (English violinist, 1744–1806)

Sainsbury identifies Fisher as the composer of four *Concerti* for the oboe, published by Clementi.

Förster, Emanuel (1748–1823)

MGG attributes to Förster five *Concerti* for oboe.

Fortunato, Ferdenando

(Six) *Romanzes*, for oboe and voice
MS A:Wn Sm 10374

Gagnebin, Henri (b. 1886)

MGG attributes to Gagnebin a *Danse montagnarde* (Paris: Henn) for oboe and piano or string orchestra.

Garnier, Joseph-Francois (1755–1825)

MGG attributes to Garnier the following works for solo oboe:
(Six) *Duos concertants* (with violin), Op. 7 (Paris: Nadermann)
(Three) *Concerti*
Symphonie concertante, Op. 4

Etudes and Caprices (Paris: Pleyel)

Methode raissonnee pour le hautbois, suivie de 55 lecons, six petits duos et six sonates (Paris: Pleyel]

Sainsbury identifies Garnier as a professor of oboe to Louis XVI and the publisher of oboe music in Paris in 1788.

Gassmann, Florian (1729–1774)

Divertimento, for oboe and strings
MS A:Wn Sm 3663

Divertimento, for oboe and strings
MS A:Wn Sm 3664

Divertimento, for oboe and strings
MS A:Wn Sm 3665

Quartet (ca. 1798), for oboe and strings
MS A:Wn Sm 11871

Quartet, for oboe and strings
MS A:Wn Sm 11872

Quartet, for oboe and strings
MS A:Wn Sm 11873

Quartet, for oboe and strings
MS A:Wn Sm 11874

Quartet, for oboe and strings
MS A:Wn Sm 11875

Quartet, for oboe and strings
MS A:Wn Sm 11876

Quartet, for oboe and strings
MS A:Wn Sm 11877

Quartet, for oboe and strings
MS A:Wn Sm 11878

Quartet, for oboe and strings
MS A:Wn Sm 11879

Quartet, for oboe and strings
MS A:Wgm XI 4643

Quartet, for oboe and strings
MS   A:Wgm XI 4644

(Six) *Quartets* for oboe and strings
MS   (Wien: Traeg's *Catalog*, 1799)

(Four) *Quintets*, for oboe and strings
MS   I:MOe Mus.D.101

Quintet, for oboe and strings
MS   I:MOe Mus.D.102

Sextet, for flute, oboe, and strings
MS   I:MOe Mus.D.100

Gayer, Johann Nepomuk (1746–1811)

MGG attributes to Gayer a *Concerto* for oboe.

Giranek, Anton (Bohemian, 1712–1760)

(Three) *Concerti* for oboe
MS   D:Ds Mus.Ms. 336

Concerto in F Major for oboe
MS   D:Ds Mus.Ms. 336/5

Concerto in Bb Major for oboe
MS   D:Ds Mus.Ms. 336/7

Godard, Benjamin Louis (1849–1895)

MGG attributes to Godard a *Scenes ecossaises* (Paris: Hamelle) for oboe.

Graff, F. H.

Quartets for oboe, bassoon and strings
MS   (Wien: Traeg's *Catalog*, 1799)

Grano, Giovanni

Solos, for flute or oboe and harpsichord
EP   (London: Walsh and Hare, ca. 1730)
    GB:Lbm G.422.j.(4.)

Graupner, Christoph (1683–1760)

Concerto in F Major for oboe
MS D:Ds Mus.Ms. 1544

Concerto for oboe
MS D:Ds Mus.Ms. 411/2

Gretsch, Johann Konrad (1710–1778)

MGG attributes to Gretsch a *Concerto* (MS, D:Rtt) for oboe and orchestra.

Griesbach, William

(Three) *Quartets*, Op. 1, for flute or oboe and strings
EP (London: Birchall, ca. 1800)
   GB:Lbm H.111.(20.)

Grosse, Samuel Dietrich (1757–1789)

MGG attributes to Grosse a lost *Concerto* for oboe.

Hamal, Henri (1747–1823)

Concerto for oboe and orchestra
MS B:Lc 86-2.L-III

Handel, Georg F. (1685–1759)

Solos, Op. 1, for flute or oboe and harpsicord
EP (London: Walsh, ca. 1733)
   GB:Lbm G.74.c.(2.)
   GB:Lbm G.74.h. [another edition]

Hanke, Karl (1750–1803)

MGG attributes to Hanke a *Concerto* for oboe.

Harrer, Johann Gottlob (1703–1755)

MGG attributes to Harrer (Three) *Trios* for oboe and strings.

Haydn, Josef (1732–1809)

Concerto for oboe and orchestra
MS A:Wgm VIII 28155

Heine, Samuel Friedrich (1764–1821)

MGG attributes to Heine two *Concerti*, in C and Eb Major, for oboe.

Heinrich, Johann Gottfried

Partia, for oboe, 2 violins, and bass
MS   P:GD Ms.4144

Herrmann, Gottfried (1808–1878)

MGG attributes to Herrmann a *Concerto*, Op. 20 (1834), for oboe and orchestra.

Hertel, Johann Wilhelm (1727–1789)

(Nine) Concerti for oboe and orchestra
MS   B:Bc Wotquenne 5562

Concerto for oboe and orchestra
MS   B:Bc Wotquenne 5563

(Three) *Partite* for oboe and organ
MS   B:Bc Wotquenne 6691

Hirich, ?

Quartet for oboe and strings
MS   (Wien: Traeg's *Catalog*, 1799)

Hoffmeister, Franz Anton (1754–1812)

Quartet, for oboe and strings
MS   A:Wn Sm 11979

Quartet, for oboe and strings
MS   A:Wn Sm 11980

Quartet, for oboe and strings
MS   A:Wn Sm 11981

Quartet, for oboe and strings
MS   A:Wn Sm 11982

Quartet, for oboe and strings
MS   A:Wn Sm 11983

Quartet, for oboe and strings
MS A:Wn Sm 11984

(Three) *Quintets* in Eb Major for oboe, 'second' horn, bassoon, and strings
MS (Wien: Traeg's *Catalog*, 1799)

(Two) *Quintets* in F and D Major for oboe, 'second' horn, bassoon, and strings
MS (Wien: Traeg's *Catalog*, 1799)

Quintet in Eb Major for oboe, bassoon, and strings
MS (Wien: Traeg's *Catalog*, 1799)

Homilius, Gottfried August (1714–1785)

MGG attributes to Homilius a *Sonata* for oboe and bass.

Hummel, Johann Nepomuk (1778–1837)

Concerto (1803) for oboe and orchestra
MS GB:Lbm Add.32227

MGG also attributes to Hummel a *Variations*, Op. 102 (Leipzig: Peters and Paris: Richault), for oboe or clarinet and orchestra.

Jadin, Louis Emmanuel (1768–1853)

MGG attributes to Jadin (Three) *Nocturnes* (Paris: Duhan) for piano and oboe and (Three) *Nocturnes sur divers airs* (Paris: Dufaut) for piano and oboe.

Janitsch, Johann Gosslich

Quartet, for oboe and strings
MS A:Wn Sm 12024

Quartet, for oboe and strings
MS A:Wn Sm 12025

Quartet, for oboe and strings
MS A:Wn Sm 12026

Sonata, for oboe, viola, cello, and bass
MS B:Bc Wotquenne 6723

Kaeberle, ?

Sainsbury identifies Kaeberle as a, 'celebrated performer on the oboe, at Beuthen on the Oder, in 1740, and composer of music for his instrument.'

Kalliwoda, Johann Wenzel (1801–1866)

Concertino in F Major, Op. 110 (1844), for oboe and orchestra
MS D:KA [cited in MGG]

Kauer, Ferdinand (1751–1831)

MGG attributes to Kauer the following works:
  Symphonie concertante for oboe and orchestra
  (Six) *Concerti* for oboe
  Concerto for piano and oboe

Klein, Jacob

Sainsbury identifies Klein as the composer of (Six) *Sonates*, Op. 1 (Amsterdam, ca. 1720) for
  oboe and continuo and a following six *Sonatas* as Op. 2.

Klemcke, Louis

Concerto for oboe and orchestra
MS A:Wgm VIII 28431

Klughardt, August Friedrich (1847–1902)

MGG attributes to Klughardt a *Konzertstuck*, Op. 18 (Leipzig: Fritzsch, 1870) for oboe.

Kospoth, Otto Karl (1753–1817)

MGG attributes to Kospoth a *Concerto* (1794) for oboe and orchestra.

Kozeluch, Johann Anton (Bohemian, 1738–1814)

Concerto for oboe and orchestra
MS CS:Pn V.F.24; and XI.C.239 [cited in MGG]

Krebs, Johann Tobias (1690–1762)

MGG attributes to Krebs a *Fantasia* (MS, D:DS) for oboe, 2 claviers and bass.

Krommer, Franz (Bohemian, 1759–1831)

Concerto in F Major, for oboe and orchestra
EP (Not given)
     A:Sca 70343

Concerto in F Major, Op. 37, for oboe and orchestra
EP (Paris: Duhan)
F:Pn Vm.24.161

(Two) *Quartets* for oboe and strings
MS A:Sca Hs. 122

Quartet for oboe and strings
MS A:Sca Hs. 1827

(Two) *Quartets* for oboe and strings
EP (Not given)
A:Sca 70247

Küffner, Johann Jakob (German, 1727–1786)

MGG attributes to Kuffner a *Concerto* (MS, D:Rtt) for oboe.

Kunzen, Adolph Carl (1720–1781)

MGG attributes to Kunzen six *Concerti* for oboe.

Lebrun, Ludwig (1752–1790)

Concerto for oboe and orchestra
MS A:Sca Hs. 96

Concerto in F Major, for oboe
MS D:Ds Mus.Ms. 1239

Quartet for oboe and strings
MS (Wien: Traeg's *Catalog*, 1799)

MGG also attributes to Lebrun the following works:
(Three) *Concerti* (Paris: Sieber, 1777–1787) for oboe
(Six) *Concerti* (Offenbach: André, 1804) for oboe
Concerto (MS, A:Wn) for oboe
(Six) *Trios* (Offenbach: André) for oboe, violin and bass
Quartet for oboe and strings (formerly MS, D:DO)
Rondo in D Major (MSS, D:SWl)

Loeillet, Jean [of Ghent] (d. 1728)

(Six) *Sonatas*, Op. 5, for flute, oboe, or violin and bc
EP (Amsterdam: Roger, ca. 1725)
GB:Lbm G.685.b.(2.) [Book 1]
GB:Lbm G.685.b.(3.) [Book 2]

Loeillet, John (of London)

Sonatas, Op. 1, 'for a Comon flute or Hoboy, also for two flutes and bc'
EP   (London: Walsh and Hare, ca. 1725)
   GB:Lbm G.685.b.(1.)
   GB:Lbm H.17.(6.) [another copy]

Malzat, Ignaz (1757–1804)

Concerto, in F Major, for oboe
MS (Wien: Traeg's *Catalog*, 1799)

(Six) *Quartets* for oboe and strings
MS (Wien: Traeg's *Catalog*, 1799)

Quintet in C Major for oboe and strings
MS (Wien: Traeg's *Catalog*, 1799)

Quintet in F Major for oboe and strings
MS (Wien: Traeg's *Catalog*, 1799)

Marcello, Alessandro (1684–1750)

MGG attributes to Marcello a *Concerto* for oboe, strings and organ.

Massonneau, Louis (1766–1848)

MGG attributes to Massonneau (Three) *Quatuors* (Hamburg: Boehme, 1798) for oboe and
strings and a lost *Concerto* for oboe.

Mathes, Carl Ludwig

Sainsbury identifies Mathes as an oboist in the court of the Margrave of Brandenburg-
Schwedt, adding, 'in [K. P. E.] Bach's *Vierlerley* two solos for the oboe.'

Mazzinghi, Joseph

Sainsbury identifies as a composer of many flute works in London at the end of the eighteenth century.

Mendelssohn, Arnold

Suite (1917) for oboe and piano
MS D:Ds Mus.Ms. 1917

Mica, Jan Adam (1746–1811)

MGG attributes to Mica three *Quartets* (MS, *CS:Pn*) for oboe and strings.

Molter, Johann Melchior (1695–1765)

MGG attributes to Molter five *Concerti* for oboe (MS, D:KA).

Mozart, Wolfgang A. (1756–1791)

Concerto, in C Major, for flute
MS (Wien: Traeg's *Catalog*, 1799)

Nanisch, Franz

Sainsbury identifies Nanischas, 'a celebrated performer on the hautboy, and composer for his instrument.' Sainsbury cautions there is a trombonist by the same in Vienna.

Necchi, Francesco Antonio

Gloria Patri, for SB, solo oboe, and violins
MS I:Bsf M.N.I-19

Pacini, Giovanni (1796–1867)

Laudamus, for Bass, oboe, and orchestra
MS I:Ls C.1

Parke, John (1745–1829)

MGG attributes to Parke a *Grand Concerto* (London: Fentum, 1805) for oboe (or flute, or clarinet).

Parma, Raffaele

(Six) *Capricci* (ded. to Prof. B. Centroni) for oboe
EP (Milano: Lucca)
    I:Bc

Pezold, Christian (1677–1733)

MGG attributes to Pezold a *Trio* in G Major for violin, oboe, and bass.

Pfeiffer, Franz Anton (1754–1787)

MGG attributes to Pfeiffer a presumed lost *Concerto* for oboe and strings.

Pfeiffer, Johann (1697–1761)

MGG attributes to Pfeiffer three *Sonatas* for cembalo, oboe or violin, and bass.

Philidor, Francois-Andre Danican (1726–1795)

MGG attributes to Philidor (Six) *Quartets* (Paris: the composer, 1755) for oboe and strings.

Pignata, Pietro

Sonata, for oboe and strings
MS   A:Wn EM 100

Pla (Plas, or Plats), ?

Sainsbury identifies two brothers by this name, Spaniards, and both oboists. After 1761 they were in the employ of the Duke of Würtemburg and apparently published some music for bassoon and for flute.

Pleyel, Ignaz (1757–1831)

Quartet, for oboe and strings
MS   I:Vmc Busta 73–93-N.93

Quintet in Eb Major for oboe and strings
MS   (Wien: Traeg's *Catalog*, 1799)

Trio, for oboe or flute, violin, and cello
MS   I:Vmc Busta 54–58-N.58

Pokorny, Franz Xaver (1729–1794)

(Two) *Concerti* for oboe
MS   D:Rtt [according to MGG]

Prati, Alessio (1750–1788)

MGG attributes to Prati a *Concerto* in F Minor for oboe.

Quantz, Johann (1697–1773)

Solos, Op. 2, for flute or oboe, with bc
EP   (London: Walsh, ca. 1730)
     GB:Lbm G.1090.(1.)

Reymann, F. G.

Concerto, in C Major, for flute
MS   (Wien: Traeg's *Catalog*, 1799)

Richter, Franz Xaver (1709–1789)

Concerto in F Major for oboe
MS D:Rtt [according to MGG]

Ristori, Giovanni Alberto (1692–1753)

Concerto in E♭ Major for oboe and orchestra
MS D:B [according to MGG]

Röllig, Johann Georg (1710–1790)

MGG attributes to Rollig two *Concerti* for oboe.

Röntgen, Julius (Dutch, 1855–1932)

MGG attributes to Rontgen a *Sonata* for oboe and piano.

Rosetti, Franz Anton (1746–1792)

Concerto for oboe and orchestra
MS A:Wgm VIII 1395.

Roslawetz, Nikolai (Ukraine, 1881–1944)

MGG attributes to Roslawetz a *Quintet* for oboe, harp and strings.

Saal, Anton Wilhelm (1763–1855)

MGG attributes to Saal a *Sonata* for piano, with oboe and violin.

San Martini, Giuseppe

(Six) *Solos*, Op. 8, for flute, violin, or oboe and bc
EP (London: Johnson, ca. 1760)
    GB:Lbm G.422.b.(8.)

Schickhard, Johann

Solos, Op. 20, for flute or oboe with bc
EP (London: Walsh and Hare, ca. 1730)
    GB:Lbm H.3055.(2.)
    GB:Lbm G.1090.(3.) [another copy]

Schimpke, ?

Concerto, in F Major, for flute
MS (Wien: Traeg's *Catalog*, 1799)

Schinn, Georg

(Ten) *Variations* (1800) for oboe and cello
MS A:Sca Hs. 721

Variations (1804) for oboe and orchestra
MS A:Sca Hs. 722

Schmittbaur, Joseph Aloys (1718–1809)

MGG attributes to Schmittbaur a *Concerto* (MS, 1781) for oboe.

Schwencke, Christian Fredrich (1767–1822)

MGG attributes to Schwencke *Concerto* (Leipzig: Hofmeister, 1803) for oboe and orchestra.

Sciroli, Gregorio (1722–1781)

Concerto for oboe and orchestra
MS I:Gl SS.A.1.19.(G.8)

Sellner, Josef (nineteenth century)

Adagio, for oboe and orchestra (ca. 1830)
MS A:Wn Sm 18424

Somis, Giovanni Battista (1686–1763)

MGG attributes to Somis a *Concerto* for oboe.

Sorge, Georg Andreas (1703–1778)

MGG attributes to Sorge a *Trio* for oboe and strings.

Stamitz, ?

Concerto, in G Major, for flute
MS (Wien: Traeg's *Catalog*, 1799)

Stamitz, Anton (1754–1809)

MGG attributes to Stamitz a *Concerto* for oboe.

Stamitz, Carl

(Five) *Quartets* for oboe, horn and strings
MS (Wien: Traeg's *Catalog*, 1799)

(Three) *Quintets* for solo oboe or violin, horn and strings
MS (Wien: Traeg's *Catalog*, 1799)

Stamitz, Johann Wenzel Anton (1717–1757)

Concerto in C Major for oboe
MS D:Rtt [according to MGG]

Stricker, Augustin Reinhard (1675–1720)

MGG attributes to Stricker (Six) Italian *Cantatas* with solo oboe.

Stölzel, Gottfried Heinrich (1690–1749)

MGG attributes to Stölzel *Concerti* in G Minor and D Major for oboe.

Stüntz, Joseph Hartman (1793–1859)

Concerto for oboe
MS D:Mbs Mus.Ms. 4022

Larghetto for oboe and piano.
MS D:Mbs Mus.Ms. 4075/7

Tacet, Joseph

(Thirty-six) *Preludes*, for flute, oboe, or violin
EP (London: Longman, Lukey, ca. 1775)
    GB:Lbm A.205.

Telemann, Georg (1681–1767)

Concerto for oboe and orchestra
MS B:Bc Wotquenne 5598

Concerto for oboe
MS D:Ds Mus.Ms. 1033/4

Concerto for oboe
MS D:Ds Mus.Ms. 1033/8

Concerto for oboe
MS D:Ds Mus.Ms. 1033/12

Concerto for oboe
MS D:Ds Mus.Ms. 1033/419

Concerto for oboe
MS D:Ds Mus.Ms. 1033/20

Concerto for oboe
MS D:Ds Mus.Ms. 1033/41

Concerto for oboe
MS D:Ds Mus.Ms. 1033/65

Concerto for oboe
MS D:Ds Mus.Ms. 1033/80

Tessarini, Carlo (1690–1776)

Solos, Op. 2, for flute or oboe
EP   (London: Walsh, 1736)
     GB:Lbm G.688

Tischer, Johann Nikolaus (1707–1774)

MGG attributes to Tischer (Six) *Concerti* for oboe and viola.

Triebensee, Joseph (1772–1846)

(Three) *Quartets* for oboe and strings
MS (Wien: Traeg's *Catalog*, 1799)

Quintet, for oboe, piano and strings
MS A:Wn Sm 11409

Triébert, Charles-Louis (1810–1867)

MGG attributes to Triebert a *Fantaisie*, Op. 14 (Paris: Costallat) for oboe and piano.

Triébert, Frederic (1813–1878)

MGG attributes to Triébert the following works for oboe:
    Air pastoral, Op. 7 (Paris: Triebert, 1858), with piano
    Reverie, Op. 13 (Paris, 1868)
    Souvenir de Picardie, Op. 12 (Paris, 1868)
    Valse concertante (Paris: Millerau, 1890), with piano

Vogel, Cajetan (1750–1794)

MGG attributes to Vogel a *Concerto* for oboe and orchestra.

Vogt, August (German organist, 1861–1926)

Aria variata for oboe and strings or piano
EP   (Paris: Louner)
    I:Bc

Fourth Concerto for oboe and orchestra and piano
EP   (Paris: Richault)
    I:Bc

Variations on an Original Theme for oboe and orchestra
EP   (Paris: Richault)
    I:Bc

Wanhal, Jan (Johann Baptist, 1739–1813)

Concerto for oboe and strings
MS   I:Gl SS.A.2.19.(H.7)

(Six) *Quartets*, Op. 7, for oboe or flute and strings
EP   (London: Welcker, ca. 1785)
    GB:Lbm G.413.(19.)

Weigl, Joseph Franz (1740–1820)

(Three) *Trios*, in G, F, and D Major for oboe and strings
MS   (Wien: Traeg's *Catalog*, 1799)

MGG attributes to Weigl six *Trios* for oboe and strings.

Weiss, Johann Sigismund (1690–1737)

MGG attributes to Weiss two *Concerti* lost in D:DS during WWII.

Wendling, Johann (1720–1797)

Concerto, for flute or oboe
EP   (London: Preston, ca. 1785)
    GB:Lbm H.3213.j.(16.)

Went (Wendt), Giovanni (1745–1809)

(Six) *Quintets* for oboe, bassoon, and strings
MS   (Wien: Traeg's *Catalog*, 1799)

Wiedner, Johann Gottlieb (1714–1783)

MGG attributes to Wiedner a *Concerto* in E♭ Major for oboe and strings.

Winter, Peter (1754–1825)

Concerto for oboe and orchestra
MS   A:Sca Hs. 397

Concerto, in F Major, for flute
MS   (Wien: Traeg's *Catalog*, 1799)

Wragg, J.

Oboe Preceptor
EP   (London: the author, 1792)
    GB:Lbm B.117.(2.)

Wranizky, ?

(Six) *Quartets* for flute or oboe and strings
MS   (Wien: Traeg's *Catalog*, 1799)

Wunderlich, Christian Friedrich (b. 1722)

Sainsbury identifies Wunderlich as an oboist in the court of the Margrave of Anspach and an 'excellent' player on the oboe and clarinet, and composer of music for both instruments between 1738–1770.

Zach, Johann (1699–1773)

MGG attributes to Zach a *Concerto* in B♭ for oboe.

Zimmermann, ?

Concerto, in C Major, for flute [originally for oboe]
MS   (Wien: Traeg's *Catalog*, 1799)

MUSIC WITH SOLO OBOE D'AMORE

Bellermann, Konstantin (1696–1758)

MGG attributes to Bellermann three *Concerti* for oboe d'amore.

Graun, August Friedrich (1698–1765)

MGG attributes to Graun (Two) *Concerti* for Oboe d'amore.

Graun, Johann (1703–1771)

Concerto in D Major for oboe d'amore
MS D:Ds Mus.Ms. 1372

Graupner, Christoph (1687–1760)

Concerto for oboe d'amore
MS D:Ds Mus.Ms. 141

Concerto for oboe d'amore
MS D:Ds Mus.Ms. 411/24

Concerto for oboe d'amore
MS D:Ds Mus.Ms. 411/40

Heinichen, David (1683–1729)

Concerto for oboe d'amore
MS D:Ds Mus.Ms. 347

Lotti, Antonio (1667–1740)

Concerto for oboe d'amore
MS D:Ds Mus.Ms. 347

Sorge, Georg Andreas (1703–1778)

MGG attributes to Sorge a *Trio* for oboe d'amore and strings.

Telemann, Georg (1681–1767)

Concerto for oboe d'amore
MS D:Ds Mus.Ms. 1033/40

Concerto for oboe d'amore
MS D:Ds Mus.Ms. 1033/46

MUSIC WITH SOLO ENGLISH HORN

Anonymous

Solo (Genova, 1801) for English horn and orchestra
MS I:Gl Sc. 41

Bach, Johann Christian (1735–1782)

Quartet for English horn and strings
MS I:Gl SS.A.2.7.(G.8)

Czerny, Gaspard

Sainsbury identifies Czerny as an excellent performer on the English horn, residing in Prague, St. Petersburg, and in 1786 in Germany, in the service of the Princess of Baden.

Draeseke, Felix (1835–1913)

MGG attributes to Draeseke a *Kleine Suite*, Op. 87 (Steingraber, 1911) for English horn or oboe.

Ferlendis, Giuseppe

Sonata for English horn and continuo
MS I:Gl M.4.31.39

Laube, Anton (1718–1784)

MGG attributes to Laube a *Concerto* for English horn.

Malzat, Ignaz (1757–1804)

Quartet for English horn and strings
MS (Wien: Traeg's *Catalog*, 1799)

Concerti in F and E♭ Major for English horn
MS (Wien: Traeg's *Catalog*, 1799) [according to MGG]

Pillotti, Giuseppe

Concerto in F Major (1811)
MS I:Bc

Reicha, Anton (1770–1836)

Andante, *Andante*, and *Adagio*, (1817–1819) for English horn, accompanied by flute, clarinet, horn, and bassoon
MS F:Pn MS.12022

MUSIC WITH SOLO CLARINET

Abraham, ? (d. 1805)

Sainsbury attributes to Abraham, 'a teacher of the clarinet at Paris, a great many airs (ca. 1788) for his instrument.'

Acerbi, Giuseppe (1773–1846)

[Solo clarinet composition]
MS I:MAc

Amon, Giovanni Andrea (1763–1825)

(Two) *Quartets*, Op. 106, for clarinet and strings
EP (Offenbach: André)
    I:Bc

Anna Amalie, Herzogia (1739–1807)

MGG attributes to this Lady a *Divertimento* (Weimar: Ambrosius) for clarinet, piano, viola and cello.

Anonymous

Compleat Instructions for the Clarionet
EP (London: Bland & Weller, ca. 1798)
    GB:Lbm B.160.g.(1.)

The Clarinet Instructor ('to which is added a Quintetto for horns, clarinets, and bassoon')
EP (London: Longman & Broderip, ca. 1780)
    GB:Lbm B.161.i.

Concerto for clarinet and orchestra
MS A:Wn Sm 5659

Concerto (1831) for clarinet and orchestra
MS A:Wn Sm 3788

Concerto for clarinet and orchestra
MS BRD:F Mus.Hs. 2347

Concerto, in B♭ Major, for clarinet
MS (Wien: Traeg's *Catalog*, 1799)

Quintet, for clarinet and strings
MS BRD:F Mus.Hs. 1958

Quintet, for clarinet and strings
MS BRD:F Mus.Hs. 1952

Quintet, for clarinet and strings
MS BRD:F Mus.Hs. 1954

Quintet, for clarinet and strings
MS BRD:F Mus.Hs. 1960

Variations for solo clarinet
MS (Wien: Traeg's *Catalog*, 1799)

Avoni, Petronio

Tema variato, 1825, for clarinet and orchestra
MS I:Bc

Backofen, Enrico (German, 1718–1839)

Quintet, Op. 15, for clarinet and strings
EP (Leipzig: Breitkopf & Härtel)
    I:Bc

Bärman, F.

Sainsbury identifies Barman as 'a celebrated performer on the clarinet in Munich. He is
    remarkable for his beautiful piano, and for his facility more than for his general tone.'

Bärmann, Carl (1810–1885)

Conzertstuck, Op. 44, for clarinet and orchestra
EP (Offenbach: André)
    I:Bc

Conzertstuck, Op. 49, for clarinet and orchestra
EP (Offenbach: André)
    I:Bc

[Untitled work], for clarinet and piano
MS BRD:F Mus.Hs. 575

Bauer, Alois (German, 1794–1872)

Offertorium, for Alto, clarinet solo, strings, and organ
MS A:Wn Sm 23923

Baumgarten, Carl F.

Concerto, for oboe, flute or clarinet and orchestra
EP (London: Longman and Broderip, ca. 1790)
GB:Lbm H.102.(3.)

Beer, Joseph (1744–1811)

Sainsbury identifies Beer as 'chamber-musician to the King of Prussia since 1792. He is
an eminent performer on the clarinet and has composed much music for the clarinet
between 1794 and 1807.'

Berr, Frederic (1794–1838)

(Three) *Air Variés*, for clarinet and piano
MS F:Pn K.1206, K. 1207, and K. 1209

There are many additional solo clarinet works in F:Pn by Berr.

Solo for clarinet and orchestra or piano
EP (Paris: Richault)
I:Bc

Blasius, Matthieu Frederic (1758–1829)

Quartet, for clarinet and strings
MS A:Wn Sm 22113

First *Concerto* for clarinet
EP (Paris: Cochet)
F:Pn Vm.7.10,526
F:Pn Vm.24.23 [another copy]

New Clarinet Method
EP (Paris: Porthaux)
F:Pn L.9954

Bochsa, Charles Nicholas (1789–1856)

Solo per la clarinet (for Bärmann, London, July 7, 1839)
MS D:Mbs Mus.Ms. 1818

Bochsa, Karl 'pere' (d. 1821)

(Three) *Quartets* for clarinet and strings
EP   (Paris: Imbault)
    F:Pn Vm.7.10,405

(Three) Quartets for clarinet and strings
EP   (Paris: Imbault)
    F:Pn Vm.7.6664bis

(Three) *Quartets*, Op. 30, for clarinet and strings
EP   (Paris: Imbault)
    F:Pn Vm.7.10,406

(Three) *Quartets* for clarinet and strings
EP   (Paris: Bochsa)
    F:Pn Vm.18.28

(Three) *Quartets* for clarinet and strings
EP   (Paris: Sieber)
    F:Pn Vmg.14905

Boscka, ?

Sainsbury identifies Boscka as a composer of some *Quartets* for clarinet and strings in Germany in 1802.

Brepsant, Engebert (nineteenth century)

6th Air Varié, for solo clarinet and band
MS F:Pn K.1182

Carafa, Michele (1787–1872)

Solo de Clarinet, (in 'Les Souvenier de Naples') accompanied by 2 clarinets, bassoon, and ophicleide
MS   F:Pn MS. 3445

Allegretto ('July 19, 1845') for solo clarinet, accompanied by 2 oboes, 3 clarinets, 2 horns, 2 bassoons, and cornet
MS F:Pn MS.3929

Castelbarco, conte Cesare

Quintet, Op. 43 (1848), for clarinet and strings
EP   (Milan: Scotti)
    I:Bc

Catel, Charles-Simon (1773–1830)

(Three) *Quartets* for clarinet and strings
EP   (Paris: l'Imprimerie du Cons. de Musique)
    F:Pn Cons.A.35.445

Crémont, Pietro d'Aurillac

Concerto, Op. 4, for clarinet and orchestra
EP   (Publisher not given)
    I:Bc

Sainsbury identifies Crémont as a German professor of clarinet, and composer for the
    instrument, in Vienna in 1825.

Crusell, Bernard, Swedish (1775–1838)

Concerto, Op. 1, for clarinet and orchestra
EP   (Leipzig: Peters)
    I:Bc

Concerto in F Major (ded. to Alexander I of Russia)
EP   (Leipzig: Peters)
    I:Bc

Concerto in B♭ Major, Op. 11, for clarinet and orchestra
EP   (Leipzig: Peters)
    I:Bc

Quartet, Op. 7, for clarinet and strings
EP   (Leipzig: Peters)
    I:Bc

Sainsbury identifies Crusell as a German clarinetist and 'his more favorite works,' as his
    Concertante, Op. 3, for clarinet, horn, and bassoon with orchestra and his *Symphonie Con-
    certante*, Op. 22, for flute, clarinet and bass, with orchestra.

David, Ferdinand

Introduction and Variations on a theme of Schubert, Op. 8, for clarinet and orchestra
EP   (Leipzig: Breitkopf & Härtel)
    I:Bc

Devienne, François (1759–1803)

(Six) *Sonatas*, Op. 28, for clarinet and bass
MS (Wien: Traeg's *Catalog*, 1799)

MGG also attributes to Devienne (Three) *Sonatas* (Paris: Sieber) for clarinet and strings.

Dotzauer, Giusto Giovanni (Italian, 1807–1865)

Divertimento, Op. 68, for clarinet and orchestra
EP   (Mainz: Schott)
    I:Bc

Duvernoy, Charles

Sainsbury identifies Duvernoy as a brother to the famous hornist, Frederic Duvernoy, and [Charles is] a 'distinguished performer on the clarinet and professor at the Paris Conservatory. He has published much music since 1795.'

Eberl, Anton Franz Josef (1765–1807)

MGG attributes to Eberl a *Quintet*, Op. 41 (1806), in G Minor for clarinet and strings.

Eberwein, Christian (1750–1810)

MGG attributes to Eberwein a *Concerto*, Op. 65, for clarinet.

Eckert, ?

Concerto for clarinet and orchestra
MS A:Wn Sm 5652

Eichner, Ernst (1740–1777)

Concerto (1798) for clarinet and orchestra
MS A:Wn Sm 5848

Elding, Johann (1754–1786)

Sainsbury identifies Elding as a clarinetist and composer of clarinet music, born in Eisenach, Saxony.

Farrenc, Jacques Hyppolite (1794–1865)

MGG attributes to Farrenc a *Trio*, Op. 44, in E♭ Major for piano, clarinet, and cello.

Fiala, Joseph (1754–1816)

MGG attributes to Fiala a *Concerto* for clarinet and viola.

Frugatta, Giuseppe (1860–1933)

MGG attributes to Frugatta a *Suite*, Op. 44, for clarinet and piano.

Frühling, Carl (1868–1937)

MGG attributes to Frühling a Trio, Op. 40, for piano, clarinet, and cello.

Fuchs, Giovanni (1752–1821)

Concerto for clarinet
MS F:Pn Ms. 1966

Concerto, Op. 14, in B♭ Major, for clarinet
MS (Wien: Traeg's *Catalog*, 1799)

(Twelve) *Duets* for clarinet and violin
MS (Wien: Traeg's *Catalog*, 1799)

Trio, for clarinet, viola and cello
MS A:Wgm XI 6237

Trio, for clarinet, viola and cello
MS A:Wgm XI 6238

Gagnebin, Henri (b. 1886)

MGGattributes to Gagnebin an unpublished *Andante and Allegro* for clarinet and orchestra.

Gänsbacher, Johann Baptist (1778–1844)

MGG attributes to Gänsbacher a *Concertino* (1819) in E♭ Major for clarinet and orchestra.

Garaude, Alexis (1779–1852)

MGG attributes to Garaude *Trois themes ou andante varies* (1810) for clarinet and strings.

Gassmann, Florian (1729–1774)

Notturno (1798) for chalamaux and orchestra
MS   A:Wn Sm 11394

Gilg, Franz

Ave Maria, for SATB, clarinet solo, and strings
MS   A:Wn Sm 242

Girschner, Christian Friedrich (1794–1860)

MGG attributes to Girschner *Vergiss mein nicht*, (Mainz: Schott) for Soprano, clarinet
and piano.

Gnecco, Francesco (Italian, b. 1769)

Notturno for clarinet and strings
MS   I:Gl SS.A.1.20.(G.8)

Quintet for clarinet and strings
MS   I:Gl N.1.7.2.(sc.16)

Quintet for clarinet and strings
MS   I:Gl N.1.7.2.(sc.26)

Goepfert, Carl Andreas (b. 1768)

Sainsbury identifies Goepfert as, 'a celebrated performer on the clarinet and has composed
much valuable music for his instrument.'

Grenser, ?

Concerto for clarinet and orchestra
MS   A:Wn Sm 5653

Haensel, Pietro

Quartet, Op. 19, for clarinet and strings
EP   (Wien: Artaria)
     I:Bc

Hanssens, Charles-Louis (1802–1871)

Concerto, Nr. 2, for clarinet and orchestra
MS   B:Bc Wotquenne 5554

Concertino for clarinet
MS   B:Bc Wotquenne 5553

Solo for clarinet and orchestra
MS   B:Bc Wotquenne 5552

Heine, Samuel Friedrich (1764–1821)

MGG attributes to Heine a *Sonata* (Hamburg: Böhme) for piano and clarinet.

Henry, Louis F. (1786–1855)

MGG attributes to Henry *Etudes en caprices*, Op. 2, for clarinet and (Three) *Duos* (Paris: Dufant & Dubois) for clarinet and guitar.

Herrmann, Gottfried (1808–1878)

MGG attributes to Herrmann the following works:
Concerto in E♭ Major for clarinet and orchestra
Am Meer in A♭ Major (Bremen: Prager & Meier, 1870), for clarinet and piano
Variation and Introduction in A♭ Major for clarinet and piano

Hoffmeister, Franz Anton (1754–1812)

Concerto for clarinet and orchestra
MS A:Wn Sm 5849

Concerto for clarinet and orchestra
MS A:Wn Sm 5850

(Two) *Concerti*, in B♭ Major, for clarinet
MS (Wien: Traeg's *Catalog*, 1799)

Quartet, Nr. 18, for clarinet and strings
MS A:Wgm XI 10742

Quartet, Nr. 21, for clarinet and strings
MS A:Wgm XI 10745

Quartet, Nr. 22, for clarinet and strings
MS A:Wgm XI 10743

Quartet, Nr. 23, for clarinet and strings
MS A:Wgm XI 10744

Quartet, Nr. 24, for clarinet and strings
MS A:Wgm XI 10741

Quartet, Nr. 26, for clarinet and strings
MS A:Wgm XI 10740

Rondo and Variations for clarinet and orchestra
MS A:Wn Sm 5852

Holmes, Augusta Mary-Anne (1847–1903)

MGG attributes to Holmes a *Fantasie* (Paris: Evette & Schaeffer, 1900) for clarinet and piano.

Hostie, ?

Sainsbury identifies Hostie as a clarinetist in the band of the Duke of Montmorency in Paris in 1788 and composer of published *Concerto* and six Duets for clarinet and other instruments.

Hummel, Johann Nepomuk (1778–1837)

Graduale, for soprano, SATB, clarinet solo, and orchestra
MS A:Wn Sm 14321

MGG also attributes to Hummel a *Variations*, Op. 102 (Leipzig: Peters and Paris: Richault), for oboe or clarinet and orchestra.

Hummel, Joseph Friedrich (1841–1919)

MGG attributes to Hummel two *Concerti* (Leipzig: Breitkopf & Härtel) for clarinet.

Jadin, Louis Emmanuel (1768–1853)

MGG attributes to Jadin a *Premiere Fantaisie concertante* for clarinet and piano (Paris: Frey) and (Three) *Nocturnes* (Paris: Besozzi) for piano and clarinet.

Kalliwoda, Johann (1801–1866)

Morceau de Salon, Op. 229, for clarinet and orchestra
EP (Mainz: Schott)
    I:Bc

Kallusch, W.

Variations on an original theme ('Pressburg, 1830'), for clarinet and orchestra
MS A:Wn Sm 2297

Kauer, Ferdinand (1751–1831)

MGG attributes to Kauer a *Symphonie concertante* for clarinet and orchestra.

Kleinheinz, Franz Xaver

Sainsbury identifies Kleinheinz as a pianist in Vienna and Budapest who composed a *Trio*, Op. 13, for violin or clarinet, piano, and bass.

Kodrin, ?

Conzert-Variationen (1886) for E♭ clarinet with band
MS A:Wn Sm 20800

Koschowitz, Josef

Serenata, for clarinet, violin, and cello
MS H:Bn Ms.Mus.1655

Kozeluch, Johann Anton (b. 1753)

Concerto for clarinet and orchestra
MS A:W*n* Sm 5853

Concerto for clarinet and orchestra
MS A:Wn Sm 5854

Kreith, Carlo (d. 1809)

Sonata in E♭, for clarinet and violin
MS A:Wgm XI 5958

Krenn, Franz (1839–1890)

Concertino (1844) for clarinet and orchestra
MS A:Wn Sm 14548

Krommer, Franz, 1759–1831

Concerto in E♭ for clarinet and orchestra
MS I:Bc

Concerto in E♭, Op. 52, for clarinet and orchestra
MS I:Bc

Concerto in F Major, Op. 36, for clarinet and orchestra
EP (Paris: Duhan)
    F:Pn Vm.24.158

Quartet, for clarinet and strings
MS A:Wgm XI 2577

Quartet, for clarinet and strings
MS A:Wgm XI 10745

Grand Quartet in B♭, Op. 83, for clarinet and strings
MS I:Bc

Quartet in B♭ for clarinet and strings
EP (Firenze: Cipriani)
  I:Bc

Quartet in E♭ for clarinet and strings
EP (Firenze: Cipriani)
  I:Bc

Krufft, Nikolaus Freiherr von (1779–1818)

Variations and Rondo, for clarinet and piano
MS A:Wgm XI 6725

MGG also attributes to Krufft a *Variations sur l'air de la Sentinelle* (Wien: Artaria, 1812) for clarinet and piano.

Küffner, Joseph (1776–1856)

Potpourri, Op. 190, for clarinet and orchestra
EP (Mainz: Schott)
  I:Bc

MGG also attributes to Küffner a *Principes elementaires … de Clarinette*.

Kurpinski, Karol Kazimierz (Polish, 1785–1857)

MGG attributes to Kurpinski a *Concerto* (1823) for clarinet and a *Trio* for clarinet, violin and cello.

Labitzky, Josef (Czech, 1802–1881)

Divertimento, for clarinet and orchestra
MS A:Wn Sm 23348

Lebrun, Ludwig (1752–1790)

MGG attributes to Lebrun a *Concerto* in B♭ (Breitkopf & Härtel, 1781) for clarinet.

Lefèvre, Jean Xavier (1763–1829)

Concerto for clarinet and orchestra
MS A:Wn Sm 5655

Sainsbury identifies Lefèvre as the first clarinet at the Opera in Paris and composer of (Five) *Concerti* (Paris, 1793–1799) for clarinet.

Lindpainter, Peter (1791–1856)

Concertino, Op. 41 (ded. to Mr. Tausch, fils), for clarinet and orchestra or piano
EP (Mainz: Schott)
  I:Bc

Concerto (ded. Bärmann) for clarinet and orchestra
EP (Mainz: Schott)
  I:Bc

Mahon, John (1746–1834)

MGG attributes to Mahon two *Concerti* (London: Bland, 1785, 1790) and *A New and Complete Preceptor* ('to which is added the gamut for the Clara Voce or Corno Bassetta,' London: Goulding, 1803).

Marty, Georges Eugene (1860–1908)

MGG attributes to Marty a *Fantaisie* (Paris: Buffet) for clarinet and orchestra.

Maurer, Ludwig Wilhelm (1789–1878)

MGG attributes to Maurer a *Concertino*, Op. 57 (Leipzig) and a *Concertino* in A♭ Major, Op. 64 (Braunschweig: Meyer) for clarinet and orchestra.

Meissner, Filippo

(Three) *Quartets*, for clarinet and strings
MS I:MOe Mus.F.729

Michel, Josef [pseud. for Michel Yost] (1754–1786)

Concerto for clarinet and orchestra
MS A:Wn Sm 5856

Concerto for clarinet and orchestra
MS A:Wn Sm 5857

Concerto for clarinet and orchestra
MS A:Wn Sm 5858

Concerto for clarinet and orchestra
MS A:Wn Sm 5859

Concerto for clarinet and orchestra
MS A:Wn Sm 5860

Concerto for clarinet and orchestra
MS A:Wn Sm 5869

Concerto, Nr. 9, for clarinet and orchestra
EP (Paris: Pleyel, ca. 1800)
      GB:Lbm H.2164.(1.)

Concerto, Nr. 10, for clarinet and orchestra
EP (Paris: Pleyel, ca. 1800)
      GB:Lbm H.2164.(2.)

Concerto, Nr.11, for clarinet and orchestra
EP (Paris: Pleyel, ca. 1800)
      GB:Lbm H.2164.(3.)

Concerto, Nr. 12, for clarinet and orchestra
EP (Paris: Pleyel, ca. 1800)
      GB:Lbm H.2189.c.(1.)

Concerto, Nr. 14, for clarinet and orchestra
EP (Paris: Pleyel, ca. 1800)
      GB:Lbm H.2164.(4.)

Quartet for clarinet and strings
MS (Wien: Traeg's *Catalog*, 1799)

According to Sainsbury, Michel also had published (Paris, 1801), *Douze Grands Solos, 'Choisis dans les Ouvrages du celebre Michel, pour servir a ceux qui veulent parvenir toutes les difficulties de cet instrument.'*

Molter, Johann Melchior (1695–1765)

MGG attributes to Molter four *Concerti* for clarinet (MS, D:KA).

Moscheles, Ignaz (1794–1870)

Fantaisie, Op. 46, for clarinet, violin, cello, and piano
EP (Paris: Richault)
      I:Bc

Müller, Iwan (1786–1854, 'Auteur de la nouvelle Clarinette')

Quartet for clarinet and strings
MS I:Bc
      I have seen an early nineteenth century engraving of Müller playing a recital before a small aristocratic gathering in Vienna which clearly shows Schubert among the listeners.

Müller, Johann Michael (1683–1736)

(Two) *Quartets*, for clarinet and strings
MS A:Wgm XI 10747

Neubauer, Johann (1760–1795)

Quartet for clarinet and strings
MS (Wien: Traeg's *Catalog*, 1799)

Nopitsch, Christoph (1758–1824)

MGG attributes to Nopitsch a *Quintetto concertante* (MS, D:NL) for clarinet and strings.

Novorks, Leopold

Quintet, for clarinet and strings
MS A:Wgm XI 38681

Oestreich, Carl (early nineteenth century)

Variationen (1822) for clarinet
MS BRD:F Mus.Hs. 678

Variationen (1822) for clarinet
MS BRD:F Mus.Hs. 733

Ottl, Josef

Ave Maria, for SATB, solo clarinet, and strings
MS A:Wn Sm 242

Pacini, Giovanni (1796–1867)

Quoniam, for Bass, clarinet and orchestra
MS I:Ls B. 102

Pechacek, Frantisek (1763–1816)

MGG attributes to Pechacek an *Adagio et Polonoise* for clarinet and orchestra.

Petricek, ?

Concerto (1810) for clarinet and orchestra
MS A:Wn Sm 610

Pfeilstuker, N.

Sainsbury identifies Pfeilstuker as a professor of clarinet, publishing in Paris, in 1802, a *Concerto* for clarinet.

Pichl, Wenzel (1741–1805)

Quartet for clarinet and strings
MS   I:Gl SS.B.1.2.(H.8)

Pillotti, Giuseppe

Concerto in B♭ Major (1815) for clarinet and orchestra
MS   I:Bc

Pleyel, Ignaz (1757–1831)

Concerto for clarinet and orchestra
MS   A:Wn Sm 5861

Concerto for clarinet and orchestra
MS   A:Wn Sm 5862

Pokorny, Franz Xaver (1729–1794)

(Two) *Concerti* for clarinet
MS   D:Rtt [according to MGG]

Polzelli, Antoine

Trio, for clarinet, viola and cello
MS   A:Wgm XI 2567

Proksch, Joseph (1794–1864)

MGG attributes to Proksch a *Concerto* for clarinet and orchestra.

Radicati, Felice

Concerto in E♭ (1816) for clarinet and orchestra.
MS   I:Bc

Rathe, ?

Sainsbury identifies Rathe as a 'celebrated clarinetist and composer for his instrument in Paris,' during the latter part of the eighteenth century.

Reinecke, Carl Heinrich (1824–1910)

MGG attributes to Reinecke a *Trio*, Op. 264, for clarinet and strings.

Reissinger, Carlo

L'Attente et l'Arrivee, (Two) Fantasies, Op. 180, for clarinet and orchestra
MS I:Bc

Riepel, Joseph (1709–1782)

Sainsbury identifies Riepel as the composer of a *Sonata*, Op. 29, for piano and clarinet, or violin.

Ries, Ferdinand (1784–1838)

MGG attributes to Ries a *Sonata*, Op. 29, for clarinet and piano.

Röder, Georg (nineteenth century)

Offertorium, for SATB, solo clarinet, and orchestra
MS A:Wn Sm 9784

Romberg, Andreas Jacob (1767–1821)

MGG attributes to Romberg a *Double Concerto* for clarinet and violin and a *Quintet* for clarinet and strings.

Ron, Jean Martin de (1789–1817)

Theme finois avec Variations for clarinet and orchestra
EP   (Leipzig)
     S:Skma [according to MGG]

Röntgen, Julius (Dutch, 1855–1932)

MGG attributes to Rontgen a *Trio* for clarinet and strings.

Rosetti, Franz Anton (1746–1792)

Concerto for clarinet and orchestra
MS A:Wn Sm 5863

Rossini, Gioacchino (1792–1868)

MGG attributes to Rossini a *Fantasia* for clarinet and piano.

Roth, Philipp Jakob (1779–1850)

MGG attributes to Roth a *Rondo* in B♭ for clarinet and orchestra.

Rudolph, Erzherzog (of Austria)

Cavatina (from Rossini's *Zelmira*), for clarinet and piano
MS   A:Wgm XI 8344
  This manuscript was owned by Beethoven.

Sonata, for clarinet and piano
MS   A:Wgm XI 15420

Variations, for clarinet
MS   A:Wgm XI 15410 [this copy is for violin]

Rudolph, Johann Joseph (1788–1831)

MGG attributes to Rudolph a *Sonata* (Wien: Steiner, 1822) for clarinet and piano.

Rummel, Christiano di Nassau

Concertino, Op. 58, for clarinet and orchestra, or band, or piano
EP   (Mainz: Schott)
  I:Bc [here only the piano version]

Schacht, Theodor Freiherr von (1748–1823)

Concerto for clarinet and orchestra
MS   D:Es [according to MGG]

Schenk, Johann Baptist (1753–1836)

MGG attributes to Schenk a *Concertante* for clarinet and orchestra.

Schindelmeisser, Louis Alexander Balthasar (1811–1864)

MGG attributes to Schindelmeisser a *Concertino* (Leipzig: Breitkopf & Härtel, 1832) for
  clarinet and orchestra.

Schmidt, ?

Concerto for clarinet and orchestra
MS   A:Wn Sm 5656

Schneider, George

Concerto, Op. 103, for clarinet and orchestra
EP   (Bonn: Simrock)
   I:Bc

Schmidt, Franz (Austrian, 1874–1939)

Quintet, for clarinet, piano, and strings
MS A:Wgm XI 50.504

Quintet, for clarinet, piano, and strings
MS A:Wgm XI 50.885

Schwindel, Friedrich (1737–1786)

MGG attributes to Schwindel a *Concerto* for clarinet.

Simon, Johann Gottfried

Concerto ('Berlin') for clarinet and orchestra
MS A:Wn Sm 5657

Solere, Étienne (1753–1817)

Sainsbury identifies Solere as a clarinetist and professor at the Paris Conservatory. He published much clarinet music between 1793–1800.

Soller, ?

(Six) *Airs Varié*, Op. 4, for clarinet and viola.
MS (Wien: Traeg's *Catalog*, 1799)

Spohr, Louis (1784–1859)

First Concerto, Op. 26, for clarinet and orchestra
MS A:Wgm VIII 1570
MS I:Bc

Second Concerto, Op. 57, for clarinet and orchestra
MS A:Wgm VIII 5207

Third Concerto, for clarinet and orchestra
MS A:Wgm VIII 28036

[Composition] for Soprano, clarinet, and piano
MS BRD:F Mus.Hs. 1790

There are additional anonymous works for the same combination under this number.

Stamitz, Johann Wenzel Anton (1717–1757)

Concerto in B♭ for clarinet
MS D:Rtt [according to MGG]

Stamitz, Karl (1745–1801)

Concerto for clarinet and orchestra
MS A:Wn Sm 5864

These four concerti in A:Wn were all composed for Josef Beer, 'Kammer mus., K. Prusse'
Concerto for clarinet and orchestra
MS A:Wn Sm 5865

Concerto for clarinet and orchestra
MS A:Wn Sm 5866

Concerto for clarinet and orchestra
MS A:Wn Sm 5867

Concerto, in E♭ Major, for clarinet
MS (Wien: Traeg's *Catalog*, 1799)

Quartet for clarinet and strings
MS (Wien: Traeg's *Catalog*, 1799)

Struck, Paul (1776–1820)

MGG attributes to Struck a *Grand Duo*, Op. 7 (Wien, 1804) for clarinet and piano.

Stüntz, Joseph Hartmann (1793–1859)

Concerto for clarinet
MS D:Mbs Mus.Ms. 4025

Süssmayer, Franz (1766–1803)

Concerto for clarinet and orchestra
MS GB:Lbm Add. 32181 [incomplete]

Täglichsbeck, Thomas (1799–1867)

MGG attributes to Täglichsbeck a *Quintet*, Op. 44, for clarinet and strings.

Tanejew, Alexander (1850–1918)

MGG attributes to Tanejew an *Arabeske*, Op. 24, for clarinet and piano.

Tausch, Franz (1762–1817)

Sainsbury identifies Tausch as a clarinetist who composed chiefly concerti.

Tobi, F.J.

Sainsbury identifies Tobi as the composer of (Three) *Trios*, Op. 1 (Paris, 1780) for clarinet, violin and bass.

Truschetzky, ? (Georg Druschetzky)

Concerto for clarinet and orchestra
MS A:Wn Sm 5658

Vocet, Jan Nepomuk (1777–1843)

MGG attributes to Vocet a Concerto for clarinet.

Vogel, Cajetan (1750–1794)

MGG attributes to Vogel a Concerto for clarinet and orchestra.

Vogel, Johann Christoff (1756–1788)

Concerto for clarinet and orchestra
MS A:Wn Sm 5869

Vols, ?

Quartet, for clarinet and strings
MS A:Wgm XI 2596

Wagner, Guillaume

Divertimento for clarinet and orchestra
MS A:Wgm VIII 20075

Walter, August (1821–1866)

MGG attributes to Walter a *Phantasie and Capriccio* (Leipzig: Breitkopf & Härtel) for clarinet and piano.

Wanhal, Jan (1739–1813)

MGG attributes to Vanhal the following works:
    Concerto for clarinet (MS, Leningrad)
    Quartet in B♭ for clarinet and strings (MS, *D:B* Ms. 22583/20)
    (Two) *Trios* (London, 1785) for clarinet and strings

Weiner, Leo

Ballade, for clarinet and orchestra
MS H:Bn Ms.Mus.1856

Wessely, Johann (1762–1810)

MGG attributes to Wessely *Eight Variations* on a Theme by Süssmayr (Leipzig: Hofmeister, 1794) for clarinet and orchestra and (Three) *Quartets* (Offenbach: André) for clarinet and strings.

Westerhoff, Heinrich Philip (1760–1806)

MGG attributes to Westerhoff two *Concerti* (Braunschweig, 1798, 1799) for clarinet and orchestra.

Wilms, Johann (1772–1847)

MGG attributes to Wilms a *Concerto*, Op. 40 (Leipzig: Kühnel) for clarinet.

Winter, Peter (1754–1825)

MGG attributes to Winter the following works:
    Rondo in F Major for clarinet and cello
    Concertino in E♭ Major for clarinet
    Quartet in E♭ Major (München: Sidler) for clarinet and strings]

Winterle, Edmund

Romanze (1843) for clarinet and piano.
MS A:Wn Sm 5130

Woldemar, N.

Sainsbury identifies Woldemar as a violinist at Paris who composed and published a *Method* for the clarinet.

Wunderlich, Christian Friedrich (b. 1722)

Sainsbury identifies Wunderlich as an oboist in the court of the Margrave of Anspach and an 'excellent' player on the oboe and clarinet, and composer of music for both instruments between 1738–1770.

Yost, Michel (see Josef Michel)

Concerto for clarinet and orchestra
MS I:Gl M.36.24.22.

MUSIC WITH SOLO BASSET HORN

Druschetzky, Georg (1745–1819)

Quartet, for basset horn and strings
MS H:Bn Ms.Mus.1552

Fuss, Johann Evangelist (1777–1819)

MGG attributes to Fuss a *Quartet*, Op. 2 (Wien: Bureau des arts et d'industrie) for basset horn and strings.

Gyrowetz, Adalbert (1763–1850)

MGG attributes to Gyrowetz a lost *Concerto* for bassett horn.

Roth, Philipp Jakob (1779–1850)

MGG attributes to Roth a *Concertino* for basset horn and orchestra.

MUSIC WITH SOLO BASSOON

Abraham, ? (d. 1805)

Sainsbury attributes to Abraham a method for the bassoon.

Almenraeder, ?

Sainsbury attributes to Almenraeder 'some music for the bassoon,' before 1822.

Anonymous

Complete Instructions for the Bassoon
EP   (London: Preston, ca. 1790)
     GB:Lbm B.160.g.(2.)

Sonata (1686) for bassoon and bass
MS   I:MOe Mus.E.316

Bach, K. P. E. (1714–1788)

Trio (1755) for bassoon, viola, and cello
MS   B:Bc Wotquenne 6365

Bertoli, Giovanni

[Solo works] for bassoon
EP   (Venetia: Vincenti, 1645)
     I:Bc

Blasius, Frédéric (1758–1829)

(Six) *Sonates*, Op. 57, for bassoon and cello
EP   (Paris: Magasin de Musique)
     F:Pn Vm.9.14903

Bohner, Johann Ludwig

Concerto (1811) for bassoon and orchestra
MS   GB:Lbm Add. 32218

Boismortier, Joseph (1691–1765)

(Five) *Sonatas*, Op. 26, for cello or bassoon
EP   (Paris: the composer, 1729)
     GB:Lbm G.11.a.(2.)

Danzi, Franz (1763–1826)

MGG attributes to Danzi unpublished *Concerti* in C and F Major for bassoon.

Delcambre, Thomas

Sainsbury identifies Delcambre as a professor of bassoon at the Paris Conservatory and composer for his instrument.

Devienne, François (1759–1803)

(Seven) *Quartets* for bassoon and strings
MS (Wien: Traeg's *Catalog*, 1799)

MGG also attributes to Devienne the following works:
(Four) *Concerti* for bassoon
(Three) *Quartets*, Op. 75 (Paris: Erard), for bassoon and strings.
(Six) *Sonates,* Op. 24 (Paris: Sieber), for bassoon and bass
(Six) *Trios* for bassoon, violin and bass

Erbach, Friedrich Karl (1680–1731)

MGG attributes to Erbach (Six) *Duets* for bassoon and cello (MS, D:Ds).

Fasch, Johann Friedrich (1688–1758)

MGG attributes to Fasch a *Sonata* in C Major for bassoon and bass.

Fortia de Piles, Alphonse-Toussaint (1758–1826)

MGG attributes to Piles a *Concerto* for bassoon.

Fougas, ?

Sainsbury identifies Fougas as a professor of bassoon in Paris and composer of bassoon music.

Gagnebin, Henri (b. 1886)

MGG attributes to Gagnebin a *Scherzetto* (Paris: Leduc) for bassoon and piano.

Galliard, Johann (1687–1749)

(Six) *Sonatas* for bassoon and harpsichord
EP (London: Walsh, 1732)
GB:Lbm F.515

Sainsbury identifies Galliard as the composer, in 1745, of 'a curious instrumental piece for twenty-four bassoons and four double basses.'

Gayer, Johann Nepomuk (1746–1811)

MGG attributes to Gayer three *Concerti* for bassoon.

Gebauer, François (1773–1844)

Quartets for bassoon and strings
MS F:Pn K.1848

Menuet du Diable (May 17, 1844), for bassoon
MS F:Pn W24.117

Gehring, Johann Wilhelm (d. 1787)

Sainsbury identifies Gehring as 'Chapelmaster at Rudolstadt after the death of Gebel, was a celebrated performer on the bassoon and composer for his instrument.'

Graun, August Friedrich (1698–1765)

MGG attributes to Graun a *Concerto* in B♭ Major for bassoon.

Hargrave, Henry

(Five) *Concerti* for bassoon
EP (London: the composer, ca. 1765)
    GB:Lbm G.32

Heine, Samuel Friedrich (1764–1821)

MGG attributes to Heine a *Variations* for bassoon and orchestra.

Herold, Nicolas (1721–1790)

MGG attributes to Herold an *Air varié* for bassoon and orchestra.

Hertel, Johann Wilhelm (1727–1789)

(Three) *Concerti* for bassoon and orchestra
MS B:Bc Wotquenne 5564

Hoffmeister, Franz Anton (1754–1812)

(Two) *Concerti*, in B♭ and F Major, for bassoon
MS (Wien: Traeg's *Catalog*, 1799)

Holzbogn, Giovanni, Georg

(Six) *Sonatas* for bassoon and bass
MS (Wien: Traeg's *Catalog*, 1799)

Hummel, Johann Nepomuk (1778–1837)

Concerto for bassoon and orchestra
MS GB:Lbm Add 32218

Hummel, Joseph Friedrich (1841–1919)

MGG attributes to Hummel a *Concerto* (Leipzig: Breitkopf & Härtel) for bassoon.

Jacobi, F.

Variations for bassoon and orchestra
MS A:Wgm VIII 30596

Kalliwoda, Johann Wenzel (1801–1866)

Variations et Rondo, Op. 57 for bassoon and orchestra
MS D:KA [cited in MGG]
EP (Leipzig: Peters, 1856)

Kauer, Ferdinand (1750–1832)

MGG attributes to Kauer three *Concerti* for bassoon.

Kopprasch, Wilhelm

Sainsbury identifies Kopprasch as a German bassoonist and composer of music for at the
end of the 18th century.

Kozeluch, Johann Anton (1738–1814)

Concerto for bassoon and orchestra
MS CS:Pn F, 380 [cited in MGG]

Krufft, Nikolaus Freiherr von (1779–1818)

MGG attributes to Krufft a *Grande Sonata*, Op. 34 (Leipzig: Breitkopf & Härtel) for bassoon
and piano.

Kummer, ?

Sainsbury identifies Kummer as a performer on the bassoon at Dresden, adding, In 1799 he was much admired at Leipzig, where he also published some music for bassoon.'

Latti, ?

Concerto, in E♭ Major, for bassoon
MS (Wien: Traeg's *Catalog,* 1799)

Laube, Anton (1718–1784)

MGG attributes to Laube an *Aria* in G Major for Tenor, solo bassoon and orchestra.

Malzat, Ignaz (1757–1804)

(Two) *Concerti*, in C and G Major, for bassoon
MS (Wien: Traeg's *Catalog,* 1799)

(Six) *Quartets* for bassoon and strings
MS (Wien: Traeg's *Catalog,* 1799)

Massonneau, Louis (1766–1848)

MGG attributes to Massonneau a lost *Concerto* for bassoon.

Mattei, Stanislao (1750–1825)

Ridicolo, Solo for bassoon, with strings ('*del Sig. Walther … Esguito dal Sig. N.N. che per li numerosi anni era ridotto ad esser privo poco meno di tutti denti*')
MS I:Bsf M.Mattei XXII-7

Mercy, Louis

(Six) *Sonatas*, Op. 3, for bassoon and bass
EP (London: Johnson, ca. 1735)
    GB:Lbm E.368.c.(8.)

Michl, Joseph (1745–1815)

MGG attributes to Michl a Concerto for bassoon and orchestra.

Molter, Johann Melchior (1695–1765)

MGG attributes to Molter two Concerti for bassoon (MS, D:KA).

Moscheles, J.

Sainsbury identifies Moscheles as the composer of a *Duet Concertante* in B♭ Major for cello and bassoon.

Ozi, Etienne (b. 1754)

F:Pn has many solo works for bassoon by Ozi, including seven *Concerti*.

Sainsbury identifies Ozi as professor of bassoon at the Conservatory and first bassoon at the academy of music. In addition to the concerti, Sainsbury mentions Ozi's *Method* for bassoon which he says is considered by far the best available until 1825.

Paxton, Stephen

(Six) *Easy Solos*, Op. 3 for bassoon or cello
EP (London: the composer, ca. 1780)
    GB:Lbm G.500.(9.)
    GB:Lbm G.24.(4.) [another edition]

Perez, Davide (1711–1778)

Miserere, for 5 voices, bassoon, and organ
MS A:Wn Fond Kiesewetter St 67 F 59

Pfeiffer, Franz Anton (1754–1787)

MGG attributes to Pfeiffer the following works:
    Concerto in C Major for bassoon
    (Eight) *Quartets* for bassoon and strings (six published by Hummel in Berlin
        and Amsterdam)
    Divertimento for bassoon, violin, and cello
    (Two) *Sonatas* for bassoon and bass

According to Sainsbury Pfeiffer was a 'celebrated' performer on the bassoon, in the of the Duke of Mecklenburg. Sainsbury maintains he died in 1792 after composing much bassoon music.

Pleyel, Ignaz (1757–1831)

Quartet for bassoon and strings
MS (Wien: Traeg's *Catalog*, 1799)

Prati, Alessio (1750–1788)

MGG attributes to Prati a *Concerto* in B♭ for bassoon.

Reicha, Anton (1770–1836)

Duo, for bassoon and piano
MS F:Pn MS.2513

Quintet, for bassoon and strings
MS F:Pn MS.12032

Quintet, for bassoon and strings
MS F:Pn MS.12012

Quintet, Nr. 4, in E Minor, for bassoon and strings
MS F:Pn 2506

Quintet, Nr. 5, in A Minor, for bassoon and strings
MS F:Pn MS.2508

Reidinger, Stanislaus (1734–1794)

Concerto for bassoon
MS A:KR [according to MGG]

Ritter, Georg Wenzel (1748–1808)

Sainsbury identifies Ritter as a 'celebrated' performer on the bassoon and composer of works for bassoon published in Paris.

Röder, Carl (b. 1812)

Fantasie, for bassoon and piano
MS A:Wgm VIII 30642

Concertino, for bassoon and orchestra (or piano)
MS A:Wgm VIII 30643

Variations, for bassoon and piano
MS A:Wgm VIII 30644

Concerto, for bassoon and piano
MS A:Wgm VIII 30645

Fantasie, for bassoon and piano
MS A:Wgm VIII 30646

Elegie, for bassoon and piano ('for H. W. Ernst')
MS A:Wgm VIII 30648

Ron, Jean Martin de (1789–1817)

Andante et Polonoise for bassoon and orchestra
EP (Leipzig: Breitkopf & Härtel)
    S:Skma [according to MGG]

Schmidtbach, C.

Variations, for bassoon and orchestra
MS A:Wgm VIII 31194

Schmitbaur, Joseph Aloys (1718–1809)

MGG attributes to Schmittbaur three *concerti* for bassoon.

Schmitt, Nicol

Sainsbury identifies Schmitt as a bassoonist and composer of bassoon music published in
    Paris between 1788–1797.

Scimpke, ?

(Four) *Concerti*, in E♭, F, B♭, and C Major, for bassoon
MS (Wien: Traeg's *Catalog*, 1799)

Tartagnini, Luigi

Adagio con variations (1815) for bassoon and orchestra
MS I:Bc

Triebensee, Georg (1746–1813)

(Twelve) *Exercises and Variations*, for bassoon accompanied by cello
MS A:Wgm VIII 25299

Wagenseil, Georg (1715–1777)

MGG attributes to Wagenseil a *Concerto* for bassoon.

Wanhal, Jan (1739–1813)

MGG attributes to Vanhal a *Concerto* for bassoon (MS, D:B).

Wassermann, Heinrich Joseph (1791–1838)

MGG attributes to Wassermann an *Air varié*, Op. 19 (Leipzig: Peters) for bassoon and orchestra.

Wenck, August Heinrich (d. 1814)

MGG attributes to Wenck a *Concerto* for bassoon.

Westerhoff, Heinrich (1760–1806)

MGG attributes to Westerhoff a *Concerto* (1794) for bassoon.

Winkler, E.

Introduction and variations, for bassoon and orchestra or piano
MS   A:Wgm VIII 30692

Winter, Peter (1754–1825)

MGG attributes to Winter the following works:
    Concertino in C Minor for bassoon
    Rondo in C Major for bassoon
    Rondo con Variations (1810) for bassoon

Zellbell, Anders (1680–1727)

MGG attributes to Zellbell a *Concerto* for bassoon.

MUSIC WITH SOLO TRUMPET

Alcock, John (1715–1806)

(Six) *Suites of Easy Lessons for the Harpsicord, or Spinnet, with a Trumpet piece*
EP   (Reading: the composer, 1741)
        GB:Lbm E.3.a.(1.)

Anonymous

Sonata (1686) for cornettino and bass
MS   I:MOe Mus.E.316

Sonate, for tromba
MS   I:MOe Mus.G.312

Stücke die ein K. K. Trompeter (for field use)
MS (Wien: Traeg's *Catalog*, 1799)

Einige Ubungen für Maschin-Trompete
MS A:Wn Sm 23813

Baldessari, Pietro

Sonatas, for cornetto
MS A:Wn E.M.97

Bitti, Martino

Concertos ('*dont il y en a un pour la Trompette ou le Haubois*')
EP (Amsterdam: Roger, ca. 1715)
  GB:Lbm G.917

Buhl, David (b. 1781)

(Two) *Methods* for trumpet
MS F:Pn Cl.10; L.10.183

Ordonnance de 1803, for one trumpet
MS F:Pn L.9.632

Ordonnance de 1806
MS F:Pn L.9.628

Ordonnances ou sonnerie de trumpet de 1825
MS F:Pn L.9814

Ordonnance de 1829, for trumpet
MS F:Pn L.9804

Busi, Alessandro

Il Carnevale di Venezia, for cornet and piano
EP (Torino: Giudici e Strada)
  I:Bc

Capanna, Alessandro (1814–1892)

Concerto, for trumpet and piano (based on Verdi's *Trovatore*)
EP (Bologna, 1868)
  I:Bsf FC.C.II.4.

Cazzati, Maurizio (1620–1677)

(Four) *Sonatas*, Op. 35, for tromba and strings
EP   (Bologna: Siluani, 1665)
    I:Bc

(Four) *Sonatas*, Op. 35, for tromba and strings
EP   (Bologna: Siluani, 1668)
    I:Bc

Dixon, William (b. 1760)

Chorister's Companion, includes 'We sing His live who once was slain , The celebrated Trumpet piece'
EP   (London: Hart & Fellows, ca. 1800)
    GB:Lbm B.511.i.(3.)

Fago, Nicola (1672–1745)

MGG attributes to Fago a *Credo* for chorus, oboe, trumpet, and organ, and a *Messa dei morti* for chorus with trumpet.

Gabrielli, Domenico (1659–1690)

MGG attributes to Gabrielli a *Concerto* a 4 and (Six) *Sonatas* for trumpet and strings (MS, I:Bsp), the latter apparently containing a picture of the composer.

Gagnebin, Henri (b. 1886)

MGG attributes to Gagnebin a *Sonata da chiesa* (Paris: Schola cantorum) for trumpet and organ.

Gottsched, Johann Christoph (1700–1766)

MGG attributes to Gottsched a *Tafelmusik fur Graf von Manteuffel* (1743), a cantata with trumpet and timpani.

Hanke, Karl (1750–1803)

MGG attributes to Hanke a Concerto for trumpet.

Heinrich, Anton Philipp (1781–1861)

MGG attributes to Heinrich a *Concerto* for the Kent Bugle.

Herrmann, Gottfried (1808–1878)

MGG attributes to Herrmann an *Andante and Polacca* (1828) for trumpet and orchestra.

Hertel, Johann Wilhelm (1727–1789)

Concerto for trumpet and orchestra
MS B:Bc Wotquenne 5565

Concerto for trumpet and orchestra
MS B:Bc Wotquenne 5566

Concerto for trumpet and orchestra
MS B:Bc Wotquenne 5567

Hillemacher, Paul Josepf (1852–1933)

MGG attributes to Hillemacher a *Solo* (Paris: Evette & Schaeffer, 1897) for trumpet and piano.

Hummel, Johann Nepomuk (1778–1837)

Concerto for trumpet and strings
MS GB:Lbm Add. 32222

Jacchini, Giuseppe Maria (d. 1727)

MGG attributes to Jacchini (Three) *Sonatas* for trumpet and strings.

Kauer, Ferdinand (1751–1831)

MGG attributes to Kauer three *Concerti* for clarino.

Kéler, Béla (1820–1882)

MGG attributes to Kéler a 'Stücke' for cornet a piston.

Kurpinski, Karol Kazimierz (1785–1857)

MGG attributes to Kurpinski a *Cavatine* for trumpet and orchestra.

Manfredini, Francesco Maria (1688–1748)

Concerto for 1 or 2 trumpets, strings, and organ
MS I:Bsp [according to MGG, which reproduces the first page on VIII, col. 1579.]

Molter, Johann Melchior (1695–1765)

MGG attributes to Molter four *Concerti* for clarino (MS, D:KA).

Morequx, ?

(Six) *Morceaux*, for Trompette de Cavalerie and piano
MS GB:Lbm R.M.21.e.4.Nr. 6.

Pacini, Giovanni (1796–1867)

Laudamus e Gratias, for Baritone, trumpet, and orchestra
MS I:Ls B. 73

Pepusch, Johann (1667–1752)

(Six) *Cantatas*, four with flute and two with trumpet and voice
EP (London?)
    GB:Lbm G.222.(2.)

Purcell, Daniel (d. 1717)

(Three) *Sonatas* for trumpet and strings
MS GB:Lbm [according to MGG]

Reali, M.

Kyrie, for TTB, clarino, and organ
MS I:Bsf FC.F.I.8

Richter, Franz Xaver (1709–1789)

MGG attributes to Richter a *Concerto* for Clarino.
MS US:Wc [according to MGG]

Rustici, Alessandro

Messa, for SATB, trumpet, and 2 organs
MS I:Ls B.130b

Schmittbaur, Joseph Aloys (1718–1809)

MGG attributes to Schmittbaur seven Concerti for trumpet.

Somis, Giovanni Battista (1686–1763)

MGG attributes to Somis four *Concerti* for trumpet.

Torelli, Giuseppe (1658–1709)

(Eleven) Sonatas for trumpet and strings
MS I:Bsp [according to MGG]

Viviani, Giovanni Bonaventura

Capricci Armonici da Chiesa (contains a *Sonate* for tromba solo)
EP(Venetia: Sala, 1678)

Weckmann, Matthias (1621–1674)

MGG attributes to Weckmann (Two) *Sonatas* for cornetto and strings and (Eight)
Sonatas for cornetto, violin, trombone, bassoon, and continuo (both MS, D:Lr).

MUSIC WITH SOLO HORN

Aghte, F. W.

Sainsbury attributes to Aghte 'music for the horn,' ca. 1822.

Andre, Johann Anton (1775–1842)

MGG attributes to Andre a *Concerto*, Op. 33, for horn and orchestra.

Anonymous

(Two) *Concerti*, in E♭ Major, for horn
MS (Wien: Traeg's *Catalog*, 1799)

(Collection) of solo works for horn, with various ensembles
MS S:L Wenster I, Nr. 1–17

Compleat Tutor for the French Horn
EP   (London: Simpson, ca. 1746)
    GB:Lbm D.47.f.(1.)

Complete Tutor for the French Horn
EP   (London: Thompson, ca. 1755)
    GB:Lbm D.47.e.

Variations in C Major, for viola, horn, and cello
MS (Wien: Traeg's *Catalog*, 1799)

Arnkiel, T.

Sainsbury attributes to Arnkiel a published treatise (1683) on the use of horns in music.

Bachelet, Alfred (1864–1944)

Lamento for viola or horn and string orchestra
MP (Paris, Leduc, 1915) [cited in MGG]

Bellonci, von Leidisdorf

Sonate for horn and piano
MS A:Wgm XI 5983

Brock, Othone von Den

Sainsbury identifies Brock as the composer of much music for the horn in Paris since 1788.

Bury, ?

Sainsbury identifies Bury as a horn player and composer for the horn in Paris, ca. 1800.

Caparelli, ?

Sainsbury identifies Caparelli as an Italian horn player and composer of horn music published in Vienna in 1799.

Carafa, Michele (1787–1872)

Solo de Cor, accompanied by 2 clarinets and bassoon;
Solo de Cor à piston, accompanied by 2 clarinets, bassoon, and ophicleide, in 'Les Souvenier de Naples.'
MS F:Pn MS.3445

Carr, John

The Huntsman, a contata with 'symphonies accompanyed with the French Horn.'
EP (London: J. Johnson, ca. 1760)
        GB:Lbm G.807.a.(3.)

Dauprat, Louis-François (1781–1868)

Solo de Cor, accompanied by 2 clarinets, bassoon, and ophicleide, in 'Les Souvenier de Naples'
MS F:Pn MS.3445

There are many solo horn works by Dauprat in F:Pn.

MGG attributes to Dauprat the following:
  Method pour cor alto et cor basse (Paris: Zetter)
  Du cor a pistons (Paris: 1829)
  (Five) *Concerti* for horn (Paris: Zetter)
  (Two) *Concerti* for horn (MS, F:Pn)
  Three *Quintets*, Op. 6, for horn and strings
  Three *Melodies*, Op. 25, for horn and orchestra or piano (Paris: Schonenberger, 1843)
  Deux *Solos* et un duo, Op. 12, for horn and piano (Paris: Frey)
  (Three) *Solos*, Op. 16, for horn and piano (Paris: Zetter)
  Air varié, Op. 22, for horn and harp (Paris: Zetter)
  Duo, Op. 7, for horn and piano (Paris: Zetter)
  (Three) *Solos*, Op. 17, for alto horn and piano (Paris: Zetter)
  (Three) *Solos*, Op. 11, for alto horn and orchestra (Paris: Frey)
  (Three) *Solos*, Op. 20, for alto horn and piano (Paris: Zetter)
  Sonata, Op. 2, for horn and piano (Paris: Bochsa)
  Tableau musical, Op. 5, for piano and horn (Paris: the composer)
  (Two) *Theme varié*, Op. 23, 24 (Paris: Zetter)
  Sonata, Op. 3, for horn and harp (Paris: Bochsa)

Dessauer, Joseph

Nocturni (1844) for horn and piano
MS A:Wgm XI 42388

Devienne, François (1759–1803)

MGG refers to a Fifth *Concerto* (Paris: Imbault) for horn, composed by both Devienne and Frederic Duvernoy.

Dominick, M.

Sainsbury identifies Dominick as a horn professor at the Paris Conservatory and composer of horn music, including a Method.

Dornaus, L.

Sainsbury identifies Dornaus as a horn professor, younger brother of the following, and composer of music for horn.

Dornaus, Philip

Sainsbury identifies Dornaus as a German horn professor and composer of horn music published in Offenbach in 1802.

Dumonchau, Charles-François (1775–1820)

MGG, citing Fetis, attributes to Dumonchau a *Concerto* for horn and orchestra.

Duvernoy, Frédéric (1765–1838)

Sainsbury identifies Duvernoy as, 'a celebrated French horn player and professor at the Paris Conservatory. He has published much horn music, including a *Method*, between 1793 and 1804.'

Fuchs, Georg (1752–1821)

Fourth Concerto for horn
EP   (Paris: Naderman)
  F:Pn K.2019

Garaude, Alexis (1821–1857)

MGG attributes to Garaude a *Fantasie et variations sur l'air de la Molinara* for horn and piano.

Gayer, Johann Nepomuk (1746–1811)

MGG attributes to Gayer 15 *Concerti* for horn.

Gebauer, François (1773–1844)

(Three) *Quartets*, Op. 37, for horn and strings
EP   (Paris: Jouve)
  I:Bc

Graun, Carl Heinrich (1703–1759)

MGG attributes to Graun a *Concerto* for horn and orchestra.

Grund, Eduard (1802–1871)

MGG attributes to Grund a *Trio de Salon*, Op. 27, for piano and horn (or cello, or viola).

Gugel, H.

Sainsbury identifies Gugel as 'a celebrated performer on the horn, and composer for his instrument … His knowledge of his instrument is said to be perfect, and his powers upon it beyond all expectations.'

Haindl, Josef

Sonate for horn and klavier
MS A:Wgm XI 38283

Hanke, Karl (1750–1803)

MGG attributes to Hanke a *Concerto* for horn.

Haupt, ?

Sainsbury identifies Haupt as having authored with Punto a *Methode pour apprendre les elemens des Premiers et Deuxiemes Cors*, published in Paris in 1796.

Haydn, Josef (1732–1809)

Concerto, in E♭ Major, for horn.
MS (Wien: Traeg's *Catalog*, 1799)

Herrmann, Gottfried (1808–1878)

MGG attributes to Herrmann an *Am See* for horn and piano.

Hirtl, H.

Concerto for horn and orchestra
MS A:Wgm VIII 22526

Hoffman, Giovanni

Serenade for horn, viola and cello
MS (Wien: Traeg's *Catalog*, 1799)

Hoffmeister, Anton (1754–1812)

Quintet for horn and strings
MS A:Wgm XI 10755

Quintet in E♭ Major for horn and strings
MS (Wien: Traeg's *Catalog*, 1799)

Hummel, Ferdinand (1855–1928)

MGG attributes to Hummel a *Nocturne*, Op. 42 (Siegel, 1885) for horn, harp (or piano) and strings and a *Sonata*, Op. 117 (Leipzig and Berlin, 1912) for horn and piano.

Jadin, Louis Emmanuel (1768–1853)

MGG attributes to Jadin the following:
18th Pot-pouri (Paris: Duhan) for piano, harp and horn
21st Pot-pouri (Paris: Duhan) for piano and horn
(Three) *Nocturnes* (Paris: Dufault) for piano and horn

Kalkbrenner, Friedrich Wilhelm (1785–1849)

MGG attributes to Kalkbrenner a *Nocturne*, Op. 95 (Leipzig: Kistner) for horn and piano.

Kalliwoda, Johann Wenzel (1801–1866)

Introduction et Rondo, Op. 51 (1834) for horn and orchestra
MS   D:KA [cited in MGG]

Kenn, ?

Sainsbury identifies Kenn as a hornist at the Opera in Paris in 1798 and composer of some published horn music.

Kowalowsky, Johann

Theme and Variations for horn and orchestra
MS   A:Sca Hs. 123

Krause, J. H. (nineteenth century)

Adagio and Polonaise for horn and orchestra
MS   A:Wgm VIII 7648

Krenn, Franz (1839–1890)

Andante and Allegretto (1841) for horn and piano
MS   A:Wn Sm 14176

Concertino (1841) for horn and orchestra
MS   A:Wn Sm 14151

(Two) *Gradualien*, for Bass, horn and orchestra
MS   A:Wn Sm 13344

(Four) *Offertorium* (1859), for Soprano, horn, organ, and strings
MS A:Wn Sm 13374; 13376–13378

Offertorium (1888), for ST soli, horn, organ, and orchestra
MS A:Wn Sm 22487

Salve Regina, for SATB, horn solo, organ, and orchestra
MS A:Wn Sm 13409

Kreutzer, Conradin (1780–1849)

Das Muhlrad, for singer, horn, and piano
MS A:Wn Sm 21133

Krufft, Nikolaus Freiherr von (1779–1818)

MGG attributes to Krufft a *Sonata* (Leipzig: Breitkopf & Härtel) and a *Variations sur la Cavatine de Der Augenarzt* (Wien: Haslinger) for horn and piano.

Kunze, Carl H.

Sainsbury identifies Kunze as the composer of horn music between 1793–1800.

Kurpinski, Karol Kazimierz (1785–1857)

MGG attributes to Kurpinski a *Nokturn* for horn and strings.

Lachnith, Ludwig (1746–1820)

MGG attributes to Lachnith three *Concerti* for horn and orchestra.

Lackner, Ignaz

Noturno for horn and piano
MS A:Wn Sm 20465

Lebrun, Jean (1759–1809)

MGG attributes to Lebrun the following works for horn:
A *Concerto*
An *Adagio*
An *Ariette with variations*
a programmatic work on the 'Hirschjage.'

Leidesdorf, Maximilian (1787–1840)

MGG attributes to Leidesdorf a *Sonata* for horn and piano.

Makoweczky, ?

Sainsbury identifies Makoweczky as a horn player in the Prussian court and a student of Punto. He published in 1802 several volumes of horn music in Leipzig

Marechal, Henri Charles (1842–1924)

MGG attributes to Marechal a *Fantaisie* (Paris: Deplaix, 1899) for horn and piano.

Matthison-Hansen, Hans (1807–1890)

MGG attributes to Matthison a manuscript Sonata for horn and piano.

Massonneau, Louis (1766–1848)

MGG attributes to Massonneau a lost *Concerto* for horn.

Meifred, Joseph (1791–1867)

MGG attributes to Meifred the *Methode pour le cor cromatique* (Paris: Costallat, 1840).

Mengal, Martin Joseph (1784–1851)

MGG attributes to Mengal three *Concerti* for horn.

Molter, Johann Melchior (1695–1765)

MGG attributes to Molter a *Concerto* for horn (MS, D:KA).

Moscheles, Ignaz (1794–1870)

MGG attributes to Moscheles an *Introduction et rondeau*, Op. 63 (Leipzig: K & S, 1821) for horn and piano.

Mozart, Wolfgang A. (1756–1791)

(Two) *Concerti*, in E♭ Major, for horn
MS (Wien: Traeg's *Catalog*, 1799)

Quintet in E♭ for horn and strings
MS (Wien: Traeg's *Catalog*, 1799)

Naderman, F. J. (b. 1780)

Sainsbury identifies Naderman as a, 'celebrated harpist, born in Prague, and the composer of a *Trio* for harp, horn, and cello.'

Neubauer, ?

Duetto for horn and viola
MS (Wien: Traeg's *Catalog*, 1799)

Nisle, Johann Friedrich (b. 1780)

Sainsbury identifies Nisle as a horn player and composer of a few works for horn after 1798.

Oestreich, Carl, Frankfurt (nineteenth century)

Adagio & Polonaise for solo horn and orchestra
MS BRD:F Mus.Hs. 679

Andante con Variations, for horn and orchestra
MS BRD:F Mus.Hs. 673

Andante con Variations ('pour le Corno 2do Principalo') for horn and orchestra
MS BRD:F Mus.Hs. 677 and Mus. Hs. 683

Concertino for Second Horn (1830)
MS BRD:F Mus.Hs. 784

Concerto for horn
MS BRD:F Mus.Hs. 676 [incomplete]

Concerto for horn and orchestra (for 'Harder in Dresden')
MS BRD:F Mus.Hs. 680

Concerto for horn and orchestra
MS BRD:F Mus.Hs. 742 [incomplete]

Larghetto for horn and orchestra
MS BRD:F Mus.Hs. 675 [incomplete]

Sextetto, for horn and strings
MS BRD:F Mus.Hs. 682

Thema con Variation ('Dresden, 1816') for horn and orchestra
MS BRD:F Mus.Hs. 685

Tiroler con Variazione for horn and orchestra
MS BRD:F Mus.Hs. 743 [incomplete]

[Unfinished sketches] for horn
MS BRD:F Mus.Hs. 799

Pacini, Giovanni (1796–1867)

Quoniam, for Tenor, horn, and orchestra
MS I:Ls B.87

Pezold, Christian (1677–1733)

MGG attributes to Pezold a *Trio* in F Major for violin, horn, and bass.

Pfeffinger, Philip Jacob (1765–1821)

MGG attributes to Pfeffinger a *Grand Trio* (Paris: Carli) for piano, horn, or violin, and cello.

Pokorny, Franz Xaver (1729–1794)

Concerto for horn
MS D:Rtt [according to MGG]

Punto (born Stich), Johann Wenzel (1755–1803)

Sainsbury identifies Punto as a horn player whose 'powers on his instrument occasioned general astonishment and admiration.' His list of works include:
    (Six) *Quintets* for horn and strings
    (Twelve) *Quartets* for horn and strings
    (Five) *Concerti* for horn

Reicha, Anton (1770–1836)

[Untitled work] for solo horn and piano
MS F:Pn MS.2500

Rheinberger, Joseph (1839–1901)

MGG attributes to Rheinberger a *Sonata* in E♭ Major, Op. 178, for horn and piano.

Richter, Franz Xaver (1709–1789)

MGG attributes to Richer (Six) lost *Concerti* for horn.

Riepel, Joseph

Sainsbury identifies Riepel as the composer of a *Sonata*, Op. 34, for piano and horn, or cello.

Ries, Ferdinand (1784–1838)

MGG attributes to Ries a *Sonata*, Op. 34, and an *Introduction and Rondeau*, Op. 113, for horn and piano.

Röser, Johann Georg (1740–1797)

MGG attributes to Röser two *Concerti* for horn and orchestra.

Rosetti, Franz Anton (1746–1792)

Concerto (for 'Second') horn and orchestra
MS A:Sca Hs. 1631

Sainsbury identifies Rosetti as the composer of three *Concerti* for horn.

Rossini, Gioacchino (1792–1868)

Prelude, Theme et Variations for horn and piano
MS F:Pn

Roth, Anton

Concerto for horn and orchestra
MS A:Wgm VIII 20055

Roth, Philipp Jakob (1779–1850)

MGG attributes to Roth a *Concerto* (1813) for horn and orchestra.

Rudolph, Joseph (1730–1812)

MGG attributes to Rudolph two *Concerti* (Paris: Sieber and Bailleaux) for horn and orchestra.

Schimpke, ?

(Two) *Concerti*, in E♭ Major, for horn
MS (Wien: Traeg's *Catalog*, 1799)

Schmittbaur, Joseph Aloys (1718–1809)

MGG attributes to Schmittbaur two *Concerti* for horn.

Schneider, Georg

Concerto, Op. 101, for horn and orchestra
EP (Bonn: Simrock)
  I:Bc

Sinigaglia, Leone (1868–1944)

MGG attributes to Sinigaglia a *Romanze*, Op. 5 (1889) and a *Noel*, Op. 7 (Lausanne: Foetisch) for horn and string quartet.

Sperger, Johann (d. 1812)

Concerto for horn and orchestra
MS A:Wgm VIII 12637

Stamitz, Carl (1745–1801)

Quartet for horn and strings
MS (Wien: Traeg's *Catalog*, 1799)

Steinmüller, ?

Sainsbury identifies three brothers of this name, all horn players in the court of Prince Esterhazy, under Haydn, and all composers of music for horn.

Storch, Anton (nineteenth century)

Theme and Variations for horn and orchestra
MS A:Wn Sm 14609

Strunz, Georg (1781–1852)

MGG attributes to Strunz a *Concerto* for horn.

Suppé, Franz von (1819–1895)

An Herrn von Puchraker, for voice, horn, and piano
MS A:Wn Sm 5358

Teyber, Anton (1756–1822)

(Two) *Concerti* for horn
MS A:Wgm [according to MGG]

Todt, Johann Christoph

MGG attributes to Todt three *Concerti* for horn.

Uber, Alexander (1783–1824)

MGG attributes to Uber a *Variations* for horn and string quartet.

Veit, Wenzel Heinrich (1806–1864)

MGG attributes to Veit an *Andante grazioso* in F Major for horn and string orchestra.

Vogel, Cajetan (1750–1794)

MGG attributes to Vogel four *Concerti* for horn and orchestra.

Wessely, Johann (1762–1810)

MGG attributes to Wessely *Das Leben ist ein Wurfelspiel*, Op. 14 (Braunschweig: Spehr) for horn and orchestra and *Ten Variations*, Op. 15 (Braunschweig: Spehr, 1802) for horn, violin and orchestra.

Witt, Friedrich (1770–1836)

MGG attributes to Witt a *Concerto* for horn.

Wolf, Friedrich Adolph (1750–1824)

Romanz, for horn, cello, and piano
MS A:Wn Sm 13130

MUSIC WITH SOLO TROMBONE

Albert, Prince Consort of England

Lebensregel, for TTBB and trombone
MS GB:Lbm R.M.18.a.7.Nr. 12

Anonymous

Sonata for tromboncino and organ
MS I:Bsf FC.A.IV.12

(Ten) *Stücke*, for trombone and orchestra
MS A:Wn Sm 15274

Carulli, Benedetto (1797–1877)

Divertimento for trombone and winds
MS I:Bsf M.C.VII-15

David, Ferdinand (1810–1873)

Concertino in E♭, Op.4 for trombone and orchestra
EP (Leipzig: Kistner) [cited in MGG]

Dressler, Johann Samuel

Sainsbury identifies Dressler as a German composer at the end of the 18th century and
adds, 'he was the first person who introduced the trombone into English orchestras.'

Friedl, Carl

Solo, for trombone and strings
MS A:Wn Sm 20462

Führer, Robert

(Two) *Libera*, for SATB, trombone and organ
MS A:Wn Sm 0161

Fux, Johann (1660–1741)

Sonatas (1726–1739) for trombone and 2 violins
MS A:Wn Sm 3630

Gagnebin, Henri (b. 1886)

MGG attributes to Gagnebin a *Sarabande* (Paris: Leduc) for trombone and piano.

Hanisch, Joseph (1812–1892)

MGG attributes to Hanisch a *Requiem*, Op. 15 (Einsiedeln, 1871) for chorus, trombone,
organ, and strings.

Heintze, Georg Wilhelm (1849–1895)

MGG attributes to Heintze unnamed works for voices, trombone, and organ.

Oestreich, Carl (Frankfurt, nineteenth century)

Concertino for 'Tenor Bass Posaune' with orchestra
MS   BRD:F Mus.Hs. 777

Quartet for trombone and strings
MS   BRD:F Mus.Hs. 817 [incomplete]

Pacini, Giovanni (1796–1867)

Virgam virtutis (1861), for Bass, trombone and orchestra
MS   I:Ls B. 123

Pfeiffer, Georges Jean (1835–1908)

MGG attributes to Pfeiffer a *Solo* (Paris: Evette & Schaeffer, 1899) for trombone.

Van Beer, ?

Concertini, for trombone and orchestra
MS   A:Wn Sm 1998

Wagenseil, Georg (1715–1777)

MGG attributes to Wagenseil a *Concerto* for trombone.

PART 2

Music With Two Wind Instruments

MUSIC WITH TWO FLUTES

Abel, Carl F. (1732–1787)

(Four) *Trios*, two are for 2 flutes with bc
EP   (London: Preston, ca. 1785)
    GB:Lbm G.420.e.(7.)

Trio in D Major for 2 flutes and bass
MS   I:Gl SS.A.1.15.(G.7)

Aber, Johann (1756–1783)

Sonata in D Major, for 2 flutes and bass
MS   I:Gl SS.B.1.8

Sonata in B♭ Major, for 2 flutes and bass
MS   I:Gl M.36.24.13

Addison, John

(Six) *Sonatas*, Op. 1, for 2 flutes or violins
EP   (Edinburgh: Johnson, 1772)
    GB:Lbm G.270.r.(1.)

Agrell, Johann (1701–1765)

(Six) *Sonatas*, for 2 flutes
EP   (London: Walsh, 1757)
    GB:Lbm G.222.b.(1.)

(Six) *Sonatas*, Op. 2, for 2 flutes ('Compos'd in a pleasing fine Taste by Giovanni Aggrell')
EP   (London: Walsh, ca. 1760)
    GB:Lbm G.280.(l.)

André, Johann Anton (1775–1842)

(Three) *Duos*, for 2 flutes
MS   A:Wgm VIII 6281

MGG attributes to Andre an *Instructive Variation*, Op 53, for 2 flutes.

Androux, Giovanni

(Six) *Trios*, for 2 flutes and bc
EP   (London: Welcker, 1765)
    GB:Lbm H.2775

Anonymous

Divertimento (1789), for 2 flutes
MS I:Vmc Busta 31-53-N.41

The Doretshire March, for 2 flutes and bc
EP   (London, ca. 1770)
    GB:Lbm H.1994.a.(177.)

Duetto, for 2 flutes
MS CH:Bu kr.IV 381, Nr. 2

Duetto, for 2 flutes
MS CH:Bu kr.IV 381, Nr. 5

Catches, for 1, 2, 3 or 4 flutes
EP   (London: Walsh and Hare, ca. 1711)
    GB:Lbm B.171.a.(1.)

Marche de Buonapart for 2 flutes
MS (Wien: Traeg's *Catalog*, 1799)

Partita for 2 flutes and continuo
MS A:Wn Sm 1013

(Thirty-six) Pieces for 2 flutes (on Weber's *Der Freischütz*)
MS A:Wn Sm 22788

Sonata in B♭ Major for 2 flutes and bass
MS S:Uu Ms. 358

Sonata for 2 flutes
MS I:Ac Mss.N.564/4, Fasciolo del sec. XVIII

(Fourteen) *Sonatas* (ca. 1760) for 2 flutes and bass
MS GB:Eu D 52–54/Nrs. 22, 26–37, 40

Theme and Variations for 2 flutes
MS A:Wn Sm 3056

Trio for 2 flutes and bass
MS CH:Bu kr.IV.381, Nr. 3

Ashley, John

(Twelve) *Duetts*, for 2 flutes
EP   (London: Preston, ca. 1795)
    GB:Lbm B.476

Astorga, Jean

(Six) *Sonatas*, for 2 flutes
EP   (London: Bremner, 1769)
 GB:Lbm G.692
 GB:Lbm H.2852.a.(3.) [another copy]

(Six) *Sonatas*, for 2 flutes
EP   (London: Preston, ca. 1790)
 GB:Lbm H.2140.k.(1.)

Aubert, Jacques (1689–1753)

MGG attributes to Aubert *Pieces*, Op. 15, for 2 flutes or violins.

Bach, Johann Christian (1735–1782)

(Four) *Quartets*, Op. 9, for 2 flutes, viola, cello; flute and strings; and flute, oboe, viola, and cello
EP   (London: Preston, ca. 1785)
 GB:Lbm G.435.(1.)
 GB:Lbm G.411.a.(1.) [a later edition, ca. 1790]

Bach, J. C. and Neubaur, Franz (1760–1795)

(Three) *Trios*, for 2 flutes and cello
EP   (London?, ca. 1800)
 GB:Lbm G.274.b.(3.)

Bach, K. P. E. (1714–1788)

Phillis und Thirsis, a Cantata for 2 voices, 2 flutes, and bc
EP   (Berlin: Winter, 1766)
 GB:Lbm H.1819.a.

Sonata for 2 flutes
MS   A:Wgm XI 36267
 This manuscript was formerly owned by Brahms.

Bach, Wilhelm Friedemann (1710–1784)

Sonata for 2 flutes and cembalo
MS   A:Wgm XI 33391

Barbandt, Carl

(Six) *Sonatas*, for 2 flutes, 2 oboes, or 2 violins
EP   (London, ca. 1755)
     GB:Lbm F.14

Bärmann, ?

(Six) *Duets* for 2 flutes
MS   (Wien: Traeg's *Catalog*, 1799)

Sainsbury identifies Bärmann as a composer of eight volumes of flute *Duets*.

Battino, ?

Duets, for 2 flutes
EP   (London: Johnson, ca. 1760)
     GB:Lbm G.218.d.(1.)

Baumberg, ?

(Six) *Trios*, Op. 1, for 2 flute and a string
MS   (Wien: Traeg's *Catalog*, 1799)

Benda, Hans George (d. 1757)

MGG attributes to Benda three *Trios* for 2 flutes and bass.

Bertie, Willoughby

(Twelve) *Country Dances* and (Three) *Capriccios*, for 2 flutes and bc
EP   (London: Monzani, ca. 1798)
     GB:Lbm G.433.d.(2.)

Besozzi, Alessandro (1702–1775)

(Eight) *Sonatas*, Op. 3, for 2 flutes and bc
EP   (London: Walsh, ca. 1760)
     GB:Lbm G.241.(1.)

(Six) *Sonatas*, Op. 5, for 2 flutes or 2 violins
EP   (London: Cox, 1764)
     GB:Lbm G.241.a.(2.)

Sonata, Op. 4, Nr. 2, for 2 flutes and bass
MS   S:Uu Ms. 25

Sonata, Op. 4, Nr. 4, for 2 flutes and bass
MS S:Uu Ms. 26

Sonata, Op. 4, Nr. 6, for 2 flutes and bass
MS S:Uu Ms. 27

Sonata, Op. 7, Nr. 2, for 2 flutes and bass
MS S:Uu Ms. 28

Sonata, for 2 flutes and bass
MS GB:Eu D 52-54, Nr. 9

Bianchi, Francesco (1752–1810)

Concertino for 2 flutes
MS I:Ac Mss.N.141/1

Binder, Christlieb (1723–1789)

MGG attributes to Binder two *Trios* for 2 flutes, keyboard, and bass.

Biscogli, Francesco

Trio in G Major, for 2 flutes and bass
MS I:Gl M.4.27.18

Bishop, John

Sainsbury identifies Bishop as organist of the Winchester Cathedral during the early days of the eighteenth century and composer of a published collection of 'asirs' for 2 flutes.

Blavet, Michel (1700–1768)

MGG attributes to Blavet six *Sonatas* for 2 flutes and bass (Paris, 1728).

Blow, John (1649–1708)

Ode on the Death of H. Purcell, for 2 contratenors, 2 flutes, and bc
MS GB:Lgc

Boccherini, Luigi (1743–1805)

Trio in A Major, for 2 flutes and cello
MS I:Gl SS.A.1.8.(G.7)

Boismortier, Joseph Bodin de (1691–1755)

MGG attributes to Boismortier the following:
  Sonatas, Op. 1 and 1 (1721), for 2 flutes
  Petites Sonates, Op. 4 (1724), for 2 flutes and bass
  Sonatas, Op. 6 and Op. 8 (1725), for 2 flutes
  Petites Sonates, Op. 13 and Op. 30 (1726), for 2 flutes
  Duos, Op. 25 (1729), for 2 flutes
  (Five) *Sonatas* (1732) for 2 flutes
  (Two) *Serenades* or '*Symphonies françoises*,' Op. 39, for 2 flutes

Bononcini, Marc Antonio (1675–1726)

Cantata for voice and 2 flutes
MS F:Pn D.1350 (5)

Bouward, ?

(Six) *Trios* for 2 flute and a string
MS (Wien: Traeg's *Catalog*, 1799)

Breunich, Michele (1699–1755)

(Six) *Sonate*, for 2 flutes and bass
MS GB:Eu D 52–54/Nrs. 10–12, 38, 39

Burney, Charles (1726–1814)

Sainsbury identifies the well-known historian as the composer of six *Duets* for 2 flutes, as well as 'A Plan of a Public Music School.'

Cambini, Giovanni (1746–1825)

Collection of French Airs, for 2 flutes
EP (London: Longman & Broderip, ca. 1788)
    GB:Lbm G.225.(1.)

(Six) *Duets*, Op. 5, for 2 flutes
EP (London: J. Bland, ca. 1790)
    GB:Lbm G.396.d.(2.)
MS (Wien: Traeg's *Catalog*, 1799)

(Six) *Duets* for 2 flutes
MS (Wien: Traeg's *Catalog*, 1799)

(Two) *Pots Pourris* for 2 flutes
MS (Wien: Traeg's *Catalog*, 1799)

(Six) *Trios*, Op. 3, for 2 flutes and bc
EP   (London: J. Bland, ca. 1790)
      GB:Lbm G.274.d.(1.)

(Twelve) *Trios* for 2 flute and a string
MS   (Wien: Traeg's *Catalog*, 1799)

Campioni, Carlo (1720–1793)

(Two) *Concerti* in D Major and G Major, for 2 flutes and orchestra
MS   I:Gl SS.A.1.15.(G.7)

(Two) *Duos* for 2 flutes or violins
MS   CH:Bu kr.50, 51

(Eight) *Sonatas*, Op. 4, for 2 flutes and bc
EP   (London: Bremner, ca. 1780)
      GB:Lbm G.420.e.(11.)

(Two) *Sonate* for 2 flutes and bass
MS   GB:Eu DD 52–54/Nrs. 16, 17

Campioni, Carlo and Ferrari, Comenico

(Six) *Sonatas*, for 2 violins or flutes and bc
EP   (London: C. and S. Thompson, ca. 1770)
      GB:Lbm H.5.a.(1.)

Canal, Giuseppe (1703–1779)

(Six) *Duos*, Op. 3, for 2 flutes
EP   (Paris: Chez de la Chevardiere, ca. 1775)
      GB:Lbm G.280.h.(3.)

(Six) *Duos*, Op. 5, for 2 flutes
EP   (Paris: Chez de la Chevardiere, ca. 1775)
      GB:Lbm G.280.h.4

(Six) *Sonatas*, Op. 2, for 2 flutes
EP   (Paris: Chez Bailleux, ca. 1775)
      GB:Lbm G.280.h.(2.)

(Two) *Sonatas* for 2 flutes and bass
MS   I:Gl N.1.6.6.(Sc.17)

Carcani, Gioseffo

Trio for 2 flutes and bass
MS   CH:Bu kr.IV 55

Carr, Robert

The Delightful Companion, lessons for one, two, and three flutes
EP   (London: J. Playford, 1686)
    GB:Lbm K.4.b.16

Cauciello, Prospero

(Six) *Duetti*, for 2 flutes
EP   (Paris: M. Garnier, ca. 1780)
    GB:Lbm 3.201.b.(4.)

Cecere, Carlo

(Twenty-four) *Duets*, for 2 flutes
EP   (London: I. Walsh, ca. 1770)
    GB:Lbm G.280.(5.)

Charles, ?

(Twelve) *Duettos* for 2 horns or 2 flutes
EP   (London?, ca. 1750)
    GB:Lbm D.379.a.(2.)

Chartrains, ?

(Six) *Duets* for 2 flutes
MS   (Wien: Traeg's *Catalog*, 1799)

Chechi (Checci?), ?

(Six) *Petit Sonates* for 2 flutes
MS   (Wien: Traeg's *Catalog*, 1799)

Cheron, Andre (1695–1766)

MGG attributes to Cheron six *Sonatas*, Op. 1, (1727), and a set of *Duets* and *Trios* for flutes, Op. 2, (1729).

Chiesa, Melchierre

Sonata in C Major, for 2 flutes and bass
MS   I:Gl M.4.31.20

Sonata in G Major, for 2 flutes and bass
MS   I:Gl M.4.31.21

Sonata in D Major, for 2 flutes and bass
MS   I:Gl M.4.31.22

Chinzer, Giovanni

(Six) *Sonatas*, for 2 flutes and bc
EP   (London: Walsh, ca. 1750)
        GB:Lbm G.241.(3.)

(Six) *Sonatas*, of which four are for 2 flutes and bc
EP   (London: Welcker, ca. 1775)
        GB:Lbm G.274.i.(1.)

Cimarosa, Domenico (1749–1801)

(Five) *Sonatas* for 2 flutes and bass
MS   I:Gl N.1.6.7.(Sc.40)

(Three) *Sonatas da Camera*, for 2 flutes and bass
MS   I:Gl N.1.6.7.(Sc.40)

MGG attributes to to Cimarosa a *Concerto* in G Major (1793) for 2 flutes.

Cocchi, Gioacchino

(Six) *Duettos*, Op. 2, for 2 voices and 2 flutes
EP   (London: Walsh, ca. 1765)
        GB:Lbm E.65

Coch, Johann

(Six) *Sonatas*, for 2 flutes and bc
EP   (London: Fentum, ca. 1775)
        GB:Lbm H.2852.a.(11.)

Cope, W.

March, for 2 flutes and piano
EP   (London: the composer, ca. 1795)
        GB:Lbm G.133.(8.)

Coreria, Cherubino

(Six) *Sonatas*, for 2 flutes and bc
EP   (London: Waylett, ca. 1740)
   GB:Lbm G.270.1.(3.)

Corrette, Michel (1709–1795)

MGG attributes to Corrette *Sonatas*, Op. 2, and Op. 21, for 2 flutes.

Courteville, Raphael (Chapel Royal of Charles II)

Sonatas, for 2 flutes
EP   (London, c. 1715)
   GB:Lbm C.105.a.(3.)

Croft, William (1678–1727) and Seignr. Pepusch

(Six) *Sonatas* for 2 flutes (by Croft) and a work for solo flute (by Pepusch)
EP   (London: Walsh and Hare, ca. 1705)
   GB:Lbm C.105.a.(1.)
EP   (London: I. Walsh, ca. 1710)
   GB:Lbm D.150.(3.)

MGG also attributes to Croft an Amsterdam edition of *Sonatas* for 2 flutes.

Dedonati, Girolamo

(Six) *Sonatas*, for 2 flutes or oboes and bc
EP   (London: R. Birchall, ca. 1790)
   GB:Lbm G.420.d.(12.)

De Fesch, Willem (Dutch, 1687–1761)

(Ten) *Sonatas*, Op. 7, for 2 flutes and bc
EP   (London: B. Cooke, ca. 1732)
   GB:Lbm G.274.g.(1.)

(Six) *Sonatas*, Op. 9, for 2 flutes
EP   (London: J. Simpson, ca. 1735)
   GB:Lbm G.280.i.(1.)

(Twelve) *Sonatas*, Op. 12, for 2 flutes and harpsichord
EP   (London: I. Walsh, ca. 1745)
   GB:Lbm G.241.(4.)

Select Lessons, for 2 flutes
EP (London?, ca. 1735)
    GB:Lbm B.30.(2.)

Demachi, ?

(Six) *Duets* for 2 flutes
MS (Wien: Traeg's *Catalog*, 1799)

Deragini, ?

Sainsbury identifies Deragini as a composer of duets for flutes published in London in 1797.

Devienne, François (1759–1803)

Collection of solos and duets, for flutes
EP (London: C. Wheatstone, ca. 1800)
    GB:Lbm G.239.b.(1.)

(Six) *Duetti* for 2 flutes
MS I:Mc [according to MGG]

Duet for 2 flutes
MS A:Wgm VIII 6567

Duet for 2 flutes
MS A:Wgm VIII 8872

Duet for 2 flutes
MS A:Wgm VIII 8873

Duet for 2 flutes
MS A:Wgm VIII 8874 [MGG cites eight *Duets* in A:Wgm]

(Six) *Duos Dialogues*, for 2 flutes
EP (Paris: Imbault, ca. 1795)
    GB:Lbm G.280.j.(4.)

(Six) *Duos*, for 2 flutes
EP (Paris: Imbault, ca. 1795)
    GB:Lbm G.280.j.(3.)

(Six) *Easy Duets*, Op. 18, for 2 flutes
EP (London: Longman & Broderip, ca. 1790)
    GB:Lbm G.225.(2.)
EP (London: Wheatstone, ca. 1800)
    GB:Lbm G.239.b.(8.)

(Twelve) *Duos*, Op. 57, for 2 flutes
EP   (London: Fentum, ca. 1800)
       GB:Lbm G.239.b.(4–7.)

(Six) *Duos*, Op. 60, for 2 flutes
EP   (Paris: Sieber, ca. 1795)
       GB:Lbm G.239.b.(11.)

(Six) *Trios*, Op. 60, for 2 flutes
EP   (London: Wheatstone, ca. 1800)
       GB:Lbm G.239.b.(10.)

(Six) *Duets* for 2 flutes
MS (Wien: Traeg's *Catalog*, 1799)

(Six) *Duets*, Op. 63, for 2 flutes
MS (Wien: Traeg's *Catalog*, 1799)

(Six) *Duets*, Op. 64, for 2 flutes
MS (Wien: Traeg's *Catalog*, 1799)

(Six) *Duets*, Op. 65, for 2 flutes
MS (Wien: Traeg's *Catalog*, 1799)

(Twenty) *Petits Airs* and (eighteen) *Duos,* Liv. 1, for 2 flutes
MS (Wien: Traeg's *Catalog*, 1799)

MGG also attributes to Devienne the following works:
   Sinfonie concertante, Op. 76 (Paris: Sieber), for 2 flutes
   (Six) *Duos*, Op. 2 (Paris: Sieber), for 2 flutes
   (Six) *Duos concertants* for flute and viola (Paris: Le Duc)
   (Six) *Duos*, Op. 5 (Paris), for 2 flutes
   (Six) *Duos*, Op. 15 (Paris: Sieber), for 2 flutes
   (Six) *Duos*, Op. 7 (Paris: Imbault), for 2 flutes
   (Three) *Duos*, Op. 8 (Paris: Pleyel), for 2 flutes
   (Six) *Duos dialogues*, Op. 10 (Paris: Imbault), for 2 flutes
   (Six) *Duos* (Paris: Gaveaux) for 2 flutes
   (Six) *Duos*, Op. 67 (Paris), for flute and violin
   (Six) *Duos*, Op. 75 (Offenbach: André) for 2 flutes
   (Three) *Duos*, Op 80 (Paris), for 2 flutes
   (Three) *Duos* (Paris: Magasin de musique) for 2 flutes
   (Six) *Dueti* (Berlin: Hummel) for 2 flutes
   (Six) *Duos* (Paris: Imbault) for 2 flageolets
   (Eighteen) *Trios* for 2 flutes and bass

Döthel, Nicolas

(Three) *Canoni* for 2 flutes
MS   I:Gl SS.A.2.5.(G.8)

(Six) *Duetts*, for flutes
EP   (London: Chapman, ca. 1760)
       GB:Lbm G.227.

(Six) *Sonatas*, Op. 3, for 2 flutes
EP   (London: C. & S. Thompson, ca. 1765)
       GB:Lbm G.227.aa.

(Nineteen) *Sonatas* for 2 flutes and continuo
MS   I:Gl SS.A.2.5.(G.8)

(Six) *Sonatas* for 2 flutes
MS   B:Bc Wotquenne 5536

(Twelve) *Sonatine Notturne*, for 2 flutes
EP   (London: J. Oswald, ca. 1753)
       GB:Lbm G.280.(7.)

(Six) *Trios*, for 2 flutes and bc
EP   (London: C. & S. Thompson, ca. 1765)
       GB:Lbm G.677.

Droste-Hulshoff, Maximilian Friedrich (1764–1840)

MGG attributes to Droste (Sixteen) *Duettini*, Op. 16, for 2 flutes.

Drouet, Louis (1792–1873)

MGG attributes to Drouet the following works:
       (Six) *Duos brillants et faciles*, Op. 74 (Paris: Gambaro) for 2 flutes
       (Six) *Duos concertants* (Paris: Richault) for 2 flutes
       (Three) *Grand duos*, Op. 204 (Paris: Richault)

Duereux, ?

(Six) *Duets*, Op. 3, for 2 flutes
MS   (Wien: Traeg's *Catalog*, 1799)

Dulon, Friedrich Ludwig (1769–1826)

MGG attributes to Dulon, *Caprices*, for one and two flutes (Leipzig, 1801), and (Three) *Duos*
(Leipzig) for 2 flutes.

Eidenbenz, ?

(Six) *Duets*, Op. 6, for 2 flutes
MS (Wien: Traeg's *Catalog*, 1799)

Enderle, Wilhelm Gottfried (1722–1790)

MGG attributes to Enderle (Eighteen) *Trios* for 2 flutes and bass.

Erbach, Friedrich Karl (1680–1731)

MGG attributes to Erbach (Twelve) *Sinfonie* for 2 flutes and bass.

Essex, Dr.

Sainsbury identifies Essex as the composer of (Six) *Duets* for 2 flutes, published
    by Millhouse.

Eyre, Joseph

(Eight) *Sonatas*, two of which are for 2 flutes and bc
EP   (London: R. Thompson, ca. 1765)
        GB:Lbm I.6

Farrenc, Jacques (1794–1865)

Sainsbury identifies Farrenc as a flutist, and student of Berbiguier, and composer of the
    'highly esteemed' *Grand Duets Concertante*.

Fawcett, John (1789–1867)

MGG attributes to Fawcett 106 *Trios* for 2 flutes (or violins) and cello.

Ferlendis, Giuseppe

(Six) *Sonatas* for 2 flutes and bass
MS I:Gl M.4.31.30

Sonata for 2 flutes and bass
MS I:Gl M.4.31.33/36

Sonata for 2 flutes
MS I:Gl M.4.31.31

Sonata for 2 flutes
MS I:Gl M.4.31.32

Sonata for 2 flutes
MS I:Gl T.c.7.1.(Sc.111)

Ferrari, Carlo (1710–1789)

MGG attributes to Ferrari (Six) *Trio Sonaten* for 2 flutes, or violins, and bass (London: Lave) and (Six) *Sonatas* for 2 flutes, or violins, and bass (London: Thompson).

Fesch, Willem de (1687–1757)

MGG attributes to Fesch the following works:
(Ten) *Sonatas* for 2 flutes (London, 1733–1736)
Concerto for 2 flutes (London, 1741)
(Thrity) *Duets* for 2 flutes (London, 1747)
(Twelve) *Sonatas* (London: Walsh, 1748) for 2 flutes.

Fisher, John Abraham

Sainsbury identifies Fisher as the composer of *Divertisements* for 2 flutes, published by Clementi.

Fiala, Joseph (1754–1816)

Duet for 2 flutes
MS A:Sca Hs. 712

Filtz, Anton (1730–1760)

(Six) *Sonatas*, Op. 2, for 2 flutes and bc
EP (London: Longman, Lukey & Co., ca. 1775)
GB:Lbm G.409.b.(1.)
EP (Paris: Chevardiere) [cited in MGG]

(Three) *Trios* for 2 flutes and bass
MS I:Gl SS.A.2.6.(G.8)

Finger, Gottfried (ca. 1660–1723)

MGG attributes to Finger the following works:
(Six) *Sonatas* for 2 flutes, Op. 2 (London: Walsh)
Sonatas for 2 flutes and bass, Op. 4 and Op. 6

Fiorillo, Fedrigo (1755–1823)

(Six) *Concerti* for 2 flutes and strings
MS B:Bc Wotquenne 5542

MGG attributes to Fiorollo the following:
   Simphonie concertante, Op. 24, for 2 flutes and orchestra (Augsburg: Gombert)
   Sinfonia concerttante (1786) for 2 flutes and orchestra (MS, A:Wgm and D:B)

Fischer, Johann (1733–1800)

(Seven) *Divertimenti*, for 2 flutes
EP   (London: Longman & Broderip, ca. 1780)
      GB:Lbm H.241.(1.)

Flath, ?

(Three) *petits Duets* for 2 flutes
MS   (Wien: Traeg's *Catalog*, 1799)

Florio, Pietro Grassi (d. 1795)

(Six) *Sonatas*, Op. 1, for 2 flutes
EP   (London: Whitaker, ca. 1765)
      GB:Lbm G.421.n.(3.)
EP   (London: C. & S. Thompson, ca. 1770)
      GB:Lbm G.421.n.(4.)

(Six) *Sonatas*, Op. 2, for 2 flutes
EP   (London: C. & S. Thompson, ca. 1765)
      GB:Lbm G.421.n.(7.)

Foinelli, ?

Sonata for 2 flutes
MS   I:Gl SS.B.1.3

Franz, Étienne

Trio for 2 flutes and viola
MS   A:Wgm XI 1560

Trio for 2 flutes and viola
MS   A:Wgm XI 6237

Frühling, Carl (1868–1937)

MGG attributes to Fruhling a *Duettino*, Op. 57, for 2 flutes.

Gabrielsky, W.

Sainsbury identifies Gabrielsky as the composer of six sets of *Duets* for flutes.

Gebauer, ?

(Two) *Pots Pourris* for 2 flutes
MS (Wien: Traeg's *Catalog*, 1799)

Sainsbury writes, 'There were four brothers of the name, resident in Paris. One of the brothers published *Sixty Methodical Lessons, as Duets, for two flutes, for the Use of Beginners*, a work which is much esteemed in Germany.'

Geminiani, Francesco (1679–1762)

MGG attributes to Geminiani (Two) *Duets* in *Apollo's Collection* (London: Oswald, 1750) for 2 violins or 2 flutes.

Gerard, James

(Six) *Sonatas*, for 2 flutes
EP   (London: Johnson, ca. 1765)
    GB:Lbm G.502.(3.)

Ghillini di Asuni, ?

(Six) *Duets*, for 2 flutes or oboes
EP   (London: Welcker, ca. 1775)
    GB:Lbm G.421.n.(1.)

Gianella, Luci

(Three) *Duos concertantes* for 2 flutes
MS A:Wgm VIII 2438

Giordani, Tommaso (1730–1806)

(Six) *Duets*, for 2 flutes
EP   (London: Preston, ca. 1785)
    GB:Lbm H.111.(10.)

(Six) *Sonatas*, for 2 flutes
EP   (London: Longman & Broderip, ca. 1780)
    GB:Lbm G.421.s.(1.)

Glachant, Antoine-Charles (1770–1851)

MGG attributes to Glachant six *Duos* (Paris: Imbault) for flutes.

Gleissner, Franz (1759–1818)

MGG attributes to Gleissner (Six) *Duos*, Op. 12 (Wien: Chemische Druckerei, 1801) for 2 flutes and (Twenty-four) *Duos* (Leipzig: Baumgartner) for flutes.

Goetzel, ?

(Six) *Duets* for 2 flutes
MS (Wien: Traeg's *Catalog*, 1799)

Graff, ?

Concerto for 2 flutes and orchestra
MS (Wien: Traeg's Catalog, 1799)

(Two) *Quartets* for 2 flutes and strings
MS (Wien: Traeg's Catalog, 1799)

(Six) *Duets* for 2 flutes
MS (Wien: Traeg's Catalog, 1799)

Granom, Lewis

(Twenty-four) *Duets*, Op. 3, for 2 flutes
EP (London: Simpson, ca. 1750)
    GB:Lbm F.54

(Twenty-four) *Duets*, Op. 11, for 2 flutes
EP (London: Bennett, ca. 1755)
    GB:Lbm E.201.a.(2.)

(Six) *Sonatas*, Op. 2, for 2 flutes
EP (London: Simpson, ca. 1756)
    GB:Lbm G.247.g.(2.)

(Six) *Sonatas*, Op. 9, for 2 flutes
EP (London: Bennett, ca. 1752)
    GB:Lbm E.201.a.(3.)

Graun, August Friedrich (1698–1765)

MGG attributes to Graun (Eight) *Sonatas* (London: Walsh) for 2 flutes.

Graun, Carl Heinrich (1703–1759)

Trio for 2 flutes and bass
MS   B:Bc Wotquenne 5547

Trio for 2 flutes and bass
MS   B:Bc Wotquenne 6610

(Two) *Trios* for 2 flutes and bass
MS   B:Bc Wotquenne 6614

Grenser, Karl Augustin III (1794–1864)

MGG attributes to Grenser (Three) *Grands Duos*, Op. 7 (Leipzig: Probst) for 2 flutes.

Griesbach, Charles

(Three) *Progressive Duetts*, Op. 4, for 2 flutes
EP   (London: Williamson, ca. 1797)
    GB:Lbm G.225.(3.)

(Three) *Concertante Duetts*, for 2 flutes
EP   (London: Fentum, ca. 1800)
    GB:Lbm G.71.e.(3.)

Groenemann, Johann

(Six) *Sonatas* for 2 flutes
EP   (London: Simpson, ca. 1745)
    GB:Lbm G.420.h.(2.)

(Six) *Sonatas*, Op. 2, for 2 flutes
EP   (London: Thompson & Son, ca. 1760)
    GB:Lbm G.446

Gualdo da Vandero, Giovanni

(Six) *Sonatas*, Op. 2, for 2 flutes and harpsichord
EP   (London: C. & S. Thompson, ca. 1765)
    GB:Lbm H.5.a.(2.)

Guillemant, Benoit

MGG attributes to Guillemant (Six) *Sonatas* (1749) for 2 flutes.

Hagen, ?

(Three) *Duets*, Liv. 1, for 2 flutes
MS (Wien: Traeg's *Catalog,* 1799)

Handel, Georg F. (1685–1759)

Concerto for 2 flute and a string
MS (Wien: Traeg's *Catalog*, 1799)

(Six) *Sonatas*, Op. 2, for 2 violins, oboes, or flutes
EP (London: Cooke, ca. 1735)
   GB:Lbm H.436.d

(Six) *Sonates*, for 2 flutes
EP (London: LeClerc, ca. 1750)
   GB:Lbm H.2681.c
   This work is now thought to be by one, G. Schultze.

Harbordt, ?

(Three) *Duets*, Op. 2, for 2 flutes
MS (Wien: Traeg's *Catalog*, 1799)

Harrer, Johann Gottlob (1703–1755)

MGG attributes to Harrer 51 now lost flute duets.

Hartmann, C.

Sainsbury identifies Hartmann as the composer of (Three) *Duos*, Op. 7 for 2 flutes, published in Paris.

Hasse, ?

Concerto for 2 flutes and strings
MS B:Bc Wotquenne 5555

Hasse, Johann Adolf (1699–1783)

(Six) *Sonatas*, Op. 1, for 2 flutes and bc
EP (London: Walsh, ca. 1740)
   GB:Lbm G.409.(4.)
   GB:Lbm G.979.(1.) [another edition]

Sonata, Op. 1, Nr. 2 (1750), for 2 flutes and bass
MS S:Uu Ms. 163

(Six) *Sonatas*, Op. 2, for 2 flutes and bc
EP (Amsterdam: Witvogel and Paris: Le Clerc) [according to MGG]

(Six) *Sonatas*, Op. 3, for 2 flutes and bc
EP (London: Oswald, ca. 1755)
  GB:Lbm G.979.(2.)

(Four) *Sonatas* for 2 flutes and bass
MS I:Gl SS.B.1.4.(H.8)

Haydn, Franz Joseph (1732–1809)

(Three) *Duos*, Op. 101, for 2 flutes
EP (Bonn: Simrock, ca. 1800)
  GB:Lbm G.280.a.(7.)

Kleines Trio (1794) for 2 flutes and cello
MS A:Wgm VIII 3

Heine, Samuel Friedrich (1764–1821)

MGG attributes to Heine (Three) *Duos*, Op. 1 (Berlin: Hummel, 1792) for 2 flutes.

Henning, Carl Wilhelm (1784–1867)

MGG attributes to Henning (Three) *Duos concertante*, Op. 3 (Berlin: Schlesinger) for
  2 flutes.

Heyne, Frederich

Sainsbury identifies Heyne as a chamber musician to the Duke of Mecklenburg-Schwerin
  and 'second husband to Madame Benda, the celebrated German singer. He has published
  Trois Duos, Op. 1 (Berlin, 1792) for 2 flutes.'

Hoffmann, L.

Divertimento for 2 flutes and a string
MS (Wien: Traeg's *Catalog*, 1799)

Hoffmeister, Franz Anton (1754–1812)

Divertimento in D Major for 2 flutes
MS A:Wgm VIII 1189

(Three) *Duets* for 2 flutes
MS A:Wgm VIII 1185

(Six) *Duets* for 2 flutes
MS A:Wgm VIII 1188

(Six) *Duets* for 2 flutes
MS A:Wgm VIII 1190

Duet in F Major for 2 flutes
MS A:Wgm VIII 8881

Duet in A Major for 2 flutes
MS A:Wgm VIII 8884

Duets for 2 flutes
MS A:Wgm VIII 8885

(Three) *Duos*, Op. 20, for 2 flutes
EP (Wien: the composer, ca. 1790)
    GB:Lbm G.225.(4.)

(Six) *Duos*, Op. 22, for 2 flutes
EP (Amsterdam: Schmitt, ca. 1795)
    GB:Lbm G.421.r.(5.)

(Six) *Duos* for 2 flutes
MS I:Gl SS.A.1.11.(G.7)

(Three) *Duets*, Op. 30, for 2 flutes
EP (London: Cahusac, ca. 1800)
    GB:Lbm H.250.b.(4.)

(Three) *Duos concertans*, Op. 37, for 2 flutes
EP (London, ca. 1800)
    GB:Lbm G.421.p.(5.)

(Six) *Duetts*, for 2 flutes
EP (London: Wheatstone, ca. 1800)
    GB:Lbm G.280.f.(10.)

(Six sets of six) *Duets* (including Op. 36 and 37) for 2 flutes
MS (Wien: Traeg's *Catalog*, 1799)

Hoffmeister, ?

(Six) *Quintets* for 2 solo flutes, bassoon and strings
MS (Wien: Traeg's *Catalog*, 1799)

Hugot, Antoine (d. 1803)

(Three) *Duos Concertants*, Op. 9, for 2 flutes
EP   (London: Wheatstone, ca. 1800)
    GB:Lbm G.280.f.(15.)

Sainsbury identifies Hugot as the composer of the following:
    (Six) *Duos Concertante*, Op. 1 (1798), for 2 flutes
    (Six) *Duos Concertante*, Op. 2, for 2 flutes
    (Six) *Duos Concertante*, Op. 3, for 2 flutes
    (Three) *Trios*, Op. 6, for 2 flutes and bass
    (Three) *Trios*, Op. 7, for 2 flutes and bass
    (Six) *Duos Concertante*, Op. 9, for 2 flutes

Hugot, F. G.

(Three) *Concertante Duetts*, Op. 1, for flutes
EP   (London: Fentus, ca. 1800)
    GB:Lbm G.71.e.(5.)

(Six) *Duos concertantes*, Op. 9, for 2 flutes
EP   (Paris: Imbault)
    I:Bc

Holzbauer, Ignaz Jakob (1711–1783)

MGG attributes to Holzbauer a *Duette* for 2 flutes.

Ivanschiz, Amandus (eighteenth century)

MGG attributes to Ivanschiz a *Trio* in G Major (MS, D:KA) for 2 flutes.

Janitzsch, ?

Quartet for 2 flutes and strings
MS (Wien: Traeg's *Catalog*, 1799)

Jenson, Niels Peter (1802–1846)

MGG attributes to Jenson (Three) *Duos*, Op. 9 (Kopenhagen: Lose) and (Six) *Duos faciles et brillants*, Op. 16 (Kopenhagen: Lose) for flutes.

Jomelli, Nicolo (1714–1774)

(Six) *Sonatas*, for 2 flutes
EP   (London: Walsh, ca. 1760)
    GB:Lbm G.990

Sonata in D Major for 2 flutes and bass
MS S:Uu Ms. 170

Sonata in D Major for 2 flutes and bass
MS S:Uu Ms. 171

Sonata for 2 flutes
MS A:Wgm VIII 9193

MGG also attributes to Jomelli (Six) *Trios* for 2 flutes and bass.

Keiser, Reinhard (1674–1739)

MGG attributes to Keiser a *Sonata* (1721) for 2 flutes and cembalo.

Kerntl, C. F.

(Six) *Duets*, for 2 flutes
EP (London: Longman, Lukey, ca. 1775)
  GB:Lbm G.421.c.(2.)

Sainsbury adds that Kerntl published two volumes of flute *Duets* in Holland in 1782.

Kertstein, ?

Sainsbury identifies Kerstein as the composer of five *Duets* (London, before 1797) for 2 flutes.

King, Robert

MGG attributes to King *Airs* (in *A Collection of Airs*, London: Weldon and Gasperini, 1703) for 2 flutes.

Knorr, Barone

Trio for 2 flutes and viola
MS A:Wgm XI 1559

Kleinknecht, Jakob Friedrich (1722–1794)

Trio for 2 flutes and bass
MS B:Bc Wotquenne 6743

MGG also attributes to Kleinknecht the following:
    (Six) *Trios* (London, 1750) for 2 flutes
    (Six) *Trios*, Op. 3 (Paris: Berault) [4 of these are in MS in D:KA]
    Sonata in C Minor for 2 flutes (MS, D:KA)

Klöffler, Johann (d. 1792)

(Six) *Sonatas*, Op. 5, for 2 flutes
EP   (Amsterdam: Hummel, ca. 1780)
GB:Lbm G.71.e.(6.)

Klöffler, G. F.

(Six) *Sonatas* for 2 flutes and bass
MS   B:Bc Wotquenne 6744

Kohler, ?

(Twelve) *Duets* for 2 flutes
MS (Wien: Traeg's *Catalog*, 1799)

Krasinsky [pseud. for Ernst Muller]

(Six) *Duos*, Op. 7, for 2 flutes
EP   (Paris: Naderman, ca. 1800)
GB:Lbm G.421.(17.)

(Six) *New Duos*, Op. 22, for 2 flutes
EP   (Paris: Naderman, ca. 1800)
GB:Lbm G.69.(16.)

Kreith, Carl (d. 1809)

(Six) *Duetts*, Op. 10, for 2 flutes
EP   (London: Fentum, ca. 1800)
GB:Lbm G.280.g.(9-10.)

(Three) Duets, Op. 24, for 2 flutes
EP   (London: Fentum, ca. 1800)
GB:Lbm G.280.g.(11.)

(Three) *Duets* for 2 flutes
MS I:Gl SS.A.1.11.(G.7)

(Three) *Duets* for 2 flutes
MS I:Gl C.2.2.32.(Sc.133)

(Eight sets of three) *Duets* for 2 flutes
MS (Wien: Traeg's *Catalog*, 1799)

(Three) *Duets*, Liv. 1, 2, for 2 flutes
MS (Wien: Traeg's *Catalog*, 1799)

(Twelve) *Polonoises*, for 2 flutes
EP   (London: Walker, ca. 1800)
    GB:Lbm G.280.g(14.)

Theme and Variations, for 2 flutes
EP   (London: Wheatstone, ca. 1800)
    GB:Lbm G.280.g.(13.)

Kremberg, Jakob (1650–1718)

Since I have seen, for recorder, flute (or violin) and cembalo
MS GB:Och Nr. 1067 [cited in MGG]

Krenn, Franz (1839–1890)

Offertorium, for Bass, 2 soli flutes, and orchestra
MS A:Wn Sm 14113

Kreusser, Georg (1743–1810)

(Three) *Duetten* for 2 flutes
MS B:Bc Wotquenne 5571

Kuhlau, Friedrich (1786–1832)

(Three) *Duos*, Op. 81, for 2 flutes
MS A:Wn Sm 22791

(Three) *Duos*, Op. 102, for 2 flutes
MS A:Wn Sm 22786

La Berre, Michel de (1675–1743)

MGG attributes to La Berre several suites and a *Duo* (MS, D:ROu) for 2 flutes.

La Maillerie, M. de

Sainsbury identifies La Maillerie as a musician of the early 18th century and composer of
(Six) *Sonatas* for 2 flutes and continuo.

Lampugnani, Giovanni (1706–1784)

Trio for 2 flutes and bass
MS CH:Bu kr.IV 175

MGG also attributes to Lampugnani two *Concerti* (MS, D:KA) for flute and orchestra.

Lapis, Santo

Trios, for 2 flutes and bass
EP   (Amsterdam, 1756)
   GB:Lbm G.213.c.(2.)

Lebrun, Ludwig (1752–1790)

MGG attributes to Lebrun (Six) *Duos faciles* (Paris: Nadermann) for 2 flutes.

Legat de Furcy, Antoine (b. 1740)

MGG attributes to Legat (Six) *Sonatas* for 2 flutes.

Leo, Leonardo (1694–1744)

Concerto for 2 flutes and orchestra
MS   A:Wn Sm 3705

Lewis, Giovanni

Duet for 2 flutes
MS   I:Gl SS.B.1.8.(H.8)

Lidarti, Christiano (1730–1793)

(Six) *Duetti notturni* for 2 flutes
MS   I:Gl SS.B.2.63.(E.5.25)

(Six) *Divertimenti* for 2 flutes
MS   I:Gl SS.B.2.63.(E.5.25)

(Six) *Sonatas*, for 2 flutes
EP   (London: Welcker, ca. 1770)
   GB:Lbm G.242.(4.)

Ling, William

(Three) *Duets*, Op. 3, for 2 flutes
EP   (London: Rolfe, ca. 1800)
   GB:Lbm G.225.(5.)

Sainsbury also cites a set of *Duets*, Op. 2.

Locatelli, Pietro (1695–1764)

(Six) *Sonatas*, Op. 4, for 2 flutes
EP   (London: Walsh, ca. 1745)
    GB:Lbm G.225.a.(2.)

(Six) *Sonatas*, Op. 5, for 2 violins or 2 flutes with bc
EP   (Amsterdam: the composer, 1736)
    GB:Lbm H.1663

EP   (London: Walsh, ca. 1745)
    GB:Lbm G.241.(5.)

Loeillet, John (of London)

Sonatas, Op. 1, 'for a Comon flute or Hoboy, also for two flutes and bc'
EP   (London: Walsh and Hare, ca. 1725)
    GB:Lbm G.685.b.(1.)
    GB:Lbm H.17.(6.) [another copy]

(Twelve) *Sonatas*, Op. 2, of which three are for 2 flutes and three are for flute and oboe.
EP   (London: Walsh and Hare, ca. 1725)
    GB:Lbm G.685.

Mancinelli, Domenico (1775–1802)

Duetto for 2 flutes
MS I:Vmc Busta 1-8-N.4

(Eight) *Duets*, Op. 2, for 2 flutes
EP   (London: Longman, Lukey & Co., ca. 1775)
    GB:Lbm G.520.(2.)

(Six) *Duets*, Op. 6, for 2 flutes
EP   (London: Babb, ca. 1780)
    GB:Lbm G.520.(3.)

(A Fifth Set of Twelve) *Easy Duets*, for 2 flutes
EP   (London: Fentum, ca. 1780)
    GB:Lbm G.520.(4.)

(Twenty-four) *Duetto*, for 2 flutes
EP   (London: Fentum, ca. 1780)
    GB:Lbm G.421.a.(7.)
EP   (Dublin: J. Lee, ca. 1785)
    GB:Lbm G.520.(6.)

(Six) *Notturnos*, for 2 flutes
EP   (London: Longman & Broderip, ca. 1780)
      GB:Lbm G.520.(1.)

Notturni, for 2 flutes and bass
MS I:Vmc Busta 1-8-N.3

Notturno for 2 flutes
MS I:Vmc Busta 31-53-N.37

(Twelve) *Notturni* for 2 flutes
MS I:Ac Mss.N.191/5

(Six) *Sonatas*, Op. 3, for 2 flutes
EP   (London: Longman, Lukey & Broderip, ca. 1778)
      GB:Lbm G.520.(5.)

Marescalchi, Luigi

Trio for 2 flutes and cello
MS I:Gl N.1.6.7.(Sc.40)

Martinn, Jacques Joseph (1775–1836)

MGG attributes to Martinn two *Symphonie concertantes* for 2 flutes and bass.

Massa, Pietro Gulielmi di

Trio for 2 flutes and bass
MS GB:Eu D 52-53/Nr. 13

Massonneau, Louis (1766–1848)

MGG attributes to Massonneau a *Concerto* in G Major, Op. 12 (Offenbach: André, 1802) for 2 flutes and orchestra.

Mattheson, Johann (1681–1764)

(Twelve) Sonatas, for 2 and 3 flutes
EP   (Amsterdam: Roger, 1708)
      GB:Lbm F.84.

Mayer, I. M.

(Six) *Duets* for 2 flutes
MS (Wien: Traeg's *Catalog*, 1799)

McGibbon, William (1690–1756)

MGG attributes to McGibbon (Six) *Sonatas* (London: Simpson, 1745) for 2 flutes.

Melegari, Andrea

Sonata for 2 flutes
MS I:Gl M.3b.24.4

Metzger, Georg (d. 1794)

Sainsbury identifies Metzger as the composer of (Six) *Duos*, Op. 3, for 2 flutes and (Three) *Concerti*, Op. 4, for 2 flutes.

Michael, ?

(Twelve) *Sonatas*, of which three are for 2 flutes and bc
EP (London: Smith, 1731)
    GB:Lbm G.951.a.(2.)

Mischel, ?

(Six) *Duets* for 2 flutes
MS (Wien: Traeg's *Catalog*, 1799)

Montéclair, Michel Pinolet (1667–1737)

MGG attributes to Monteclair *Concerts a deux flutes traversieres* (Paris: the composer) for 2 flutes.

Monzani, Tebaldo (1762–1839)

(Four) *Trios*, Op. 7, for 2 flutes and piano
EP   GB:Lbm G.409.a.(7.)

(Three) *Trios*, Op. 9, for 2 flutes
EP (London: Culliford, Rolfe & Barrow, ca. 1798)
    GB:Lbm G.222.(5.)

(Three) *Duetts*, Op. 10, for 2 flutes
EP (London: Preston, ca. 1800)
    GB:Lbm G.280.h.(6.)

Morgan, ?

Sonata, for 2 flutes and bc
EP   (London: Walsh and Hare, ca. 1697)
   GB:Lbm K.2.i.21.

Morgerotti, Carlo

Sainsbury identifies Morgerotti as the composer of *Amusement de Musique Nocturne* (Augsburg, 1753) consisting of six *Duets* for 2 flutes.

Mueller, ?

(Six) *Duos*, Op. 8, for 2 flutes
EP   (Lyon: Guera, ca. 1770)
   GB:Lbm G.106.

Mühling, Heinrich (1786–1847)

MGG attributes to Muhling (Three) *Duos concertants*, Op. 16 (Leipzig) for 2 flutes.

Müller, August Eberhart (1767–1817)

(Six) *Grands Duos Concertante*, Op. 2, for 2 flutes
MS (Wien: Traeg's *Catalog*, 1799)

Nardini, Pietro (1722–1793)

(Two) *Duetti* for 2 flutes
MS I:Gl M.3b.23.30/31

(Six) *Sonatas*, for 2 flutes and bc
EP   (London: Bremner, ca. 1770)
   GB:Lbm H.2852.a.(7.)

(Three) *Trii* for 2 flutes and bass
MS I:Gl M.3b.23.27/29

(Three) *Trii* for 2 flutes and bass
MS I:Gl M.3b.23.35.40 e 41

Negri, Giacomo

[Unfinished work]
MS A:Wgm VIII 1764

Neilson, Laurence Cornelius

Sainsbury identifies Neilson as the composer of (Three) *Original Duets* (London: Preston) and (Twelve) Duets [based on Clementi] for 2 flutes.

Nichelmann, Christoph (1717–1762)

MGG attributes to Nichelmann (Three) *Trios* (MS, D:DS) for 2 flutes and bass.

Nicholls, George

(Twenty-five) *Divertimenti*, for 2 flutes
EP   (Cambridge: the composer, ca. 1792)
    GB:Lbm G.225.(7.)

(Six) *Divertimenti*, Op. 2, for 2 flutes and piano
EP   (London: Preston, ca. 1780)
    GB:Lbm H.120.(15.)

Noferi, Giovanni Battista

MGG attributes to Noferi (Six) *Sonatas*, Op. 4 (Den Haag: Hummel, 1763) for 2 violins or 2 flutes.

Paisible, James

Six Setts of Aires, for 2 flutes and bc
EP   (London: Walsh and Hare, ca. 1706)
    GB:Lbm H.23.

(Six) *Sonatas*, Op. 1, for 2 flutes
EP   Walsh and Hare, ca. 1705)
    GB:Lbm C.105.a.(4.)

Palladino, Giuseppe

Deus exaudi (1747), for SSBB, flutes, and organ
MS   I:Bsf Mss. 51

Parcham, Andreas (d. 1730)

Sainsbury identifies Parcham as the composer of (Two) *Caprices*, Op. 1, for 2 flutes and bass.

Park, John (1745–1829)

MGG attributes to Parke (Three) *Duetts* (London: Longman & Broderip) for 2 flutes.

Parke, William

(Three) *Duetts*, for 2 flutes
EP   (London: Longman and Broderip, ca. 1793)
   GB:Lbm G.225.(9.)

(A Second Set of Three) *Duetts*, for 2 flutes
EP   (London: Longman and Broderip, ca. 1795)
   GB:Lbm G.225.(8.)

Parry, John (b. 1776)

Sainsbury identifies Parry as a composer of *Duets* for flutes.

Patoni, Giovanni

(Six) *Sonatas*, Op. 1, for 2 flutes
EP   (London: Simpson's Musick Shop, ca. 1750)
   GB:Lbm G.70.c.(3.)

Peraut, ?

Sainsbury identifies Peraut as the composer of (Three) *Duos Concertant*, Op. 1, Part I, for 2 flutes.

Pez, Johann (1664–1716)

Sonata da Camera, for 2 flutes and bc
EP   (London: Walsh, Randall, and Hare, ca. 1710)
   GB:Lbm D.150.

Philidor, Pierre Dancan (1681–1731)

MGG attributes to Philidor four *Suites* and a *Trio* , for 2 flutes, together with the suggestion that similar works are likely to be found in F:V in manuscript.

Pla, Jose (1728–1762)

(Six) *Sonatas*, for 2 flutes and bc
EP   (London: Welcker, ca. 1770)
   GB:Lbm H.2852.a.(9.)

(Six) *Sonatas*, for 2 flutes, violins, or oboes with bc
EP   (London: Hardy, ca. 1760)
   GB:Lbm F.23.

Pleyel, Ignaz (1757–1831)

Duet in A Minor for 2 flutes
MS A:Wgm VIII 6134

Duet in C Major for 2 flutes
MS A:Wgm VIII 6135

Duet in D Major for 2 flutes
MS A:Wgm VIII 6136

Duet in F Major for 2 flutes
MS A:Wgm VIII 6138

Duet in E Minor for 2 flutes
MS A:Wgm VIII 6139

Duet in G Major for 2 flutes
MS A:Wgm VIII 6140

(Six) *Duets* for 2 flutes
MS A:Wgm VIII 9232

(Six) *Duetts Concertante*, for 2 flutes
EP (London: Fentum, ca. 1795)
     GB:Lbm H.250.b.(15.)
     GB:Lbm H.2140.a.(7.) [another edition]
     GB:Lbm G.421.p.(8.) [another edition]

(Three) *Duetts*, for 2 flutes
EP (London & Edinburgh: Corri, Dussek, ca. 1797)
     GB:Lbm G.225.(10.)

(Six) *Duetti* for 2 flutes
MS I:Gl N.1.7.2.(Sc.16)

(Three) *Duetti* for 2 flutes
MS I:Gl T.C.7.1. Sc.III)

(Eighteen) *Duets* for 2 flutes
MS (Wien: Traeg's *Catalog*, 1799, as well as another fifty-four duets arranged by Andre, Hoffmeister, Hagen, etc.)

(Six) *Trios*, for 2 flutes and viola
EP (Paris: Le Duc, ca. 1790)
     GB:Lbm G.414.(3.)

Sainsbury was familiar with (Six) *Duos*, Op. 24 (Offenbach) and (Six) *Sonatines*, Liv. 1, 2 (Offenbach) for 2 flutes.

Prota, Tomaso

(Six) *Sonatas*, for 2 flutes and bc
EP   (London: Chapman, ca. 1760)
GB:Lbm G.222.(6.)

Sonata for 2 flutes and bass
MS   GB:Eu D 52–54, Nr. 21

Pucolas, ?

(Six) *Duets*, Op. 6, for 2 flutes
MS   (Wien: Traeg's *Catalog*, 1799)

Pujolas, J.

Concertante Duettos, for 2 flutes
EP   (London: Wragg, ca. 1800)
GB:Lbm H.250.b.(12.)

Purcell, Daniel (1664–1717)

Sonata, for 2 flutes
EP   (London?, ca. 1708)
GB:Lbm B.171.a.(2.)

MGG attributes to Purcell four *Sonatas* for 2 flutes and bass, 1707–1710.

Quantz, Johann (1697–1773)

(Six) *Duetti*, Op. 2, 1759, for 2 flutes
EP   (Berlin: Winter)
I:Bc

(Six) *Duets* for 2 flutes
MS   (Wien: Traeg's Catalog, 1799)

(Six) *Sonatas*, Op. 1, for 2 flutes
EP   (Amsterdam, 1740)
GB:Lbm G.281.a.

(Six) *Sonatas,* Op. 3, for 2 flutes
EP   (London: Walsh, 1733)
GB:Lbm G.241.(7.)

(Six) *Sonatas*, Op. 5, for 2 flutes
EP   (London: Walsh, ca. 1760)
GB:Lbm G.280.b.(9.)

Sonata for 2 flutes and bass
MS   GB:Eu D 52–54, Nr. 18

Rabboni, Giuseppe (1800–1856)

(Three) *Duets* for 2 flutes
MS   A:Wgm VIII 26427
    A:Wgm has 32 early prints of other Rabboni flute works.

Racca, Antonio

Sonata in C Major for 2 flutes
MS   I:Gl M.4.28.21

Sonata in C Major for 2 flutes
MS   I:Gl M.4.28.22

Rathe, ?, (eighteenth century)

(Five) *Trios*, for 2 flutes and bc
MS   GB:Lbm R.M.21.b.8.

Rault, Felix

(Three) *Duetts concertanti*, Op. 1, for 2 flutes
EP   (London and Edinburgh: Corri, Dussek, ca. 1797)
    GB:Lbm G.225.(11.)

(Six) *Easy Duetts*, for 2 flutes
EP   (London & Edinburgh: Corri, Dussek, ca. 1797)
    GB:Lbm G.225.(12.)

(Six) *Duets* for 2 flutes
MS   (Wien: Traeg's Catalog, 1799)

Sainsbury identifies Rault as the composer of four sets of (Six) *Duos*, Op. 5–8 for 2 flutes.

Reinards, William

Amusement, Op. 1, for 2 flutes.
EP   (Amsterdam: Hummel, ca. 1775)
    GB:Lbm B.72.(1.)

(Six) *Duets*, for 2 flutes.
EP   (London: Welcker, 1768)
    GB:Lbm H.2140.d.(4.)
    GB:Lbm G.421.a.(2.) [another copy]

Duets, for 2 flutes
EP (London: Welcker, ca. 1770)
  GB:Lbm G.421.a.(3.)

Duets, Op. 4, for 2 flutes
EP (London: Welcker, ca. 1772)
  GB:Lbm G.421.a.(4.)

(Six) *Sonatines*, Op. 4, for 2 flutes
EP (Amsterdam: Hummel, ca. 1775)
  GB:Lbm B.72.(2.)

Rhein, Ferdinand

(Three) *Duets* for 2 flutes
MS A:Wgm VIII 1207

(Six) *Duets* for 2 flutes
MS (Wien: Traeg's *Catalog*, 1799)

Sainsbury identifies Rhein as a flutist in Paris who published there (Three) *Duos*, Op. 1, for 2 flutes.

Ricci, Francesco (1733–1800)

MGG attributes to Ricci a *Sonata* in C Major and a *Trio* in C Major (both, MS, D:KA) for 2 flutes.

Riedt, Friedrich (1710–1783)

MGG attributes to Riedt the following works:
  Trio (Leipzig: Breitkopf & Härtel, 1758) for 2 flutes and bass
  Trio (Leipzig: Breitkopf & Härtel, 1761) for 2 flutes and cembalo
  Duet (Berlin: Birnstiel, 1760) for 2 flutes
  Duett (Berlin: ?) for 2 flutes

Rolla, Alessandro (1757–1841)

MGG attributes to Rolla (Three) *Trios* (Zurich: Nageli) for 2 flutes and viola.

Romano, L. H.

Sainsbury identifies Romano as the composer of two sets of (Twelve) *Sonatas* for 2 flutes.

Rossini, Gioacchino (1792–1868)

MGG attributes to Rossini (Twelve) Walzer (1827) for 2 flutes.

Rozelli, ?

(Ten) *Duets*, Op. 2, for 2 flutes
EP   (London: Thompson, ca. 1764)
    GB:Lbm G.225.a.(3.)

Ruge, Filippo

(Six) *Duetti* for 2 flutes
MS I:Ac Mss.N.476/8

Salulini, Paolo

(Six) *Sonatas* in C Major for 2 flutes and bass
MS S:Uu Ms. 276–281

Sammartini, Giovanni (1698–1775)

Sonata a tre, for 2 flutes and bass
MS CH:Bu kr.IV 300

Sonata a tre, for 2 flutes and bass
MS CH:Bu kr.IV 301

MGG attributes to Sammartini (Six) *Sonatas or Duets* Op. 4 (London: Walsh, 1748)
    for 2 flutes, followed by Op. 5 (1756), Op. 7 (1757) and Op. 10 (1763).

Sammartini, Giuseppe (1693–1751)

MGG attributes to Sammartini (Twelve) *Sonatas* (London: Walsh, 1738) and (Six) *Sonatas or Duets*, Op. 1 (London: Oswald, 1750) for 2 flutes.

San Martini, Giovanni

(Six) *Sonatas*, Op. 4, for 2 flutes
EP   (London: Walsh, ca. 1750)
    GB:Lbm G.421.n.(3.)
    GB:Lbm G.421.h.(1.) [another copy]

(Six) *Sonatas*, Op. 5, for 2 flutes
EP   (London: Walsh, ca. 1755)
    GB:Lbm G.70.c.(6.)

(Six) *Sonatas*, Op. 7, for 2 flutes
EP (London: Walsh, ca. 1755)
   GB:Lbm G.280.b.(11.)

(Six) *Sonatas*, Op. 10, for 2 flutes
EP (London: Walsh, ca. 1760)
   GB:Lbm G.280.b.(12.)

San Martini, Giuseppe

(Twelve) *Sonatas*, for 2 flutes
EP (London: Walsh, 1738)
   GB:Lbm G.241.(9.)

(Twelve) *Sonatas*, for 2 flutes and bc
EP (London, ca. 1740)
   GB:Lbm H.39.

Sonata a Solo, Op. 1, for 2 flutes and bc
EP (London: the composer, ca. 1735)
   GB:Lbm G.86.b.

(Six) *Sonatas*, Op. 1, for 2 flutes
EP (London: Oswald, ca. 1750)
   GB:Lbm D.161.a.(6.)

(Six) *Sonatas*, Op. 6, for 2 flutes and bc
EP (London: Walsh, ca. 1745)
   GB:Lbm G.242.(5.)

Scaglies, Angelo

Tantum ergo for Soprano, 2 flutes and continuo
MS I:Ac Mss.N.480/7

Scarlatti, Pietro Alessandro (1660–1725)

MGG attributes to Scarlatti the following works:
   Augellin vago e canoro (1699) for Soprano and 2 flutes
   Filli, Tu sai s'io t'amo (1701) for Soprano and 2 flutes
   Sonata for 2 flutes and bass

Schetky, ?

(Six) *Duets*, Op. 5, for 2 flutes
MS (Wien: Traeg's *Catalog*, 1799)

(Six) *Sonatas* for 2 flute and a string
MS (Wien: Traeg's *Catalog,* 1799)

Schmitt, Joseph (1734–1791)

(Six) *Trios,* Op. 7, for 2 violins or flutes with bc
EP (Amsterdam: the composer, ca. 1785)
    GB:Lbm H.2852.a.(6.)

MGG also attributes to Schmitt a *Concertino,* Op. 15 (Amsterdam, 1782) for 2 flutes
and orchestra.

Schmittbaur, Joseph Aloys (1718–1809)

MGG attributes to (Three) *Trii* (Speyer: Bossler, 1783) for 2 flutes and violin.

Schultz, Lebrecht (eighteenth century)

Sonata in G Major for 2 flutes and cello, or bassoon
MS D:KA Ms. 897 [according to MGG]

Schultze, J. C.

Sonata for 2 flutes and bass
MS B:Bc Wotquenne 7049

Schwartzkopff, Theodor (1659–1732)

MGG attributes to Schwartzkopff *Sonates* for 2 flutes and cembalo.

Schwindl, Friedrich (1737–1786)

(Twelve) *Duetts,* Op. 4, for 2 flutes
EP (London: Goulding, ca. 1800)
    GB:Lbm B.71.

(Six) *Duets* for 2 flutes
MS (Wien: Traeg's *Catalog,* 1799)

(Six) *Trios,* Op. 10, for 2 flutes and bc
EP (London: Goulding, ca. 1800)
    GB:Lbm H.1522.a.

(Six) *Sonatas,* Op. 3, for 2 flutes and bc
EP (London: Welcker, ca. 1770)
    GB:Lbm G.71.f.(6.)

Shield, William (1748–1829)

(Six) *Duetts*, Op. 1, of which one is for 2 flutes
EP (London: Napier, ca. 1775)
    GB:Lbm G.421.q.(4.)

Sixt, Giovanni (1757–1797)

Duet for 2 flutes
MS I:Gl T.C.7.1.(Sc.111)

(Six) *Duets*, Op. 3, for 2 flutes
MS (Wien: Traeg's *Catalog*, 1799)

(Six) *Duetti*, Op. 3, for 2 flutes
MS D:DO [according to MGG]

Sorge, Georg Andreas (1703–1778)

MGG attributes to Sorge a *Trio* for 2 flute douces and bass and (Six) *Trios* for 2 flutes
    and bass.

Sperger, Johann (d. 1812)

(Six) *Divertimenti* for 2 flute and a string
MS (Wien: Traeg's *Catalog*, 1799)

Stabingher, Mathias (1750–1815)

(Six) *Duets* for 2 flutes
MS I:Gl M.4.29.40

Duetti, Nr. 6, for 2 flutes
MS I:Vmc Busta 31-53-N.44

MGG attributes to Stabingher the following works:
    (Six) *Duos*, Op. 1 (Paris, 1776), for 2 flutes
    (Six) *Sonatas*, Op. 2 (Paris, 1776), for 2 flutes
    (Six) *Duos concertants*, Op. 7 (Venedig, 1792), for 2 flutes
    (Two) *Duetti* (MS, *I:Mc*) for flutes
    Duetti (MS, *I:Pci*) for flutes

Stadler, J. Dominicus, Abbé (Austrian, 1748–1833)

(Three) *Serenate* for 2 flutes and bass
MS GB:Eu D 52–54/Nrs. 23–25

Stamitz, Carl

(Six) *Duetts,* for 2 flutes
EP (London: Gardom, ca. 1785)
    GB:Lbm G.421.r.(11.)

(Six) *Duetts*, Op. 27, for 2 flutes
EP (London: Preston, ca. 1785)
    GB:Lbm G.280.b.(14.)

(Nine) *Duets* for 2 flutes
MS (Wien: Traeg's *Catalog*, 1799)

Stamitz, Johann Wenzel Anton (1717–1757)

MGG attributes to Stamitz two *Trios* for 2 flutes and bass (MS, D:HR and B:Bc).

Steinfeld, Albert Jacob (1741–1815)

(Six) *Duets*, Op. 4, for 2 flutes
MS (Wien: Traeg's *Catalog*, 1799)
EP (Hamburg, 1797) [according to MGG]

Süssmayr, Franz Xaver (1766–1803)

MGG attributes to Sussmayr a *Duett* for 2 flutes.

Telemann, Georg (1681–1767)

(Six) *Duets* for 2 flutes
MS (Wien: Traeg's *Catalog*, 1799)

(Six) *Sonatas*, Op. 2, for 2 flutes
EP (London: Walsh, ca. 1740)
    GB:Lbm G.401.a.(2.)

(Six) *Sonatas* 'a Canone,' for 2 flutes
MS I:Gl SS.B.1.8.(H.8)

Sonata for 2 flute and a string
MS (Wien: Traeg's Catalog, 1799)

Tessarini, Carlo (1690–1766)

(Six) *Sonatas*, for 2 flutes
EP (London: Walsh, ca. 1752)
    GB:Lbm G.409.k.(3.)

Sonate, Op. 12, for 2 flutes
EP   (Paris: Boivin, ca. 1745)
      GB:Lbm G.274.c.(7.)

MGG also attributes to Tessarini (Six) *Sonatas* (Amsterdam, 1732) for 2 flutes and bass.

Todt, Johann Christoph (1833–1900)

MGG attributes to Todt three *Concerti* for 2 flutes.

Toeschi, Johann [Giovanni] (1735–1800)

Trio for 2 flutes and bass
MS   B:Bc Wotquenne 7130

Torti, Giuseppe

(Two) *Trios* for 2 flutes and bass
MS   GB:Eu D 52–54/Nrs. 19, 20

Valentine, Robert (1680–1735)

(Six) *Setts of Aires*, for 2 flutes
EP   (London: Walsh and Hare, ca. 1715)
      GB:Lbm H.250.c.(6.)

(Seven) *Sets of Aires*, Op. 10, for 2 flutes
EP   (London: Wright, ca. 1720)
      GB:Lbm G.297.(3.)

(Six) *Sonatas*, Op. 4, for 2 violins, oboes, or flutes
EP   (London: Wright, ca. 1715)
      GB:Lbm H.11.f.
EP   (London: Walsh, ca. 1715)
      GB:Lbm H.11.c.(2.) [for 2 flutes]

(Six) *Sonatas*, Op. 6, for 2 flutes
EP   (London: Walsh, ca. 1720)
      GB:Lbm G.71.f.(7.)

(Six) *Sonatas*, Op. 7, for 2 flutes
EP   (London: Wright, ca. 1720)
      GB:Lbm G.297.(1.)

Vannacci, Biago

Sonata for 2 flutes
MS   I:Gl SS.A.1.20.(G.8)

Vern, Auguste

(Three) *Duos* for 2 flutes
MS   A:Wgm VIII 6314

MGG attributes to Vern the following works:
    (Six) *Grand Duos Concertans*, Op. 6 (Paris, 1810), for 2 flutes
    (Three) *Duets*, Op. 7 (London: 1830), for 2 flutes
    (Three) *Grands Duos*, Op. 9 (Leipzig), for 2 flutes
    (Three) *Grand Duos*, Op. 10 (Bonn and Köln), for 2 flutes

Vogel, Johann Christoph (1758–1788)

(Six) *Duets*, Op. 35, for 2 flutes
MS   (Wien: Traeg's *Catalog*, 1799)

MGG also attributes to Vogel a *Simphonie concertante*, Op. 20 (Augsburg: Gombart) for 2
    flutes and orchestra.

Walckiers, ?

(Three) *Duos*, Op. 27, for 2 flutes
EP   (Milano: Lucca)
    I:Bc

Wanhal, Jan (1793–1813)

(Three) *Duetts*, for 2 flutes, one of which is by Wanhal
EP   (London: Fentum, ca. 1795)
    GB:Lbm G.421.p.(4.)

(Six) *Duets* for 2 flutes
MS   (Wien: Traeg's *Catalog*, 1799)

MGG attributes to Vanhal (Six) *Duetts* (London, 1780) and a *Duet* in G Major (MS, CS:Pnm
    XXVII B. 124) for 2 flutes.

Weideman, Charles (d. 1782)

(Six) *Sonatas*, Op. 3, for 2 flutes and bc
EP   (London: the composer, 1751)
    GB:Lbm G.674.b.

(Six) *Duets*, Op. 4, for 2 flutes
EP   (London: the composer, 1751)
       GB:Lbm G.674.c.

(Six) *Duets*, Op. 6, for 2 flutes
EP   (London: Walsh, ca. 1765)
       GB:Lbm G.674.c.(3.)

Weiss, Carl R.

Sainsbury identifies Weiss as the composer of a number of works for 2 flutes.

Weiss, Franz (1778–1830)

MGG attributes to Weiss *Duetti* (Wien, 1804) and *Preludi* (Mailand: Riccordi) for 2 flutes.

Weiss, Johann Sigismund (1690–1737)

MGG attributes to Weiss a *Sonata* in D Major for 2 flutes and bass.

Weiss, Karl II (1777–1845)

MGG attributes to Weiss *Studies on Modulation*, Op. 2, and a *Duette* for 2 flutes.

Weldon, John (1676–1736)

MGG attributes to Weldon a *Collection of Aires* (London: Walsh & Hare, 1703) for 2 flutes.

Wendling, Johann (1720–1797)

(Six) *Duettes*, Op. 4, for 2 flutes.
EP   (Amsterdam: Hummel, ca. 1780)
       GB:Lbm H.2140.a.(10.)

(Six) *Duetts*, Op. 6, for 2 flutes.
EP   (London: Napier, ca. 1775)
       GB:Lbm G.421.s.(8.)

(Six) *Duos,* Op. 9, for 2 flutes.
EP   (Amsterdam: Schmitt, ca. 1790)
       GB:Lbm G.280.b.919.)

(Six) *Duetts*, for 2 flutes.
MS I:MOe Mus.D.552–557

(Six) *Sonatas*, Op. 1, for 2 flutes.
EP   (London: Longman, Lukey and Co., ca. 1775)
       GB:Lbm G.225.a.(4.)

(Two) *Sonatas* for 2 flutes
MS   A:Wgm VIII 5220

Sonata for 2 flutes
MS   I:Gl SS.B.1.8.(H.8)

Wenkel, Johann Friedrich (1734–1792)

MGG attributes to Wenkel four Duetts (Berlin: Bock, 1772), for flutes.

Wendt, Giovanni (1745–1809)

(Six) *Duets* for 2 flutes
MS   (Wien: Traeg's *Catalog*, 1799)

Wessely, Johann (1762–1810)

MGG attributes to Wessely *Twelve Variations* (Leipzig: Joachim) for 2 flutes and orchestra.

Westerhoff, Heinrich (1760–1806)

MGG attributes to Westerhoff (Three) *Trios* (Kassel, ca. 1800) for 2 flutes and viola.

Willman, Samuel David

Sainsbury identifies Willman as the composer of (Four) *Duets* (Berlin, 1797) for 2 flutes.

Worgan, James ('the Younger')

Sonata, Op. 1, for piano with 2 flutes ad lib
EP   (London: Longman & Broderip, ca. 1785)
   GB:Lbm G.222.(3.)

Wragg, J.

(Three) *Duettos*, Op. 5, for 2 flutes
EP   (London: the composer, ca. 1800)
   GB:Lbm G.225.(14.)

Wranitzky, ?

Concerto for 2 flutes and orchestra
MS   (Wien: Traeg's *Catalog*, 1799)

(Six) *Duets* for 2 flutes
MS   (Wien: Traeg's *Catalog*, 1799)

(Six) *Duets*, Op. 33, for 2 flutes
MS (Wien: Traeg's *Catalog*, 1799)

Wraniczky, Paul (1756–1808)

Duets for 2 flutes
MS A:Wgm VIII 1223

(Six) *Duos concertants*, Op. 13, for 2 flutes
EP   (Paris: Sieber, ca. 1790)
     GB:Lbm G.280.j.(10.)

(Six) *Duos Concertants*, Op. 33, for 2 flutes
EP   (Augsbourg: Gombart, ca. 1800)
     GB:Lbm G.280.b.(21.)

Wunderlich, Johann Georg (1755–1819)

MGG attributes to Wunderlich (Six) *Duos* for 2 flutes.

Zanetti, Francesco (b. 1740)

Concertino for 2 flutes and orchestra
MS I:Ac Mss.N.349/3

Zarth, Georg (1708–1778)

MGG attributes to Zarth a *Trio* in G Major (MS, B:Bc) for 2 flutes and continuo.

Zinck, Bendix Friedrich (1743–1801)

MGG attributes to Zinck (Six) *Sonatas*, Op. 1 (Berlin: Hummel, 1782), for 2 flutes.

Zuckert, Johann

(Eight) *Sonatas*, for 2 flutes and bc
EP   (London: the composer, 1770)
     GB:Lbm G.420.g.(6.)

Zumsteeg, Johann Rudolf (1760–1802)

MGG attributes to Zumsteeg a *Concerto* in D Major for 2 flutes and orchestra.

MUSIC WITH FLUTE AND OBOE

Anonymous

Trio, for flute, oboe, and cello ('as performed by Messrs. Weiss, Fischer, & Crosdil …')
EP   (London: Longman & Broderip, ca. 1790)
    GB:Lbm G.420.d.(13.)

Atys, ?

(Six) *Sonates*, Op. 4, 'en Duo,' for 'flute, Haut-bois, Pardessus de Viole a cinq Cordes, Violon, Bassoon, et Violoncelle'
EP   (Paris: the composer, ca. 1770)
    GB:Lbm E.201.b.(1.)

Bach, Johann Christian (1735–1782)

(Four) *Quartets*, Op. 9, for 2 flutes, viola, cello; flute and strings; and flute, oboe, viola, and cello
EP   (London: Preston, ca. 1785)
    GB:Lbm G.435.(1.)
    GB:Lbm G.411.a.(1.) [a later edition, ca. 1790]

(Six) *Quintets* for flute, oboe, and strings
MS   (Wien: Traeg's *Catalog*, 1799)

Quintet in C Major for violin or flute solo, oboe, and strings
MS   (Wien: Traeg's *Catalog*, 1799)

Chédeville, Nicholas

(Six) *Sonatas*, for flute, oboe, and bc
EP   (Paris: the composer, ca. 1740)
    GB:Lbm K.7.f.15.(5.)

Dornel, Antoine (1685–1765)

MGG attributes to Dornel, *Sonates en trio*, Op. 3, 1713, for flute, oboe, and violin.

Fasch, Johann Friedrich (1688–1758)

MGG attributes to Fasch a *Sonata* in B♭ for oboe, flute a bec, violin, and cembalo.

Fischer, Johann (1733–1800)

Trio, for flute, oboe and cello ('as performed by Weiss, Fischer, & Crosdil')
EP   (London: Longman & Broderip, ca. 1790)
    GB:Lbm G.420.d.(13.)

Fortia de Piles, Alphonse-Toussaint (1758–1826)

MGG attributes to Piles quintets for flute, oboe and strings.

Gautier, Pierre (1643–1697)

MGG attributes to Gautier a *Recueil de trio nouveaux* (Paris, 1699) for violin, oboe, and flute.

Gluck, Christoph (1714–1787)

Sextet, for flute, oboe, and strings
MS   I:MOe Mus.E.62

Graun, August Friedrich (1698–1765)

MGG attributes to Graun the following works:
    Concerti grossi with flute and oboe (or flute) as concertino
    Concerto a tre, with flute, violin (or flute) and oboe as concertino

Hoffmeister, ?

(Three) *Duets*, Op. 38, for flute and oboe
MS   (Wien: Traeg's *Catalog*, 1799)

Janitzsch, ?

(Two) *Quartet* for flute, oboe, and strings
MS   (Wien: Traeg's *Catalog*, 1799)

Kleinknecht, Jakob Friedrich (1722–1794)

MGG attributes to Kleinknecht a *Sonata* in C Minor (MS, D:KA) for flute, oboe (or violin)
    and bass.

Konink, Servas de (d. 1717)

MGG attributes to Konink *Trios*, Op. 1 (Amsterdam: Delorme & Roger, 1696) and *Trios*,
    Op. 4 (Amsterdam, Roger, 1700) for flute, oboe, and violin.

Krommer, Franz (1759–1831)

Concerto for flute and oboe and orchestra
MS I:PAc F.V.7

Loeillet, John (of London)

(Twelve) *Sonatas*, Op. 2, of which three are for 2 flutes and three are for lute and oboe.
EP (London: Walsh and Hare, ca. 1725)
    GB:Lbm G.685.

Mica, Jan Adam (1746–1811)

MGG attributes to Mica a *Sextet* (MS, CS:Pn) for flute, oboe and strings.

Morawetz, Giovanni

Sainsbury identifies Morawetz, a musician in Vienna in 1799, as the composer of a *Sextet* for oboe, flute, and strings.

Pleyel, Ignaz Joseph (1757–1831)

MGG attributes to Pleyel (Three) *Quintets* for flute, oboe, and strings; Sainsbury indicates these were published in Offenbach.

Salieri, Antonio (1750–1825)

MGG attributes to Salieri a *Concerto* (1774) for flute and oboe with orchestra.

Schickhard, Johann

(Six) *Sonatas*, Op. 14, for flute, oboe, and bc
EP (Amsterdam: Roger, ca. 1712)
    GB:Lbm G.274.c.(3.)

Süssmayer, Franz (1766–1803)

Quintet, for flute, oboe, and strings
MS A:Wgm XI 23524

Vincent, Thomas II (1720–1783)

MGG attributes to Vincent (Six) *Solostücke*, Op. 1 (London: the composer, 1748) and (Six) *Solostücke*, Op. 2 (London, 1755) for oboe, flute, violin and cembalo.

Westenholz, Friedrich (1756–1802)

MGG attributes to Westenholz a *Sinfonie concertante*, Op. 6, for flute and oboe with orchestra.

Wolf, E. G.

Quartet for flute, oboe, and strings
MS (Wien: Traeg's *Catalog*, 1799)

Wragg, J.

A Fifth Solo, for flute or oboe, with bassoon
EP (London: the composer, ca. 1800)
    GB:Lbm G.221.(10.)

Wraniczky, Paul, 1756–1808

(Four) *Quintets*, Op. 3, for oboe, flute, and strings
EP (Berlin: Hummel, ca. 1790)
    GB:Lbm H.2828.a.

MUSIC WITH FLUTE AND ENGLISH HORN

Anonymous

Variazione, for flute, English horn, violin, viola, and piano
MS I:OS Ms. Musiche B. 4749/ a,b

Pugni, Cesare, 19th Century

Quintet for flute, English horn, piano, and strings
MS I:Mc Mss. 32/1

Zucchi, Giacomo (early nineteenth century)

Settimino, for flute, English horn, piano, and strings
MS I:Mc Da Camera MS. 30/2

MUSIC WITH FLUTE AND CLARINET

Danzi, Franz (1763–1826)

MGG attributes to Danzi a *Concerto* for flute and clarinet (Offenbach: André).

Fröhlich, Franz Joseph (1780–1862)

MGG attributes to Fröhlich a *Serenade*, Op. 20 (Augsburg: Gombert) for flute, clarinet and strings.

Fuchs, Giovanni

(Three) *Duets* for flute and clarinet
MS (Wien: Traeg's *Catalog*, 1799)

Quintet, for flute, clarinet, violin, viola, cello
MS A:Wgm XI 2548

Kerstein, ?

Sainsbury identifies Kerstein as the composer of a *Duet* (London, before 1797) for flute and clarinet.

Kreutzer, Conradin (1780–1849)

Quintet, for flute, clarinet, viola, cello, and piano
MS A:Wgm XI 4731

Monteilli, ?

(Three) *Trios* (1824) for flute, clarinet, and viola
MS A:Sca Hs. 236

(Three) *Trios*, Op. 1, for flute, clarinet, and viola
MS (Wien: Traeg's *Catalog*, 1799)

According to Sainsbury, Montelli published three Trios, Liv. 1 (Paris, 1796) for flute, clarinet, and viola.

Vanderhagen, Armand Jean (1753–1822)

MGG attributes to Vanderhagen *Duos* for flute and clarinet, or horn.

MUSIC WITH FLUTE AND BASSOON

Fasch, Johann Friedrich (1688–1758)

MGG attributes to Fasch a *Sonata* in D Major for flute, violin, bassoon, and cembalo.

Fischer, Thomas (?)

Duetto, for flute and bassoon
MS A:Wgm VIII 1181

Foerster, Emmanuel (1748–1823)

Concerto, for flute, bassoon and orchestra
MS A:Wn Sm 1200 ch XIX 8 fol.

Hoffmann, Karl (?)

Divertimento, for flute and bassoon
MS A:Wgm VIII 9270

Leo, Leonardo (1694–1744)

MGG attributes to Leo a *Sonata* (London: Bland, 1795) for flute, violin, and bassoon.

Molter, Johann Melchior (1695–1765)

MGG attributes to Molter a *Concerto* for flute and bassoon (MS, D:KA).

Myslivecek, Josef (1737–1781)

MGG attributes to Myslivecek (Three) *Trios* (London: Bland, 1795) for flute, violin and bassoon.

Pepusch, Johann (1667–1752)

Solos for flute and bassoon and harpsichord
EP (London: Walsh, Randall, and Hare, ca. 1710)
    GB:Lbm H.250.c.(2.)

Ruge, ?

Sonata for flute and bassoon
MS B:Bc Wotquenne 5586

MUSIC WITH FLUTE AND TRUMPET

Graupner, Christoph (1683–1760)

MGG attributes to Graupner (Five) *Sonatas* (MS, D: KA) for flute, trumpet, viola d'amore and continuo.

MUSIC FOR FLUTE AND HORN

Candeille, Pierre-Joseph (1744–1827)

MGG attributes to Candeille a lost *Concerto* for piano, horn and flute (1789).

Droste-Hulshoff, Maximilian F. (1764–1840)

MGG attributes to Droste a *Fantasie* for flute, viola, horn, cello and orchestra.

Hoffmeister, Franz Anton (1754–1812)

Notturno, for flute d'amore, horn, and viola
MS A:Wgm XI 1558

Kozeluch, Leopold Anton (1747–1818)

Serenata in E♭ Major for flute, horn and strings
MS D:W [cited in MGG]

Poessinger, Franz (1767–1827)

MGG attributes to Poessinger a *Trio*, Op. 28 (Wien: Artaria, 1806) for flute, horn, and viola.

Punto, Johann Wenzel (1757–1803)

Sainsbury identifies Punto as the composer of (Three) *Quintets* for horn, flute and strings.

Süssmayr, Franz Xaver (1766–1803)

MGG attributes to Süssmayr a *Serenade* for flute, horn, and viola.

Wolf, Friedrich Adolph (Viennese, 1828–1887)

Serenade, for flute, horn, cello, and piano
MS A:Wn Sm 13128

Abendlied, for flute, horn, cello, and piano
MS A:Wn Sm 13129

MUSIC WITH TWO OBOES

Barbandt, Carl

(Six) *Sonatas*, for 2 flutes, 2 oboes, or 2 violins
EP (London, ca. 1755)
GB:Lbm F.14

Bochsa, Charles (Karl)

(Three) *Duos concertants* for 2 oboes
EP (Paris: Schonenberger)
I:Bc

Bokemeyer, Heinrich (1679–1751)

Me miserum!, for Tenor and 2 oboes
MS D:B [cited in MGG]

Braun, Guillaume

Grand Duo, Op. 23, for 2 oboes
EP (Leipzig: Breitkopf & Härtel)
I:Bc

Castnis, Fran. de

Sonata, for 2 oboes
MS A:Wn EM 76

Dedonati, Girolamo

(Six) *Sonatas*, for 2 flutes or oboes and bc
EP (London: R. Birchall, ca. 1790)
GB:Lbm G.420.d.(12.)

Fasch, Johann Friedrich (1688–1758)

MGG attributes to Fasch a *Trio* in E Minor and a Sonata in G Minor for 2 oboes and continuo.

Ghillini di Asuni, ?

(Six) *Duets*, for 2 flutes or oboes
EP   (London: Welcker, ca. 1775)
   GB:Lbm G.421.n.(1.)

Graupner, Christoph (1687–1760)

Concerto for 2 oboes
MS D:Ds Mus.Ms. 1541

Concerto for 2 oboes
MS D:Ds Mus.Ms. 411/12

Concerto for 2 oboes
MS D:Ds Mus.Ms. 411/30

Handel, Georg F. (1685–1759)

(Six) *Sonatas*, Op. 2, for 2 violins, oboes, or flutes
EP   (London: Cooke, ca. 1735)
   GB:Lbm H.436.d

Haydn, Josef (1732–1809)

(Three) *Duetti* for 2 oboes
MS I:Mc A/33/16/2

(Six) *Duetti* for 2 oboes
MS I:Mc A/33/16/1

Lettorio, Marino

Sainsbury identifies Lettorio as a musician who 'acquired notoriety in Paris,' and composer of (Six) *Duos*, Op. 2 (Paris, 1801), for 2 oboes.

Malzat, Ignaz (1757–1804)

Concerto in C Major for 2 oboes
MS A:KR [cited in MGG]

Marcello, Alessandro (1684–1750)

MGG attributes to Marcello (Six) *Concerti* (Augsburg, 1738) for 2 oboes and orchestra.

Pez, Johann Christoph (1664–1716)

Concerto grosso in A Major for 2 oboes in the concertino
MS   D:Dlb [according to MGG]

Pfeiffer, Franz Anton (1754–1787)

MGG attributes to Pfeiffer a presumed lost *Sonata* for 2 oboe d'amore, 2 viola di braccio and bass.

Pfeiffer, Johann (1697–1761)

MGG attributes to Pfeiffer a *Sonata* for 2 oboe d'amour and strings.

Pla, Jose

(Six) *Sonatas*, for 2 flutes, violins, or oboes with bc
EP   (London: Hardy, ca. 1760)
        GB:Lbm F.23.

Platti, Giovanni Benedetto (1700–1763)

MGG attributes to Platti a *Sonata* for 2 oboes and bass.

Romhild, Johann Theodor (1684–1756)

Das neue Jahr, solo cantata for Bass, 2 oboes, and continuo
MP   (Kasel, 1951) [cited in MGG]

Schiassi, Maria

Concerto for two oboes and orchestra
MS   A:Wgm VIII 2839

Sellner, Joseph (German oboist, 1787–1843)

(Twelve) *Duets*
MS   A:Wgm VIII 41531

Stölzel, Gottfried Heinrich (1690–1749)

MGG attributes to Stolzel a *Concerto* in D Major for 2 oboe d'amore.

Telemann, Georg (1681–1767)

Concerto for 2 oboes
MS   D:Ds Mus.Ms. 1033/44

Concerto for 2 oboes
MS   D:Ds Mus.Ms. 1033/51

Concerto for 2 oboes
MS   D:Ds Mus.Ms. 1033/56

Concerto for 2 oboes
MS   D:Ds Mus.Ms. 1033/81

Valentine, Robert (1680–1735)

(Six) *Sonatas*, Op. 4, for 2 violins, oboes, or flutes
EP   (London: Wright, ca. 1715)
    GB:Lbm H.11.f.
EP   (London: Walsh, ca. 1715)
    GB:Lbm H.11.c.(2.) [for 2 flutes]

Vogt, August

Duo for 2 oboes and orchestra
EP   (Paris: Richault)
    I:Bc

MUSIC WITH OBOE AND ENGLISH HORN

Graupner, Christoph (1687–1760)

Concerto for oboe, English horn, and viola d'amore
MS   D:Ds Mus.Ms. 1540

Süssmayr, Franz Xaver (1766–1803)

MGG attributes to Süssmayr a *Quintet* for oboe, English horn, guitar, and strings.

MUSIC WITH OBOE AND CLARINET

Sinigaglia, Leone (1868–1944)

MGG attributes to Sinigaglia (Twelve) *Variations on a Theme of Schubert*, Op. 19, for oboe, clarinet and piano.

Szabo, Xaver

Romeo und Julie, for oboe, clarinet, harp, and piano
MS   H:Bn Ms.Mus. 344

MUSIC WITH OBOE AND BASSOON

Besozzi, Alessandro (1702–1775)

Sonata in F Major for oboe and bassoon
MS   I:Gl SS.A.1.16.(G.8)

Brod, Henri

Fantasie on a theme of Rossini, Op. 21, for oboe, bassoon, and piano
EP   (Paris: Frere)
    I:Bc

Corrette, Michel (1709–1795)

MGG attributes to Corrette a work entitled, *La Gamme du hautbois et du bassoon* of 1776.

Desehaye, ?

(Eight) *Duets* for oboe and bassoon
MS   (Wien: Traeg's *Catalog*, 1799)

Devienne, François (1759–1803)

MGG attributes to Devienne a *Sinfonie concertante* for oboe, or clarinet, and bassoon with orchestra.

Fasch, Johann Friedrich (1688–1758)

MGG attributes to Fasch a *Sonata* in F Major for violin, oboe, bassoon, and cembalo.

Fiala, ?

(Six) *Duets* for oboe and bassoon
MS (Wien: Traeg's *Catalog*, 1799)

MGG attributes to Fiala a *Duo Concertant* (Regensburg: Reitmayr, 1806) for oboe or flute and bassoon.

Graff, F. H.

Quartets for oboe, bassoon and strings
MS (Wien: Traeg's *Catalog*, 1799)

Heine, Samuel Friedrich (1764–1821)

MGG attributes to Heine a double *Concerto* for oboe and bassoon.

Malzat, Ignaz (1757–1804)

(Two) *Concerti* for oboe and bassoon and orchestra
MS (Wien: Traeg's *Catalog*, 1799)
MS A:KR [according to MGG]

Massonneau, Louis (1766–1848)

MGG attributes to Massonneau a lost *Concerto* for oboe and bassoon.

Morigi, Angelo

Duetto for oboe and bassoon
MS I:Gl M.3.23.10

Pfeiffer, Franz Anton (1754–1787)

MGG attributes to Pfeiffer a *Concerto* for bassoon and oboe with orchestra.

Quantz, Johann (1697–1773)

Sonata in G Major, for oboe, bassoon, and continuo
MS GB:Lbm R.M.21.b.7.

Schubert, Johann Fredrich (1770–1811)

MGG attributes to Schubert a *Symphonie concertante*, Op. 4 (Leipzig: Peters) for oboe and bassoon.

Stegmann, Carl David (1751–1826)

Concerto for oboe and bassoon with orchestra
MS B:Bc [according to MGG]

Tadolini, Giovanni (1793–1872)

Concertone in E♭ Major for oboe and bassoon and orchestra
MS I:Bc

MGG also attributes to Tadolini a *Trio* for piano, oboe, and bassoon.

Wagner, Karl Jakob (1772–1822)

MGG attributes to Wagner a *Concertante* for oboe and bassoon.

Wendt, Johann

(Three) *Quintets*, for oboe, bassoon and strings
MS A:Wgm XI 1033

Westenholz, Friedrich (1756–1802)

MGG attributes to Westenholz a *Sinfonie concertante*, Op. 7, for oboe and bassoon
with orchestra.

MUSIC WITH OBOE AND TRUMPET

Torelli, Giuseppe (1658–1709)

(Eight) *Sinfonie Concertante* for oboe and trumpet and strings.
MS I:Bsp [according to MGG]

MUSIC WITH OBOE AND HORN

Fasch, Johann Friedrich (1688–1758)

MGG attributes to Fasch a *Quartet* in F Major for violin, oboe (or oboe d'amore), horn
and bass.

Herzogenberg, Heinrich (1843–1900)

MGG attributes to Herzogenberg a *Trio* in D Major, Op. 61 (1889), for piano, oboe, and horn.

Müller, W.

Concerto for oboe and horn and orchestra
MS (Wien: Traeg's *Catalog*, 1799)

Reinecke, Carl Heinrich (1824–1910)

MGG attributes to Reinecke a *Trio*, Op. 188, for oboe, horn, and a string.

Schacht, Theodor Freiherr von (1748–1823)

MGG attributes to Schacht a *Quintet* for violin, oboe, horn, viola and cello.

Spandau, ?

Trio in C Major for horn, oboe, and bass
MS (Wien: Traeg's *Catalog*, 1799)

Stamitz, Karl (1745–1801)

(Three) *Quartets* for oboe, horn, 2 violas, and cello
MS I:Gl M.4.25.37

Stoelzel, ?

Sonata for oboe, horn, violin, and bass
MS B:Bc Wotquenne 7108

MUSIC WITH TWO CLARINETS

Anonymous

Lumen, for SATB, 2 clarinets
MS A:Wn Sm 0314 ch XIX 5 fol.

Pange lingua, for SSAATB, 2 clarinets
MS A:Wn Sm 21803

Osterlied, for SATB, 2 clarinets
MS A:Wn Sm 0309 ch XIX 8 fol.

Osterlied, for SAB, 2 clarinets, and organ
MS A:Wn Sm 680

Toddtenlied, for SATB and 2 clarinets
MS A:Wn Sm 0380

Bach, K. P. E. (1714–1788)

Duo, for 2 clarinets
MS A:Wn Sm 5520

Blasius, Fr.

(Six) Duets for 2 clarinets
MS (Wien: Traeg's *Catalog*, 1799)

(Six) *Duets*, Op. 39, for 2 clarinets
MS (Wien: Traeg's *Catalog*, 1799)

Devienne, François (1759–1803)

(Three) *Duos*, Op. 67, for 2 clarinets
EP (London: Preston, ca. 1790)
    GB: Lbm H.2143.a.(1.)

MGG also attributes to Devienne the following works:
    Sinfonie concertante, Op. 25 (Paris, 1794), for 2 clarinets and orchestra
    (Six) *Duos concertants*, Op. 65 (Paris: Sieber), for 2 clarinets
    (Three) *Sonatas*, Op. 28 (Paris: Porthaux), for 2 clarinets and bass
    Sonatas (Paris: Sieber) for 2 clarinets and bass

Dumonchau, Charles François (1775–1820)

(Three) *Duos*, Op. 18, for 2 clarinets
EP (Paris: Pollet)
    I:Bc

Gayer, Johann Nepomuk (1746–1811)

MGG attributes to Gayer six *Concerti* for 2 clarinets.

Gebauer, ?

(Three) *Duets*, Liv. 2, for 2 clarinets
MS (Wien: Traeg's *Catalog*, 1799)

Grossmann, ?

(Three) *Quartets* for 2 clarinets and strings
MS (Wien: Traeg's *Catalog*, 1799)

Henry, Louis F. (1786–1855)

MGG attributes to Henry *Duos*, Op. 4 (Paris: Sieber) for clarinets.

Hoffmeister, Franz Anton (1754–1812)

Concerto, for 2 clarinets and orchestra
MS A:Wn Sm 5851

Khym, ?

(Three) *Duets*, Op. 2, for 2 clarinets
MS (Wien: Traeg's *Catalog*, 1799)

Kreutzer, Conradin (1780–1849)

Duet ('a Comte Kinsky'), for 2 clarinets
MS A:Wgm VIII 2518

Trio, for 2 clarinets and viola
MS A:Wgm XI 2568

Krommer, Franz (1759–1831)

Concerto in F Major, Op. 35, for 2 clarinets and orchestra
EP   (Paris: Duhan)
       F:Pn Vm.24.157

Concerto in E♭ for 2 clarinets and orchestra
MS I:Bc

(Eight) *Pieces*, Op. 47, for 2 clarinets and viola
MS F:Pn LA.34.547

Küffner, Joseph (1776–1856)

MGG attributes to Küffner 24 *Duos* (Mainz: Schott) for 2 clarinets.

Labitzky, Josef (1802–1881)

Variations (1848), for 2 clarinets and orchestra
MS A:Wn Sm 15290

Mahon, John (1746–1834)

MGG attributes to Mahon (Four) *Duetts* (London: Clementi, 1803) for 2 clarinets.

Michel, 'Celebre' [probably same person as the following]

Duo concertante, for 2 clarinets
MS   A:Wgm VIII 2520

Michel, J. (pseud. for Michel Yost, 1754–1786)

(Six) *Duos*, Op. 6, for 2 clarinets
EP   (London: Broderip & Wilkinson, ca. 1800)
      GB:Lbm H.3212.b.(4.)

(Six) *Duets*, OP. 12, for 2 clarinets
EP   (London: Kohler, ca. 1800)
      GB:Lbm H.2189.c.(4.)

(Six) *Duets* for 2 clarinets
MS (Wien: Traeg's *Catalog*, 1799)

According to Sainsbury, Michel published 54 *Duets*, Op. 1–9, and *Petits Airs variés*, for
      2 clarinets.

Michel & Vogel

(Twelve) *Quartets* for 2 clarinets and strings
MS (Wien: Traeg's *Catalog*, 1799)

Müller, Iwan

Concertante, Op. 23, for 2 clarinets and orchestra
EP   (Milano: Ricordi)
      I:Bc

Neubauer, Giovanni

Concerto for 2 clarinets and orchestra
MS (Wien: Traeg's *Catalog*, 1799)

Pinsuti e Liverani

Grand Duet for 2 clarinets and orchestra
MS I:Bc

Reitter, ?

(Six) *Duets*, Op. 2, for 2 clarinets
MS (Wien: Traeg's *Catalog*, 1799)

(Six) *Sonatas* for 2 clarinets
MS I:Gl M.4.29.26/31

Schnyder von Wartensee, Franz Xaver (1786–1868)

MGG attributes to Wartensee a *Concerto* (Winterthur, 1941) for 2 clarinets.

Spaet (Spath?), Andrea

Sinfonia concertante, Op. 103, for 2 clarinets and orchestra
EP (Mainz: Schott)
     I:Bc

Tausch, Franz (German, 1762–1817)

Concerto for 2 clarinets and orchestra
MS A:Wn Sm 5122

Vanderhagen, Armand (1753–1822)

(Six) *Duets* ('dedicated to 'Monsieur de la Verneville') for 2 clarinets
MS I:Gl M.4.27.5

Vern, A. G.

MGG attributes to Vern (Three) *Duos Concertans* (1810) for 2 clarinets.

Vogel e Mic.

(Six) *Duos*, Op. 10, for 2 clarinets
EP (Bonn: Simrock)
     I:Bc

Vogel, ?

(Six) *Quartets* for 2 clarinets and strings
MS (Wien: Traeg's *Catalog*, 1799)

Walter, ?

(Two) *Pot-Pouri* for 2 clarinets
MS (Wien: Traeg's *Catalog,* 1799)

Walter, Johann Ignaz (1755–1822)

MGG attributes to Walter a *Concerto* for 2 clarinets.

Weber, Ludwig

(Three*) Pieces*, for clarinet and bass clarinet
MS   A:Wgm VIII 46.525

Weiss, Franz (1778–1830)

MGG attributes to Weiss a *Concertant-Duett* for 2 clarinets.

Yost, Michel [see also J. Michel, above]

(Six) *Duetti con molto variazioni*; and, (Six) *Duets*, for 2 clarinets
MS   I:Gl SS.B.1.9.(H.8)

MUSIC WITH CLARINET AND BASSOON

Bach, K. P. E. (1714–1788)

(Six) *kleine Sonaten* for clarinet, bassoon and klavier
MS   B:Bc Wotquenne 6359

Danzi, Franz (1763–1826)

MGG attributes to Danzi a *Concerto*, Op. 47, for clarinet and bassoon (Leipzig: Breitkopf & Härtel).

Devienne, François (1759–1803)

MGG attributes to Devienne (Six) *Duos concertants*, Op. 21 (Paris: Sieber) and two *Duos Concertants* (Paris: Sieber) for clarinet and bassoon.

Graupner, Christoph (1683–1760)

MGG attributes to Graupner a *Sonata* (MS, D:KA) for bassoon and Chalumean with continuo.

Hummel, Johann Nepomuk (1778–1837)

MGG attributes to Hummel a *Grande Serenade*, Op. 63 (Wien: Artaria) for piano, violin, clarinet, bassoon, and guitar.

Hurlstone, William Yeates (1876–1906)

MGG attributes to Hurlstone a *Trio* (1900) for clarinet, bassoon and piano.

Kreutzer, Konrad (1780–1849)

MGG attributes to Kreutzer a *Trio* in E♭ Major, Op. 43 (Leipzig: Peters) for clarinet, bassoon, and piano.

Kurzweil, ?

Trio in E♭ Major for clarinet, bassoon, and viola
MS (Wien: Traeg's *Catalog*, 1799)

Lefevre, Xavier (1763–1829)

Sinfonie Concertante for clarinet and bassoon [cited by Sainsbury]

Ozi, Etienne (b. 1754)

Sainsbury identifies Ozi as the composer of (Three) *Sinfonie concertante*, Op. 5, 7, and 10 (Paris, to 1798) for clarinet and bassoon.

Payer, ?

Grand Trio, for clarinet, bassoon, and piano
MS A:Wgm XI 10896

Pleyel, Ignaz (1757–1831)

(Six) *Sonatas* for clarinet, bassoon, and viola
MS I:Gl N.2.1.27.(Sc.119)

Rudolph, Erzherzog (of Austria)

Variations on 'Vous me quittez pour aller a la guerre,' for clarinet, bassoon, viola, and guitarre
MS A:Wgm XI 15421

Serenade, for clarinet, bassoon, viola, and guitarre
MS A:Wgm XI 15442

Schubert, Johann Fredrich (1770–1811)

Concerto, for clarinet and bassoon with orchestra
MS A:Wgm VIII 2510

Schwencke, Christian Fredrich (1767–1822)

MGG attributes to Schwencke a *Concerto* in B♭ Major for piano, clarinet and bassoon.

Tucsek, Vincenz

Concertstück for clarinet, bassoon and orchestra
MS H:Bn Ms.Mus. 1313

Vogel, Johann Christoph (1758–1788)

MGG attributes to Vogel a *Simphonie concertante* (Paris: Boyer) for bassoon and clarinet with orchestra.

Westerhoff, Heinrich (1760–1806)

MGG attributes to Westerhoff a *Symphonie concertante* for clarinet and bassoon.

MUSIC WITH CLARINET AND HORN

Alexander, Friedrich (Landgraf von Hessen)

Trio, for clarinet, horn, and piano
MS A:Wgm VIII 36751
     This manuscript was once owned by Brahms.

Benda, ?

Quintet in E♭ for clarinet, horn and strings
MS (Wien: Traeg's *Catalog*, 1799)

Eberl, Anton Franz Josef (1765–1807)

MGG attributes to Eberl a *Sextet*, Op. 47 (1800), in E♭ Major, for clarinet, horn, and strings.

Frugatta, Giuseppe (1860–1933)

MGG attributes to Frugatta a *Quintet* (1899) for piano, clarinet, horn and strings.

Gänsbacher, Johann Baptist (1778–1844)

MGG attributes to Gansbacher an *Introduction and Variations* for clarinet and horn.

Lachner, Franz (1803–1890)

MGG attributes to Lachner a *Trio* in B♭ Major (1830) for piano, clarinet and horn.

Moscheles, Ignazio (1794–1870)

Septet, Op. 88, for clarinet, horn, violin, viola, cello, bass, and piano
EP (Leipzig: Kistner)
    I:Bc

Reinecke, Carl Heinrich (1824–1910)

MGG attributes to Reinecke a *Trio*, Op. 274, for clarinet, horn, and a string.

Schenk, Johann Baptist (1753–1836)

MGG attributes to Schenk a *Konzert-Satze* for clarinet and horn.

MUSIC WITH TWO BASSET HORNS

Anonymous

Duet for 2 basset horns
MS (Wien: Traeg's *Catalog*, 1799)

(Fourteen) *Pieces* for 2 basset horns
MS (Wien: Traeg's *Catalog*, 1799)

(Three) *Parthias* for 2 basset horns
MS (Wien: Traeg's *Catalog*, 1799)

MUSIC WITH TWO BASSOONS

Blasius, Frederic (1758–1829)

(Three) *Duos*
MS A:Wgm VIII 25284

(Three) *Duos concertantes*
MS A:Wgm VIII 25285

Boismortier, Joseph (1691–1765)

(Six) *Sonates*, Op. 40, for 2 bassoons
EP   (Paris: the composer, 1732)
     GB:Lbm G.11.a.(3.)

(Six) *Sonates*, Op. 14, for 2 bassoons
EP   (Paris: the composer, 1726)
     GB:Lbm G.11.a.(1.)

(Six) *Sonates*, Op. 50, for 2 bassoons and bass
EP   (Paris: the composer, 1734)
     GB:Lbm G.11.a.(4.)

Petites Sonates, Op. 66, for 2 bassoons
EP   (Paris: the composer, 1737)
     GB:Lbm G.11.a.(5.)

Devienne, François (1759–1803)

MGG attributes to Devienne (Six) *Duos concertants*, Op. 3 (Paris: Sieber), for 2 bassoons.

Dietter, Chr. Ludwig (1757–1822)

(Three) *Sonatas*
MS A:Wgm VIII 25286

(Three) *Sonatas*
MS A:Wgm VIII 25287

Dotzauer, I. F.

(Three) *Duos concertantes*
MS A:Wgm VIII 25288

Dumonchau, Charles-François (1775–1820)

MGG attributes to Dumonchau, *Duos*, Op. 27 (Paris) for 2 bassoons.

Fesch, Willem de (1687–1757)

MGG attributes to Fesch, *Sonatas* (Paris: Le Clerc, 1738) for 2 celli or bassoons.

Gebauer, ?

(Three) *Duets*, Liv. 1, 2, for 2 bassoons
MS (Wien: Traeg's *Catalog*, 1799)

Gebauer, Josef (1763–1812)

Aria Variés
MS A:Wgm VIII 27267

Guillemant, Benoit

(Fifty) *Studies*
MS A:Wgm VIII 25289

MGG attributes to Guillemant *Pieces*, Op. 3 (EP, Paris) for 2 bassoons.

Ibotte, ?

Sainsbury identifies Ibotte as the composer of six *Duos* (Leipzig, before 1801) for 2 bassoons.

Johnsen, Heinrich Philip (1717–1779)

MGG attributes to Johnsen a *Concerto* (1751) for 2 bassoons and strings.

Kauer, Ferdinand (1751–1831)

MGG attributes to Kauer a *Duett-Konzertante* for 2 bassoons.

Kleinknecht, Johann Wolfgang (1715–1786)

MGG attributes to Kleinknecht (Three) *Sonates* (London: Thompson, 1774) for 2 bassoons or 2 celli.

Köcken, ?

(Three) *Duos concertantes*
MS A:Wgm VIII 25290

Muthel, Johann Gottfried (1728–1788)

MGG attributes to Muthel a Concerto (MS, *D:B*) for 2 bassoons and strings.

Ozi, Étienne

Sonatas
MS A:Wgm VIII 25293

(Six) *Duos facile*
MS A:Wgm VIII 25294

Sainsbury identifies Ozi as the composer of (Twenty-four) *Duos* (Paris, to 1798) for 2 bassoons.

Pleyel, Ignaz (1757–1831)

(Six) *Duos*
MS A:Wgm VIII 25295

(Four) *Duets*
MS A:Sca Hs. 308

Simonet, F. M.

(Six) *Duos*
MS A:Wgm VIII 25296

Supries, Joseph (1761–1822)

MGG attributes to Supries church *Masses* for choir, 2 bassoons, and organ.

Tartagnini, Luigi

(Four) *Duets*
MS A:Wgm VIII 27264

Vogel, J.

(Five) *Duos*
MS A:Wgm VIII 25300

Zimmermann, ?

Concerto for 2 bassoons and orchestra
MS (Wien: Traeg's *Catalog*, 1799)

MUSIC WITH TWO TRUMPETS

Anonymous

Duetti, for 2 tromba
MS I:MOe Mus.G.301

Sonate, for 2 trombe
MS I:MOe Mus.F.1529

Sonate, for 2 clarini
MS I:MOe Mus.G.297

Sonate, for 2 trombe
MS I:MOe Mus.G.314

Sonata for 2 trombe
MS A:Wn E.M. 93

Suonatine, for 2 clarini
MS I:MOe Mus.G.332

Bach, K. P. E. (1714–1788)

Duet for clarines
MS B:Bc Wotquenne 5522

Bach, Otto

Missa Solemnis in C Major (1852), for chorus, 2 trumpets, and timpani
MS A:Wn Sm 9358

Erlebach, Philipp Heinrich (1657–1714)

MGG attributes to Erlebach a *Cantata* in F:Sm for four voices, 2 trombetti, and continuo.

Glete, Johann

Musica Genialis Latino-Germanica, '2 Sonaten and 36 Trombeterstücklen auff 2 Trombe-
ten Marinen.'
EP (Augsburg: Erffürt, 1675)
    GB:Lbm C.196

Iacchini, Giuseppe

Trattentimenti per camera e due Trombe, Op. 5
EP   (Bologna: Accademico Filarmonico, 1703)
  I:Bc

Jacchini, Giuseppe Maria (d. 1727)

MGG attributes to Jacchini (Two) *Sinfonias* (1695) for 2 trumpets and strings.

Jacobi, Michael (1618–1663)

MGG attributes to Jacobi the *Das Friedejauchzende Teutschland* (Nurnberg, 1653) for singers, 2 trumpets and bass.

Morin, Jean-Baptiste (1677–1754)

MGG attributes to Morin, *Nouvelles fanfares a 2 trompes pour sonner en concert* ... (Paris: Prault, 1734).

Torelli, Giuseppe (1658–1709)

(Nine) *Sonatas* for 2 trumpets and strings
MS I:Bsp [according to MGG]

Sonata (1726) for 2 trombe and strings
MS A:Wn Sm 3740

Umstatt, Joseph (d. 1762)

MGG attributes to Umstatt two *Partitas* (MS, D:KA) for 2 violins and 2 trumpets.

Wenusch, Stanislaus (nineteenth century)

(Fifteen) *Stücke* for 2 trumpets
MS A:Wn Sm 21797

MUSIC WITH TRUMPET AND BASSOON

Oestreich, Carl (nineteenth century)

Potpouri, for posthorn and bassoon ('for Wittel & Lindner')
MS BRD:F Mus.Hs. 671

MUSIC WITH TRUMPET AND TROMBONE

Pacini, Giovanni (1796–1867)

Qui tollis, for Tenor, trumpet, trombone and orchestra
MS I:Ls B. 72

MUSIC WITH TWO HORNS

Agnola, Giacomo (1761–1845)

I:Vsmc contains a number of church works with 2 horns.

Anonymous

Forest Harmony, 'Together with several Curious Pieces out of the Water Musick,' for
   2 horns
EP   (London: Walsh, 1733)
      GB:Lbm B.4

Lass mich deine Leiden, for SA, 2 horns, and organ
MS A:Wn Sm 9675

Tantum ergo, for TB, 2 horns, and organ
MS I:Vcr Busta III N.47

Asioli, Bonifazio (1769–1832)

MGG attributes to Asioli a set of horn duets.

Bazin, Francois (1816–1878)

Melodie (1840), for 2 horns, accompanied by flute, 2 oboes, 2 clarinets, and 2 bassoons
MS F:Pn MS. 3214

Blasius, Frederic (1758–1829)

Symphonie concertante for 2 horns and orchestra
MS F:Pn A.33440

Caparelli, ?

(Twenty-four) *Duos* for 2 horns
MS (Wien: Traeg's *Catalog*, 1799)

Carafa, Michele (1787–1872)

Serenata in D Major, for voices, horns and harp
MS I:Bc

Charles, ?

(Twelve) *Duettos* for 2 horns or 2 flutes
EP (London?, ca. 1750)
    GB:Lbm D.379.a.(2.)

Corrette, Michel (1709–1795)

MGG attributes to Corrette, *Divertissements,* Op. 7, as well as an edition of hunting signals, for 2 horns or 2 trumpets.

Dauprat, Louis François (1781–1868)

MGG attributes to Dauprat the following for 2 horns:
    Twenty *Duos,* Op. 14 (Paris: Zetter)
    (Two solos and a) *Duo,* Op. 12 (Paris: Frey)
    Trios, Op. 15, for 2 horns and piano (Paris: Zetter)
    Canon (MS, F:Pn)

Dittersdorf, Karl (1739–1799)

MGG attributes to Dittersdorf a *Cassatio* in D for 2 horns and strings of 1769.

Fiala, Joseph (1754–1816)

MGG attributes to Fiala a *Concerto* for 2 horns.

Fiorollo, Federigo (1755–1823)

MGG attributes to Fiorollo a *Duett Concertante,* Op. 43 (London: Birchall, 1808) for piano and violin or flute with 2 horns ad lib and a *Duet* (London: Birchall, 1810) for harp and piano, with 2 horns ad. lib.

Fuetsch, Joachim Joseph (Austrian, 1766–1852)

Etudes for 2 horns
MS A:Sca Hs. 666

Gatti, Luigi

(Two) *Offerterium de St. Sacramento* (1813), one for SSS, 2 horns; one for SSB, 2 horns
MS   A:Wn Sm 13876

Offertorium, ('O Jesu, Du mein einziger') for SS, 2 horns, and organ
MS   A:Sca Hs. 1703

Gleissner, Franz (1759–1818)

MGG attributes to Gleissner (Twenty-four) *Duos faciles* (München: Falter) for 2 horns.

Gruber, Franz Xaver (1787–1863)

Deutsche Lytanei (1836), for 2 voices, 2 horns, and organ
MS   A:Wn Sm 9613

Graupner, Christoph (1683–1760)

MGG attributes to Graupner (Three) *Sonatas* (MS, D:KA) for 2 horns and strings.

Hanke, Karl (1750–1803)

MGG attributes to Hanke four *Concerti* and many duets for 2 horns.

Hausler, Ernst (1760–1837)

MGG attributes to Hausler a song, *Die Tonkünst*, Op. 36, for singer and piano or 2 horns.

Haydn, Josef (1732–1809)

Andante, for 2 horns
MS   I:Tf 11.II.1–12, 5

Messe in E♭ Major, for SATB, 2 horns, and organ
MS   A:Wn Sm 20287

Himmel, Frederick Heinrich (1765–1814)

Sainsbury identifies Himmel as composer of a *Grande Sestetto* (Leipzig: Kuhnel, 1802) for
   piano, 2 violas, 2 horns, and cello.

Hoffmeister, Franz Anton (1754–1812)

(Two) *Concerti* for 2 horns and orchestra
MS   (Wien: Traeg's *Catalog*, 1799)

Holmes, Valentine

(Twenty-four) *Duetts* for 2 horns
EP (London: Fentum, ca. 1765)
   GB:Lbm E.108.a.(6.)

Hummel, Ferdinand (1855–1928)

MGG attributes to Hummel a *König Eriks Genesung*, Op. 87 (Leipzig, 1905) for male chorus, AT solo, harp, and 2 horns; and a *Sangers Tod. Altnordische Ballade*, Op. 121 (Heidelberg: Hochstein, 1912) for TB solo, male chorus, harp and 2 horns.

Hummel, Johann Nepomuk (1778–1837)

MGG attributes to Hummel a *Notturno*, Op. 99 (Leipzig: Peters, 1824) for piano four-hand and 2 horns.

Hyrtner, Giovanni

Concerto for 2 horns and strings
MS I:Gl SS.B.1.5.(H.5)

Jam, ?

Concerto in D Major, for 2 horns and strings
MS I:Gl M.3b.24.14.

Jenson, Adolf (1837–1879)

MGG attributes to Jenson a song *der Nonnen* for Soprano, female choir 2 horns and harp and a *Brautlied*, Op. 10 (Hamburg: Schuberth) for mixed-chorus, 2 horns and harp.

Kalliwoda, Johann Wenzel (1801–1866)

Divertissement, Op. 59, for 2 horns
MS D:KA [cited in MGG]

Kauer, Ferdinand (1751–1831)

MGG attributes to Kauer a Concerto for 2 horns.

Kayser, Phillipp Christoph (1755–1823)

MGG attributes to Kayser a *Lieber reiner schoner blauer Himmel* (Wintherthur: Pfenninger, 1792) for singers, piano, and 2 horns.

Kliebenschadl, Josef

Ave Maria, for SSB, 2 horns, and organ
MS A:Wn Sm 20309

Kracher, Jose Matthias (1752–1827)

Deutsche Messe in F Major (1817) for AB, 2 horns, and organ
MS A:Sca [cited in MGG]

Labarbiera, Baldassare

Concerto for 2 horns and strings
MS I:Gl SS.A.1.10.(G.7)

Mattel, Padre Stanislao

(Three) *Domine* for TTTTBB, horns, and organ
MS I:Bc

Meifred, Joseph (1791–1867)

MGG attributes to Meifred (Twelve) *Duos* (Paris: Zelter) for 2 horns and *Melodies en duos faciles et progressifs* (Paris: Troupenas, 1842) for 2 horns.

Mengal, Martin Joseph (1784–1851)

MGG attributes to Mengal a *Symphonic Concertante* for 2 horns.

Moscheles, J.

Sainsbury identifies Moscheles as the composer of a *Grand Sextuor*, Op. 35, for piano, 2 horns and strings.

Oestreich, Carl (nineteenth century)

Concerto for 2 horns
MS BRD:F Mus.Hs. 817 [incomplete]

Concertino ('Frankfurt a/M, 1822') for 2 horns and orchestra
MS BRD:F Mus.Hs. 794

Duetten for 2 waldhorn
MS BRD:F Mus.Hs. 788

Pokorny, Franz Xaver (1729–1794)

(Three) *Concerti* for 2 horns
MS D:Rtt [according to MGG]

Punto, Johann Wenzel (1755–1893)

Sainsbury gives the following duets for horns by Punto:
    24 *Petits Duos* (Paris, 1793)
    Duos d'Airs (Paris, 1793)
    8 *Duos* (Paris, 1800)

Röllig, Carl Leopold

Ballo, for 2 horns and orchestra
MS A:Wn Sm 18565

Concerto for 2 horns and orchestra
MS A:Wn Sm 18557

Concerto for 2 horns and orchestra
MS A:Wn Sm 18562

Concerto for 2 horns and orchestra
MS A:Wn Sm 18566

Romberg, Bernhard Heinrich (1767–1841)

MGG attributes to Romberg a *Concertino*, Op. 41, for 2 horns.

Rossini, Gioacchino (1792–1868)

MGG attributes to Rossini lost *Duetti* (1805) for 2 horns.

Schwindel, Friedrich (1737–1786)

MGG attributes to Schwindel a *Concerto* for 2 horns.

Spergher, Ignaz

Laudate pueni (1792), for SSA, 2 horns, and continuo
MS A:Wn Sm 16556

Stamitz, Fr.

Divertimento for 2 horns
MS (Wien: Traeg's *Catalog*, 1799)

Starzer, Josef (1726–1787)

Duetto for 2 horns
MS (Wien: Traeg's *Catalog*, 1799)

Struck, Paul (1776–1820)

MGG attributes to Struck a *Sonata*, Op. 17 (Leipzig: Breitkopf & Härtel) for piano and 2 horns.

Suppé, Franz von (1819–1895)

Das is mei Osterreich, for SATB and 2 horns.
MS A:Wn Sm 5337

Todt, Johann Christoph

Concertino for 2 horns and orchestra.
MS D:SWl [according to MGG, which cites another three *Concerti* for 2 horns in manuscript.]

Torelli, Giuseppe (1658–1709)

Sinfonia in F Major for 2 horns and strings
MS I:Bsp [according to MGG]

Tuch, Heinrich (1766–1821)

MGG attributes to Tuch twenty-four works for 2 horns.

Turrschmiedt, Carl (1753–1797)

(Fifty) *Duets*, Op. 3, for 2 horns
EP (Berlin: the composer, 1795)
   GB:Lbm B.86

MGG attributes to Turrschmidt another 106 editions (Paris and Bonn) of duets for 2 horns.

Wagner, Karl Jakob (1772–1822)

MGG attributes to Wagner 40 *Duos*, Op. 5 (1796, perhaps now lost) for 2 horns.

Winkler, Johann

Todten Aria, for SATB and 2 horns
MS A:Wn Sm 2790

Witt, Friedrich (1770–1836)

(Three) *Concerti* for 2 horns and orchestra
MS A:Wn Sm 5253–5255

MUSIC WITH HORN AND BASSOON

Devienne, François (1759–1803)

MGG attributes to Devienne a *Sinfonie concertante*, Op. 1 (Paris, 1797) for horn and bassoon with orchestra.

Droste-Hulshoff, Maximilien-Frederic

Duo Concertant I, for horn, bassoon and orchestra
MS B:Lc 273-2.L-VI

Kauer, Ferdinand (1751–1831)

Concerto for horn and bassoon and orchestra
MS (Wien: Traeg's *Catalog*, 1799)

Kurpinski, Karol Kazimierz (1785–1857)

MGG attributes to Kurpinski a *Pausage music* (Leipzig: Breitkopf & Härtel) for horn and bassoon.

Punto, Johann Wenzel (1757–1803)

Sainsbury identifies Punto as the composer of (Three) *Duos* (1802) for horn and bassoon.

Roth, Philipp Jakob (1779–1850)

MGG attributes to Roth a *Concertante* for solo horn and bassoon and orchestra.

MUSIC WITH HORN AND TRUMPET

Müller, Adolph, Jr.

Posthornklang (1856), for singer, trumpet, horn, and piano
MS A:Wn Sm 14637

MUSIC WITH HORN AND TROMBONE

Vogel, Friedrich Wilhelm (1807–1892)

MGG attributes to Vogel a Concertino (Erfurt, Körner) for organ with trombone and horn.

MUSIC WITH TWO TROMBONES

Croce, Giovanni

Laudate pueri in Ecce (1636) for four choruses, 2 trombones, continuo.
MS A:Wn Fond Diesewetter St 68 Aa 100

Haydn, Michael, 1737–1806

Graduale, for SATB, 2 trombones, and organ.
MS A:Wn Sm 866

Tenebrae, for STAB, 2 trombone, and organ.
MS A:Wn Sm 830

Hoffman, Leopold, 1738–1793

Fi Homonatus (1766), for SATB, 2 trombones, and organ.
MS A:Wn Sm 22660

PART 3

Music With Three
Wind Instruments

MUSIC WITH THREE FLUTES

André, Johann Anton (1775–1842)

MGG attributes to Andre a *Trio*, Op. 29, in G Major, for 3 flutes.

Anonymous

Catches, for 1, 2, 3 or 4 flutes
EP   (London: Walsh and Hare, ca. 1711)
      GB:Lbm B.171.a.(1.)

Trio for 3 flutes
MS   A:Wn Sm 3058

Boismortier, Joseph Bodin de (1691–1755)

MGG attributes to Boismortier, *Sonates*, Op. 7 (1725) for 3 flutes.

Burrowes, John Freckleton (b. 1787)

Sainsbury identifies Burrowes as the composer of a *Trio*, Op. 12, for 3 flutes.

Carr, Robert

The Delightful Companion, lessons for one, two and three flutes
EP   (London: J. Playford, 1686)
      GB:Lbm K.4.b.16

Corrette, Michel (1709–1795)

MGG attributes to Corrette eighteen *Concerti* for 3 flutes.

Demanchi, Giuseppe

(Three) *Trios*, for 3 flutes
EP   (London: J. Fentum, ca. 1800)
      GB:Lbm G.274.d.(4.)

Devienne, François (1759–1803)

(Three) *Trios* for 3 flutes
MS   A:Wgm VIII 6233

MGG attributes to Devienne nine *Trios* for 3 flutes.

Dietter, Christian

(Twelve) *Pieces concertantes*, Op. 26, for 3 flutes
EP   (Leipzig: Breitkopf & Härtel, ca. 1800)
   GB:Lbm H.2140.(7,8.)

Döthel, Nicholas (1721–1810)

(Two) *Sonatas* for 3 flutes
MS I:Gl SS.A.2.5.(G.8)

(Four) *Sonatas* for 3 flutes
MS I:Gl T.C.1.(Sc.111)

Droste-Hulshoff, Maximilian F. (1764–1840)

MGG attributes to Droste a *Trio concertante* for 3 flutes and orchestra.

Enderle, Wilhelm Gottfried

MGG attributes to Enderle a *Trio* for 3 flutes (MS, D:KA).

Fasch, Johann Friedrich (1688–1758)

MGG attributes to Fasch a *Sonata* in G Major for flute, 2 flutes a bec, and cembalo.

Ferdinandes III, Kaiser (1608–1657)

Hymnus de Nativitate (1649)
MS A:Wn Sm 16042
   The 1st, 3rd, 5th, and 7th movements are *Sonatas* for 3 flutes.

Finger, Gottfried (ca. 1660–1723)

MGG attributes to Finger *Sonatas* for 3 flutes (MS, GB:Lbm)

Frühling, Carl (1868–1937)

MGG attributes to Frühling unnamed works for 3 flutes and piano.

Haydn, Josef (1732–1809)

(Three) *Trios* for 3 flutes
MS (Wien: Traeg's *Catalog*, 1799)

Hook, James (1746–1827)

(Six) *Trios*, Op. 83, for 3 flutes
EP   (London: Bland & Weller, 1797)
    GB:Lbm G.222.(3.)

Kalik, ?

(Six) *Trios* for 3 flutes
MS (Wien: Traeg's *Catalog*, 1799)

Kremberg, Jacob

Collection of Aires ('to which is added an Overture and Passacaille for Three Flutes')
EP   (London: Walsh and Hare, ca. 1710)
    GB:Lbm B.2.

Krufft, Nikolaus Freiherr von (1779–1818)

MGG attributes to Krufft an *Andante* (Wien: Leidesdorf, 1831) for 3 flutes and piano.

Kummer, Gaspard

Trio for 3 flutes (ded. to Henri Fischer)
MS A:Wn Sm 5839

Mattheson, Johann (1681–1764)

(Twelve) *Sonatas*, for 2 and 3 flutes
EP   (Amsterdam: Roger, 1708)
    GB:Lbm F.84.

Mersenne, Martin (1588–1648)

[Untitled group of compositions] for 3, 4, and 6 flutes
MS A:Wn Sm 1573

Poessinger, Franz Alexander (1767–1827)

(Twelve) *Divertimenti* for 3 flutes
MS A:Wgm VIII 6242

MGG attributes to Poessinger *Pieces*, Op. 5 (Wien: Kunst- u. Industrie …) for 3 flutes.

Porta, Bernardo (1758–1829)

MGG attributes to Porta (Three) *Trios*, Op. 1 (Paris, 1790) for 3 flutes; Sainsbury adds (Three) *Trios*, Op. 2 (Paris, 1798).

Praeger, Heinrich Aloys (1783–1854)

MGG attributes to Praeger *Duos*, Op. 23, for 2 flutes.

Pranzer, Giuseppe

Trio for 3 flutes
MS I:Vmc Busta 31–50-40

Quantz, Johann (1697–1773)

Sonata for 3 flutes
MS B:Bc Wotquenne 6950

Rohde, Michael

Jesu, Jesu (Communion piece) for Soprano, 3 flutes, and organ
MS S:L Wenster A, Nr. 23 [one flute part is in bass clef!]

Jesu Komm (Communion piece) for Soprano, 3 flutes, and organ
MS S:L Wenster A, Nr. 25

Ich wil euch tragen, for Bass, 3 flutes, and organ
MS S:L Wenster A, Nr. 30

Rozelli, ?

(Two) *Sonatas*, Op. 5, for 3 flutes
EP (London: C. & S. Thompson, ca. 1766)
   GB:Lbm G.418.(3.)

Scarlatti, Pietro Alessandro (1660–1725)

MGG attributes to Scarlatti a *Sonata* for 3 flutes and bass.

Schmidt, ?

(Eight) *Divertimenti* for 3 flutes
MS (Wien: Traeg's *Catalog*, 1799)

Schmugel, Johann Christoph (1727–1798)

> *Sonata* for 3 flutes
> MS B:Bc Wotquenne 5592

Weiss, Carl R.

Sainsbury identifies Weiss as the composer of a large number of *Trios* for 3 flutes.

Weiss, Karl II (1777–1845)

MGG attributes to Weiss (Seven) *Trios*, Op. 29 and Op. 39, for 3 flutes.

MUSIC WITH TWO FLUTES AND ENGLISH HORN

Triebensee, Joseph (1772–1846)

> (Six) *Variations on a Theme of Haydn*, for 2 flutes and English horn
> MS A:Wgm VIII 1228

Wendt, Johann (1745–1809)

> *Serenade*, Nr. 2, for 2 flutes and English horn
> MS A:Wgm VIII 1229

MUSIC WITH TWO FLUTES AND BASSOON

Baumberg, J. C.

> (Six) *Trios*, Op. 1, for 2 flutes and bassoon
> EP (Amsterdam: Hummel, 1783)
>   GB:Lbm H.36

Cormier, Carlo

> *Notturni*, Nr. 1, for 2 flutes and bassoon
> MS I:Vmc Busta 54–58-N.57

> (Six) *Suonatine*, for 2 flutes and bassoon
> MS I:Vmc Busta 54–58-N.56

Hoffmeister, ?

(Six) *Quintets* for 2 solo flutes, bassoon and strings
MS   (Wien: Traeg's *Catalog*, 1799)

Myslivecek, Josef (1737–1781)

MGG attributes to Myslivecek (Three) *Trios* (London: Bland, 1795) for 2 flutes and bassoon.

Piazzi, Gaetano

(Three) *Sonate*, for 2 flutes and bassoon
MS   I:Vmc Busta 73–93-N.77, 78, 79

Rault, Felix (b. 1736)

Sainsbury identifies Rault as the composer of (Six) *Trios*, Op. 25, 25 (Paris and Offenbach) for 2 flutes and bassoon.

MUSIC WITH TWO FLUTES AND TROMBONE

Nicolai, Johann Michael (1629–1685)

MGG attributes to Nicolai (Two) *Sonatas* (MS, S:Uu) for 2 flutes, violin, viola da gamba or trombone and continuo.

MUSIC WITH FLUTE, OBOE, AND CLARINET

Fumagalli, Polibio (1830–1901)

Gran terzetto di Concerto, Op. 40, for flute, oboe, and clarinet
EP   (Milano: Canti)
   I:Bc

Weissheimer, Wendelin (1838–1910)

MGG attributes to Weissheimer five church *Sonnette* (Leipzig: Thiel, 1880) for singer, flute, oboe, clarinet, Pyrophon (Fire ogran), and piano.

MUSIC WITH FLUTE, OBOE, AND BASSOON

Anonymous

Sinfonia a 4, for flute, oboe, bassoon, and viola (?)
MS   P:GD Ms.4177

Chedeville, Nicholas

(Six) Sonatas for flute, oboe, and bassoon
EP   (Paris: the composer, c. 1740)
    GB:Lbm K.7.f.15.(5.)

Davaux, Jean-Baptiste (1742–1822)

MGG attributes to Davaux, a *Simphonie concertante* (Paris, 1785) for flute, oboe, and bassoon.

Dumonchau, Charles-François (1775–1820)

MGG, citing Fetis, attributes to Dumonchau a *Symphonie concertante* for flute, oboe, and bassoon with orchestra.

Holzbauer, Ignaz Jakob (1711–1783)

MGG attributes to Holzbauer a *Sextet*, Op. 5 (Paris: Sieber) for flute, oboe, bassoon, and strings.

Widerkehr, Jacob (1759–1823)

Concertante, for flute, oboe, bassoon and orchestra
EP   (Paris: Erard, c. 1800)
    GB:Lbm H.2136.a.

Wilms, Johann (1772–1847)

MGG attributes to Wilms a *Symphonie Concertante* in F Major, Op. 35 (Berlin and Amsterdam: Hummel, 1814) for flute, oboe or clarinet, bassoon or horn, and orchestra.

Wolf, Ernst Wilhelm (1735–1792)

Quartet (c. 1798), for flute, oboe, bassoon, and continuo
MS A:Wn Sm 15909

Quartet, for flute, oboe, bassoon, and continuo
MS A:Wn Sm 15956

MUSIC WITH FLUTE, OBOE, AND TRUMPET

Weiss, Franz (1778–1830)

MGG attributes to Weiss a *Trio-Rondo* for flute, oboe, and trumpet.

MUSIC WITH FLUTE, OBOE, AND HORN

Fasch, Karl Friedrich Christian (1736–1800)

MGG attributes to Fasch a *Cantata* (Potsdam, 1756) for choir, flute, oboe, and horn.

Hurlstone, William Yeates (1876–1906)

MGG attributes to Hurlstone an unpublished *Quartet* for flute, oboe, horn, and piano.

Pfeiffer, Johann (1697–1761)

MGG attributes to Pfeiffer a *Sonata* for flute, oboe, horn, and bass.

MUSIC WITH FLUTE, ENGLISH HORN, AND BASSOON

Savinelli, Angelo

Quintet for flute, English horn, bassoon, viola, and cello
MS I:OS Mss. Musiche B. 1318

MUSIC WITH FLUTE, CLARINET, AND BASSOON

Devienne, François (1759–1803)

(Six), *Trios*, Op. 61, Liv. 1, 2, for flute, clarinet and bassoon
MS (Wien: Traeg's *Catalog*, 1799)

MGG attributes to Devienne a *Sinfonie concertante*, Op 22 (Paris, 1793) for flute, clarinet, bassoon and orchestra and six *Trios* for flute, clarinet and bassoon.

Eler, Andreas Andre-Frederic

(Three) *Trios* for flute, clarinet, and bassoon
MS F:Pn Mss.1930

Foy, James

Sainsbury identifies Foy as the composer of a *Quartet* for harp, flute, clarinet, and bassoon.

Gagnebin, Henri (b. 1886)

MGG attributes to Gagnebin a *Pastorale* for flute, clarinet, bassoon, and harp.

Mayr, Johannes Simon (1763–1845)

(Twelve) *Bagatellen* for flute, clarinet, bassoon or basset horn.
MS D:Mbs Mus.Ms.App.2033

Widerkehr, Jacob (1759–1823)

Sinphonie Concertante, for clarinet, flute, bassoon and orchestra.
EP (Paris: Erard, ca. 1800)
      GB:Lbm H.2136.b.

Wilms, Johann (1772–1847)

MGG attributes to Wilms a *Symphonie Concertante* in C Major (1814) for flute, clarinet, bassoon and strings.

MUSIC WITH FLUTE, HORN, AND BASSOON

Kreutzer, Konrad (1780–1849)

Divertimento, Op. 37, for flute, horn, bassoon, and bass
MS A:Wgm XI 14588
EP (Augsburg: Gombart)

MUSIC FOR THREE OBOES

Telemann, Georg (1681–1767)

Concerto for 3 oboes
MS D:Ds Mus.Ms. 1033/86

MUSIC WITH TWO OBOES AND FLUTE

Schickhard, Johann

(Six) *Sonates*, Op. 5, for flute, 2 oboes, viole de gambe and bc
EP   (Amsterdam: Roger, ca. 1710)
   GB:Lbm G.1054.

(Six) *Sonatas*, Op. 5, for flute, 2 oboes, bc
EP   (London: Walsh and Hare, ca. 1730)
   GB:Lbm H.250.c.(4.)

MUSIC WITH TWO OBOES AND ENGLISH HORN

Moser, Franz (d. 1930)

Trio, Op. 38 (1923), for 2 oboes and English horn.
MS   A:Wn Sm 21203

MUSIC WITH TWO OBOES AND BASSOON

Fasch, Johann Friedrich (1688–1758)

Sonata in D Minor for 2 oboes, bassoon, and cembalo
MS   D:Ds Mus.Ms. 297/5

Sonata in F Major for 2 oboes and bassoon
MS   D:Ds Mus.Ms. 298/4

Sonata in D Minor for 2 oboes, bassoon, and cembalo
MS   D:Ds Mus.Ms. 298/8

MGG also attributes to Fasch *Quartets* in F and Bb Major, and G Minor, for 2 oboes and bassoon.

Handel, Georg F. (1685–1759)

Sonata for 2 oboes and bassoon
MS   P:GD Ms.4048

Hasse, Gio. Adolfo [Johann] (1699–1783)

Crucifixus, for Countertenor, Tenor, 2 oboes, bassoon, and organ
MS   I:Vcr Busta VII N.121

Malzat, Ignaz (1757–1804)

Divertimento for 2 oboes and bassoon
MS (Wien: Traeg's *Catalog*, 1799)

Salieri, Antonio (1750–1825)

(Three) *Trios*, for 2 oboes and bassoon
MS A:Wn Sm 3768

Schelle, Johann (1648–1701)

MGG attributes to Schelle *Uns ist ein Kind* (Mugeln, 1716) for 2 Tenors, 2 oboes, bassoon
and continuo.

MUSIC WITH OBOE, ENGLISH HORN AND BASSOON

Triébert, Frédéric (1813–1878)

MGG attributes to Triebert a *Doglianza, melodie*, Op. 10 (Paris, 1859) for oboe, English horn,
bassoon (or clarinet) and piano.

MUSIC WITH OBOE, CLARINET, AND BASSOON

Devienne, François (1759–1803)

Synphonie concertante, for oboe, clarinet, bassoon, and orchestra.
MS A:Wgm VIII 6152

Hoffmeister, ?

(Three) *Quintets* in E♭ Major for oboe, 'second' horn, bassoon, and strings
MS (Wien: Traeg's *Catalog*, 1799)

(Two) *Quintets* in F and D Major for oboe, 'second' horn, bassoon, and strings
MS (Wien: Traeg's *Catalog,* 1799)

Pleyel, Ignaz (1757–1831)

Quartetto, for oboe, clarinet, bassoon, and clavicembalo.
MS A:Wgm XI 10984

MUSIC WITH OBOE, BASSOON, AND TRUMPET

Biscogli, Francesio

Concerto for oboe, trumpet and bassoon, with violin and continuo
MS F:Pn D.4892

Buhl, David (b. 1781)

Fantasie (arr. Henri Brod) for trumpet, oboe, bassoon, and piano
EP (Paris: Frey)
   I:Bc

Necchi, Francesco Antonio (nineteenth century)

Magnificat, for STB, oboe, bassoon, trumpet, continuo
MS I:Bsf M.N.III-I

MUSIC WITH OBOE, HORN, AND BASSOON

Baxberg, C. L.

Concert a 4 (Festa S.S. Trimitate), for Soprano, oboe, horn, and bassoon
MS S:L Wenster M, Nr. 11

Dominica, for Soprano, oboe, horn, and bassoon
MS S:L Wenster M, Nr. 13

Eberwein, Christian (1750–1810)

MGG attributes to Eberwein a *Concertante*, Op. 47, for oboe, horn, and bassoon (Breitkopf
   & Härtel, 1820).

Eberwein, Traugott-Maximilien

Concertante, Op. 47, for oboe, horn, and bassoon
EP (Leipzig: Breitkopf & Hartel)
   I:Bc

Fasch, Karl Friedrich Christian (1736–1800)

MGG attributes to Fasch a *Cantata* for choir, oboe, horn, and bassoon.

Graun, Carl H.

(Two) *Trios* for oboe d'amour, horn, and bassoon
MS   B:Bc Wotquenne 6612

Hoffmeister, Franz Anton (1754–1812)

Quintet, for oboe, horn, bassoon, and 2 violas
MS   A:Sca Hs. 1698

(Six) *Quintets*, for oboe, horn, bassoon, viola and bass
MS   I:MOe Mus.F.581

Mengal, Martin Joseph (1784–1851)

MGG attributes to Mengal a *Concertante* (Gent: Geyaert) for oboe, horn, and bassoon.

Röllig, Johann Georg (1710–1790)

MGG attributes to Röllig nine *Trios* for oboe, horn, and bassoon.

Stamitz, Carl

Quartet, for oboe, horn, bassoon, and viola
MS   A:Wgm XI 10720

Ursino, H. F.

Cantata (1731) for Soprano, oboe, horn, bassoon, and continuo
MS   P:GDj Ms.Joh.95

MUSIC WITH THREE CLARINETS

Hummel, Johann Nepomuk (1778–1837)

(Three) *Trios*, for 3 clarinets
MS   A:Wgm VIII 28673

MUSIC WITH TWO CLARINETS AND FLUTE

Praeger, Heinrich Aloys (1783–1854)

MGG attributes to Praeger a *Quintet,* Op. 12, for 2 clarinets, flute, viola and bass.

MUSIC WITH TWO CLARINETS AND BASSOON

Alessio, Francesco (eighteenth century)

CS:Pnm has numerous works for 2 clarinets and bassoon.

Blasius, F. (1758–1829)

Tercetto, for 2 clarinets and bassoon
MS A:Wgm VIII 2560

(Three) *Trios*, for 2 clarinets and bassoon
EP (Paris: Porthaux)
   A:Wgm VIII 2559

Devienne, François (1759–1803)

(Six) *Trios* for 2 clarinets and bassoon
MS I:Gl SS.A.2.16

MGG attributes to Devienne twelve *Trios* for 2 clarinets and bassoon.

Fucik, Julius (b. 1872)

Fantasie for 2 clarinets and bassoon
MS CS:Pnm VII D. 117

Humoreska, for 2 clarinets and bassoon
MS CS:Pnm V.F.163

Symphonie Scandaleuse for 2 clarinets and bassoon
MS CS:Pnm V.F.159

CS:Pnm has additional works for 2 clarinets and bassoon under the numbers: V.F.160, 161, 162, 164, 165, and 166.

Lefèvre, Jean (1763–1829)

Trio, for 2 clarinets and bassoon
MS A:Wgm VIII 2561

Sainsbury identifies Lefevre as the composer of two sets of six *Trios*, Op. 5 and 9, (Paris, 1793–1797) for 2 clarinets and bassoon.

Pleyel, Ignaz (1757–1831)

(Three) *Trios*, for 2 clarinets and bassoon
MS A:Wgm VIII 2562

(Three) *Trios*, for 2 clarinets and bassoon
MS A:Wgm VIII 9205

Pranzer, Giuseppe

(Six) *Trios* for 2 clarinets and bassoon
MS I:Gl SS.B.1.15.(H.8)

Senfer, Luigi

(Six) *Trios*, for 2 clarinets and bassoon
MS A:Wgm VIII 21590

Stamitz, Anton (1754–1809)

(Six) *Trios* for 2 clarinets and bassoon
MS (Wien: Traeg's *Catalog*, 1799)

Wolfl, Joseph (1773–1812)

MGG attributes to Wolfl two *Trios* for 2 clarinets and bassoon.

Wranitzky, Wenzel (eighteenth century)

Trios, for 2 clarinets and bassoon
MS *I:UDricardi* MS. 99

Trios, for 2 clarinets and bassoon
MS *I:UDricardi* MS. 100

Trios, for 2 clarinets and bassoon
MS *I:UDricardi* MS. 101

MUSIC WITH TWO CLARINETS AND HORN

Umlauff, Michael (1781–1842)

Graduale, for voice, 2 clarinets, and horn
MS A:Wn Sm 5800

Graduale, for voice, 2 clarinets, and horn
MS A:Wn Sm 5803

MUSIC WITH CLARINET, HORN, AND BASSOON

Candeille, Pierre-Joseph (1744–1827)

MGG attributes to Candeille a lost *Symphonie concertante* (1786) for clarinet, bassoon, horn, and piano.

Chiesa, Natale

Trio for clarinet, horn, and bassoon
MS I:Mc Da Camera Ms. 6.2

Devienne, François (1759–1803)

(Three) *Trios* for clarinet, horn, and bassoon
MS I:Gl SS.A.2.16

Trio for clarinet, horn, and bassoon
MS A:Sca Hs. 386

Fritz, Ernst Paul

Serenata, for 4 voices, clarinet, horn, bassoon, harp, and continuo
MS A:Wn Sm 15312

Gevhart, Francois-August (1828–1908)

MGG attributes to Gevhart a manuscript *Quartet* for clarinet, horn, bassoon, and piano.

Grutsch, Franz Seraph

Divertimento, for clarinet, horn, bassoon, and orchestra
MS A:Wn Sm 3690 [score]; Sm 3691 [parts]

Haydn, Michael (1737–1806)

Quintet for violin, clarinet, 'second' horn, bassoon, and viola
MS (Wien: Traeg's *Catalog,* 1799)

Lickl, Georgio (Hungarian, 1769–1843)

Trio, for clarinet, horn, and bassoon
EP (Wien: Eder)
    A:Wgm VIII 5227

Trio, for clarinet, horn, and bassoon
MS A:Sca Hs. 386

(Three) *Trios,* in E♭, B♭, and D Major, for clarinet, horn, and bassoon
MS (Wien: Traeg's *Catalog,* 1799)

Oestreich, Carl (nineteenth century)

[Untitled work] for clarinet, horn, and bassoon
MS BRD:F Mus.Hs. 819 [incomplete]

Punto, Johann Wenzel (1757–1803)

Sainsbury identifies Punto as the composer of a *Sextet,* Op. 34 (1802) for horn, clarinet, bassoon and strings.

Ries, Ferdinand (1784–1838)

Octet, Op. 128, for clarinet, horn, bassoon, and strings
EP (Leipzig: Probst)
    I:Bc

Winter, Peter (1754–1825)

MGG attributes to Winter a *Sinfonie concertante* for violin, clarinet, bassoon, horn and orchestra.

MUSIC WITH CLARINET, TRUMPET, AND TROMBONE

Puccini, Michele (Italian, 1813–1864)

Gratias, for Bass, clarinet, trumpet, trombone soli with orchestra
MS I:Ls B. 172

MUSIC WITH THREE BASSET HORNS

Anonymous

Trio for 3 basset horns
MS (Wien: Traeg's *Catalog*, 1799)

Martin, ?

Una Cosa rara, arranged for 3 basset horns
MS (Wien: Traeg's *Catalog*, 1799)

Mozart, Wolfgang A. (1756–1791)

Zauberflötte, arranged for 3 basset horns
MS (Wien: Traeg's *Catalog*, 1799)

MUSIC WITH TWO BASSET HORNS AND CLARINET

Zaluzan, Johann

Variations, for clarinet, basset horns, and piano
MS A:Wgm XI 10915

MUSIC WITH TWO BASSET HORNS AND HORN

Anonymous

Trio for 2 basset horns and horn
MS (Wien: Traeg's *Catalog,* 1799)

Turck, ?

(Eighteen) *Pieces* for 2 basset horns and horn
MS (Wien: Traeg's *Catalog,* 1799)

MUSIC WITH TWO BASSOONS AND HORN

Herold, Nicolas (1721–1790)

MGG attributes to Herold a *Trio* for 2 bassoons and horn.

MUSIC WITH THREE TRUMPETS

Anonymous

(Three) *Aufzüge*, for 3 clarini
MS   A:Wn Sm 0349 ch XIX 9 fol.

(Four Part-Books) for 3 trumpets and timpani
MS   S:L Wenster Ö, Nr. 4

Aufzug, for 3 trumpets and timpani
MS   S:L Engelhart 146

Baumgarten, ?

(Thirty) *Aufzuge* for 3 trumpets and timpani
EP   (Amsterdam: Hummel)
     S:L Wenster Ö, Nr. 8

Ferdinandes III, Kaiser (1608–1657)

Hymnus de Nativitate (1649)
MS   A:Wn Sm 16042
     The 11th and 13th movements are *Sonatas* for 3 trumpets.

MUSIC WITH TWO TRUMPETS AND CLARINET

Anonymous

Litanei, for SATB, clarinet, 2 clarini, timpani, and organ
MS   A:Wn Sm 0413 ch XIX 15 fol.

MUSIC WITH TWO CORNETTI AND BASSOON

Reuschel, Johann

Decas Missarum Sacra, for chorus, 2 cornetto, bassoon, continuo
EP   (Freyberggae: Beutheri, 1667)
     GB:Lbm H.3242

MUSIC WITH THREE HORNS

Artot, ?

(Twenty-four) *Trios* for horns
MS   B:Bc Wotquenne 6346

Dauprat, Louis François (1781–1868)

Trios, for horns
EP   (Paris: l'Auteur)
     F:Pn L.4461

Trios, for horns
EP   (Paris: l'Auteur)
     F:Pn L.4565

MGG also attributes to Dauprat, (Three) Trios, Op. 4 (Paris: Zetter) and *Grand Trio*, Op. 26
   (Paris: Schönenberger) for horns.

Kauer, Ferdinand (1751–1831)

MGG attributes to Kauer a *Concerto* for 3 horns.

Oestreich, Carl (nineteenth century)

Trio ('Nr. 8') for 3 horns
MS   BRD:F Mus.Hs. 791

Trio ('Nr. 12') for 3 horns
MS   BRD:F Mus.Hs. 792

(Six) *Trios* for 3 horns
MS   BRD:F Mus.Hs. 790

Punto, Johann Wenzel (1757–1803)

Sainsbury identifies Punto as the composer of some thirty-two *Trios* for horns.

Richter, Anton

(Six) *Quintets* and *Trios* for Waldhorner
MS   A:Wgm VIII 38519

Rudolph, Joseph (1730–1812)

MGG attributes to Rudolph 24 *Fanfares* (Paris: Bailleaux) for 3 horns.

Winter, Peter (1754–1825)

MGG attributes to Winter *Das Waldhorn* (Leipzig: Breitkopf & Härtel) for chorus, 3 horns, and orchestra.

MUSIC WITH TWO HORNS AND FLUTE

Mazzinghi, Joseph (1765–1844)

Sainsbury identifies Mazzinghi as the late eighteenth century composer of *Air for Harp*, with piano, flute, and 2 horns.

Moscheles, Ignazio

Sextet, Op. 35, for flute, violin, 2 horns, cello, and piano
EP (Leipzig: Hoffmeister)
   I:Bc

Mozart, Carl Thomas (1784–1858)

MGG attributes to Mozart's son (Six) *Stücke,* Op. 11 (Wien: Chem. Druckerei) for flute and 2 horns.

Struck, Paul (1776–1820)

MGG attributes to Struck a *Quartet,* Op. 5 (Wien: Mollo) for piano, flute and 2 horns.

Wanhal, Jan (1739–1813)

MGG attributes to Vanhal the following:
   Cassatio in D Major (MS, CS:Pnm XLII E. 174) for flute, 2 horns, viola, and bass
   (Five) *Notturni* (MS, CS:Pnm XXVII B. 95–99) for flute, 2 horns, viola, bass

MUSIC WITH TWO HORNS AND OBOE

Vinci, ?

Aria (for Easter, 1760), for Soprano, oboe, and 2 horns
MS S:L Kraus 222b

MUSIC WITH TWO HORNS AND ENGLISH HORN

Nicolini, Giuseppe

Quintet for 2 horns, English horn, violin, and cello
MS I:Gl T.C.3.3.(Sc.26 e 27)

MUSIC WITH TWO HORNS AND CLARINET

Oestreich, Carl (nineteenth century)

Adagio & Lied, for clarinet and 2 horns
MS BRD:F Mus.Hs. 776

Spohr, Luigi (1784–1859)

Octet, Op. 32, for clarinet, 2 horns, and strings
EP (Bonn: Simrock)
       I:Bc

MUSIC WITH TWO HORNS AND BASSOON

Baldan, Angelo (1747–1804)

Kyrie e Gloria (1789), for TB, 2 horns, bassoon, and organ
MS I:Vmc N.53

Emmert, Adam Joseph

Harmonieen, for 2 horns and bassoon
EP (Salzburg, ca. 1805)
       A:Sca 20707

Hausler, Ernst (1760–1837)

MGG attributes to Hausler a *Kirchengesung*, for singers, 2 horns and bassoon.

Müller, ?

Trio for 2 horns and bassoon
MS (Wien: Traeg's *Catalog*, 1799)

MUSIC WITH TWO HORNS AND TRUMPET

Quilici, Domenico (nineteenth century)

O Lingua, for SATB, trumpet, 2 horns, and bass
MS I:PAc

Singer, Pater Peter

Lobgesang, for SATB, 2 horns, Maschintrumpet, organ
MS A:Wn Sm 13891

WORKS WITH TWO HORNS AND TROMBONE

Scherr, L.

Deutsches Requiem, for SATB, 2 horns, trombone, and organ
MS A:Wgm I 44379

Zwyssig, Alberich (1808–1854)

MGG attributes to Zwyssig *O quam glorifica* (1855) for chorus, 2 horns, trombone, and organ.

MUSIC WITH TWO HORNS AND TUBA

Hupauf, Johann Peregrin

Lateinische Messe, for Soprano, 2 horns, bombardon, and organ
MS A:Wn Sm 23900

MUSIC WITH THREE TROMBONES

Anonymous

Pange lingua, for SATB, 3 trombones and organ
MS A:TU *439*

Duhoslav, ?

Requiem (1897), for TTBB, 3 trombones, and organ
MS A:Wn Sm 2577

Eberlin, Ernst

in Coena Domini, for SATB, 3 trombones, and continuo
MS   A:Wn Sm 22383

Erban, Franz

(Two) *Fanfares* for 3 trombones
MS   A:Wn Sm 23538

Förster, Josef (1838–1917)

Messe for choir, 3 trombones, and organ
MS   A:Wn [according to MGG]

Gleissner, Franz (1759–1818)

MGG attributes to Gleissner a manuscript in the Dombibliothek in Regensburg, the *Christus factus est* for chorus and 3 trombones.

Gregora, Franz (1819–1887)

MGG attributes to Gregora a *Mass* with 3 trombones and *Fugues* for trombones.

Haydn, Michael (1737–1806)

Libera, for SATB, 3 trombones, and organ
MS   A:TU 174

Kammerlander, Carl

Libera, for TTBB, 3 trombones, and organ
MS   A:Wn Sm 22480

Schicht, Johann

Motette, for SATB and 3 trombones
MS   A:Wgm V 1954 Rev: 2331

Starker, Liberato

Todten Arie, for SATB, 3 trombones, and organ
MS   A:Wn Sm 2784

Winkler, Johann (nineteenth century)

(Two) *Trauer Arien*, for SATB and 3 trombones
MS A:Wn Sm 2792

MUSIC WITH TWO TROMBONES AND CORNETTO

Krottendörffer, Josef

Graduale and Offertorum (1793), for SATB, 2 trombones, cornetto, and organ
MS A:Wn Sm 22493

Graduale and Offertorum (1793), for SATB, 2 trombones, cornetto, and organ
MS A:Wn Sm 22495

Graduale and Offertorum (1793), for SATB, 2 trombones, cornetto, and organ
MS A:Wn Sm 22496

PART 4

Music With Four
Wind Instruments

MUSIC WITH FOUR FLUTES

Anonymous

Catches, for 1, 2, 3 or 4 flutes
EP   (London: Walsh and Hare, ca. 1711)
    GB:Lbm B.171.a.(1.)

Variations for 4 flutes
MS   A:Wgm VIII 8920

[Untitled work] for 3 flutes and flute d'amour
MS   A:Wgm VIII 6254

Brunetti-Pisano, August (1870–1943)

Quartet for 4 flutes
MS   A:Sca Hs. 1177

Gabrielsky, Jean

Quartet for 4 flutes
MS   A:Wn Sm 5838

Graff, ?

Quartet for 4 flutes and strings
MS   (Wien: Traeg's *Catalog*, 1799)

Mersenne, Martin (seventeenth century)

Untitled group of compositions for 3, 4, and 6 flutes
MS   A:Wn Sm 1573

Reicha, Anton (1770–1836)

Sonata for 4 flutes
MS   A:Wgm VIII 8913

MUSIC WITH THREE FLUTES AND CLARINET

Haydn, Josef (1732–1809)

Quartet for 3 flutes and clarinet
EP   (Hamburg: Böhme)
   S:L Wenster Ö Nr. 1
   In this copy the clarinet part is missing and is replaced by a manuscript part for cello.

MUSIC WITH THREE FLUTES AND BASSOON

Druschetzky, Georg (1745–1819)

Quodlibet, for 3 flutes, bassoon, and cello
MS   H:Bn Ms.Mus.1573

MUSIC WITH TWO FLUTES, OBOE, AND BASSOON

Rohde, Michael

Jesu Klaeffet an, for Soprano, 2 flutes, oboe, and bassoon
MS   S:L Wenster F, Nr. 2

MUSIC WITH TWO FLUTES, CLARINET, AND BASSOON

Rohde, Michael

Aria, for SB, 2 flutes, clarinet, and bassoon
MS   S:L Wenster M, Nr. 50

MUSIC WITH TWO FLUTES AND TWO CORNETTI

Anonymous

Sonata for organ, with flutes and cornetti
MS   I:Bsf FC.A.IV.11

MUSIC WITH TWO FLUTES AND TWO HORNS

Domenichini, Antonio

(Two) *Notturni* for 2 flutes, 2 horns, viola, and bass
MS I:Gl SS.B.1.4

Morawetz, Giovanni

Sainsbury identifies Morawetz as the composer of (Eight) *Notturni* for flute, flute d'amore, 2 horns, and three strings.

MUSIC WITH FLUTE, OBOE, ENGLISH HORN, AND BASSOON

Catel, Charles-Simon (1773–1830)

(Three) *Grand Quartets* for flute, oboe, English horn, and bassoon
MS F:Pn L.2547 (1–4)

Gebauer, Francois (1773–1844)

(Three) *Quartets,* Op. 27, for flute, oboe, English horn, and bassoon
MS F:Pn L.2552 (1–4)

MUSIC WITH FLUTE, OBOE, CLARINET, AND BASSOON

Moser, Franz (d. 1930)

Zwei Impressonen, Op. 66, for flute, oboe, clarinet, bassoon, and piano
MS A:Wn Sm 21286

Grotesken in Perpetenmobile, for flute, oboe, clarinet, bassoon, and piano
MS A:Wn Sm 21302

Weigl, Joseph Franz (1740–1820)

MGG attributes to Weigl a *Concertino* for flute, oboe, clarinet, bassoon, and harp.

298 WIND REPERTOIRE FOR ONE TO FIVE PLAYERS

MUSIC WITH FLUTE, OBOE, AND TWO BASSET HORNS

Hoffmeister, ?

(Two) *Quintet* in F Major for oboe, flute, 2 basset horns, and viola
MS (Wien: Traeg's *Catalog,* 1799)

MUSIC WITH FLUTE, OBOE, BASSOON, AND TRUMPET

Sangiorgi, Filippo

Piccolo Quartet, for flute, oboe, trumpet, bassoon, and piano
EP (Milano: Lucca)
    I:Bc

MUSIC WITH FLUTE, OBOE, HORN, AND BASSOON

Devienne, François (1759–1803)

MGG attributes to Devienne a *Sinfonie concertante,* Nr. 4 (Paris, 1794), for flute, oboe, horn, bassoon and orchestra and a [Second] *Sinfonie Concertante* (Paris: Osi, 1800) for the same.

Droste-Hulshoff, Maximilian F. (1764–1840)

MGG attributes to Droste a *Grand Quantuor concertant* for flute, oboe, horn, bassoon and orchestra.

Haydn, Michael (1737–1806)

Quartet Nr. 12, for flute, oboe, horn, and bassoon
MS A:Wn Sm 11944

Divertimento, for flute, oboe, horn, and bassoon
MS A:Wgm VIII 8886 [photocopy of the autograph]

Hurlstone, William Yeates (1876–1906)

MGG attributes to Hurlstone a *Quintet* (MS, 1904) for flute, oboe, horn, bassoon, and piano.

Tadolini, Giovanni (1793–1872)

Quintet in F Major, for flute, oboe, horn, bassoon, and piano
MS I:Bc

MUSIC WITH FLUTE, CLARINET, HORN, AND BASSOON

Catel, Charles-Simon (1773–1830)

(Three) *Quartets* for flute, clarinet, horn, and bassoon
EP (Paris: l'Imprimerie du Cons. de Musique)
    F:Pn Cons. A.35.444

Eler, André-Frédéric (1764–1820)

(Three) *Quartets*, Op. 6, for flute, clarinet, horn, and bassoon
MS D:Mbs Mus Ms 8308

(Three) *Quartets* for flute, clarinet, horn, and bassoon
MS F:Pn Ms. 1928

(Three) *Quartets* for flute, clarinet, horn, and bassoon
EP (Paris: Pleyel)
    F:Pn A.33.900

(Three) *Quartets* for flute, clarinet, horn, and bassoon
MS (Wien: Traeg's *Catalog,* 1799)

Fiala, ?

(Three) *Quartets* for flute, clarinet, horn, and bassoon
MS (Wien: Traeg's *Catalog,* 1799)

Fiorollo, Federigo (1755–1823)

MGG attributes to Fiorollo a *Grand Duet*, Op. 38 (London: Birchall, 1806) for harp and
    piano, with ad. lib flute clarinet, horn, and bassoon parts.

Gambaro, Vincenzo

(Three) *Quartets* for flute, clarinet, horn, and bassoon
EP (Leipzig: Breitkopf & Härtel)
    I:Bc

Kreith, Carlo (d. 1809)

(Three) *Quartets,* for flute, clarinet, horn, and bassoon
EP (Wien: Traeg)
    A:Wgm VIII 30821

Onslow, Georg (1784–1853)

Grand Sextet, for flute, clarinet, horn, bassoon, piano, and bass
MS A:Wgm XI 26132
EP (Leipzig: Kistner)
    I:Bc

Reymann, F. G.

(Three) *Quartet* for flute d'amore, clarinet, horn, and bassoon
MS (Wien: Traeg's *Catalog,* 1799)

Ron, Jean Martin de (1789–1817)

Quintet for piano, flute, clarinet, horn, and bassoon
EP (Leipzig: Breitkopf & Härtel)
    S:Skma [according to MGG]

Rossini, Gioacchino (1792–1868)

Tema con variazioni for flute, clarinet, horn, and bassoon
MS F:Pn

Rubinstein, Anton (nineteenth century)

Quintet, for flute, clarinet, horn, bassoon, and piano
EP (Leipzig: Schuberth)
    A:Wgm XI 25992

Spohr, Luigi (1784–1859)

Quintet, Op. 52, for flute, clarinet, horn, bassoon, and piano
EP (Bonn: Simrock)
    I:Bc

MUSIC WITH FLUTE, TWO ENGLISH HORNS AND BASSOON

Schenk, Johann Baptist (1753–1836)

MGG attributes to Schenk a *Quartet* for flute, 2 English horns, and bassoon.

MUSIC WITH FLUTE, TRUMPET, HORN, AND TROMBONE

Mabellini, Teodulo (1817–1897)

MGG attributes to Mabellini a *Gran Fantasia* (Florence, 1846) for flute, horn, trumpet, trombone and orchestra.

MUSIC WITH FLUTE, TWO TRUMPETS, AND HORN

Puccini, Michele

Concertone (1808) for flute, clarino, tromba, horn with orchestra
MS I:Ls B. 164

MUSIC WITH FLUTE, TWO HORNS, AND BASSOON

Grimm, Anton

(Two) *Pastoral-Graduale*, for SATB, flute, 2 horns, bassoon, and organ
MS A:Wgm I 3193

Kozeluch, Leopold (1752–1818)

Quintet in D Major for flute, violin, 2 horns, and bassoon
MS (Wien: Traeg's *Catalog,* 1799)

Quintet in E♭ Major for flute, violin, 2 horns, and bassoon
MS (Wien: Traeg's *Catalog,* 1799)

MUSIC WITH TWO OBOES AND TWO BASSOONS

Fasch, Johann Friedrich (1688–1758)

Sonata in F Major for 2 oboes and 2 bassoons
MS D:Ds Mus.Ms. 298/9

Schubert, Ferdinand (brother to Franz Schubert, 1794–1859)

Lied (1844), for SATB, 2 oboes, 2 bassoons, or organ
MS   A:Wgm I 42257

MUSIC WITH TWO OBOES AND TWO TRUMPETS

Tag, Christian G. (1735–1811)

Kantate, 'Schaffe in mir Gott ein neues Herz' for SATB, 2 oboes, 2 trumpets, and organ
MS   P:GDj Ms.Joh.422

Kantata, '*Man singet mit Freuden,*' for Soprano, 2 oboes, 2 trumpets, timpani, and organ
MS   P:GDj Ms.Joh.423

Zabala, Nicola

Missa for SSAT and SATB, with oboes and trumpets
MS   I:Bsf M.Z.1–5

MUSIC WITH TWO OBOES AND TWO HORNS

Anonymous

Suite, for 2 oboes and 2 horns
MS   A:Wn Sm 3038

MUSIC FOR OBOE, CLARINET, HORN, AND BASSOON

Grund, Eduard (1802–1871)

MGG attributes to Grund a *Quintet,* Op. 8, in Eb Major, for oboe, clarinet, horn, bassoon, and piano.

Gyrowetz, Adalbert (1763–1850)

Divertimento concertante, for oboe, clarinet, horn, bassoon, and orchestra
MS   A:Wgm VIII 644

(Three) *Quartets* oboe, clarinet, horn and bassoon
MS   (Wien: Traeg's *Catalog,* 1799)

Henneberg, J.

Quintet, for oboe, clarinet, horn, bassoon, and viola
MS A:Wgm XI 2549

Herzogenberg, Heinrich (1843–1900)

MGG attributes to Herzogenberg a *Quintet*, Op. 43 (Leipzig, 1888), for piano, oboe, clarinet, horn, and bassoon.

Hoffmeister, ?

Quintet in D Major for oboe, clarinet, horn, bassoon, and viola
MS (Wien: Traeg's *Catalog,* 1799)

Quintet in B♭ Major for oboe, clarinet, horn, bassoon, and viola
MS (Wien: Traeg's *Catalog,* 1799)

Kalkbrenner, Friedrich (1785–1849)

Grand Septet, for oboe, clarinet, horn, bassoon, cello, bass, and piano
EP (Paris: Schlesinger)
      I:Bc

Lickl, F. Georg (1769–1843)

Sainsbury identifies Lickl as the composer of a *Cassatio* (Wien), for oboe, clarinet, bassoon, and horn.

Moser, Franz (d. 1930)

Nocturne, Op. 64, for oboe, clarinet, horn, bassoon, and piano
MS A:Wn Sm 21281

Capriccio, Op. 64, for oboe, clarinet, horn, bassoon, and piano
MS A:Wn Sm 21282

MUSIC WITH OBOE, CLARINET, AND TWO HORNS

Fanucchi, Domenico (nineteenth century)

Aria con cori, for SAB, oboe, clarinet and 2 horns
MS I:Ls B. 41

MUSIC WITH OBOE, TWO HORNS, AND BASSOON

Anonymous

Gratias, for Tenor, oboe, 2 horns, bassoon, and organ
MS I:Vcr Busta II N.27

Baldan, Angelo

Credo, for TTB, oboe, 2 horns, bassoon, and organ
MS I:Vcr Busta III N. 53

Bertoni, Fernando (1725–1813)

Credo, for TTB, oboe, 2 horns, bassoon, and organ
MS I:Vcr Busta IV N. 62

Haussler, Ernst

Kirchen-Musik for SATB, oboe, 2 horns, bassoon, and cello
MS D:Mbs Mus.Ms.

MUSIC WITH FOUR CLARINETS

Diabelli, Anton (1781–1858)

Missa solemnis (1852) for SATB, 2 clarinets in C, 2 clarinets in D, timpani, and organ
MS A:Wn Sm 20278 [only the organ part is extant here]

Schindelmeisser, Louis Alexander Balthasar (1811–1864)

MGG attributes to Schindelmeisser a *Concertante* (Leipzig: Breitkopf & Härtel, 1833) for 4
clarinets and orchestra.

MUSIC WITH TWO CLARINETS AND TWO BASSOONS

During, J. C. (arr.)

Collection of opera movements (Mozart, Rossini, and Weber) for 2 clarinets and 2 bassoons
MS BRD:F Mus.Hs. 1799

Mendelssohn, Felix (1809–1847)

Ave Maria, for SSAATTBB, 2 clarients, 2 bassoons, and organ
EP   (London: Novello)
I:Bc

MUSIC WITH TWO CLARINETS AND TWO HORNS

Anonymous

Todtenlied, for SATB, 2 clarinets and 2 horns
MS A:Wn Sm 0375

Todtenlied, for SATB, 2 clarinets and 2 horns
MS *A:Wn* Sm 0378

Toten Aria, for SATB, 2 clarinets and 2 horns
MS A:Wn Sm 0369

Toten Aria, for SATB, 2 clarinets and 2 horns
MS A:Wn Sm 0371

Trauergesang, for SATB, 2 clarinets, and 2 horns
MS A:Wn Sm 0374

Bassus, Jean M.

Sextet in D Major, for 2 clarinets, 2 horns, viola, and bass
MS D:Mbs Mus.Ms. 5507

Hausler, Ernst (1760–1837)

MGG attributes to Hausler a manuscript *Fantasie* for singer, 2 clarinets and 2 horns.

Lidmanzky, Franz

Stiller Kirchhof, for SSAATB, 2 clarinets and 2 horns
MS A:TU 272

Puschmann, Giuseppe (eighteenth century)

(Three) *Quartets* for 2 clarinets and 2 horns
MS (Wien: Traeg's *Catalog,* 1799)

Steinfeld, Albert (1741–1815)

MGG attributes to Steinfeld (Six) *Quartets,* Op. 20 (Offenbach: André) for 2 clarinets, 2 horns and ad lib. timpani and (Three) *Airs variés,* Op. 23 (Offenbach: André) for 2 clarinets and 2 horns.

Umlauff, Michael (1781–1842)

Offertorium, 'Lauda anima mea,' for voices, 2 clarinets, and 2 horns
MS   A:Wn Sm 5802

Offertorium, 'Deus qui sedes super Thronum,' for voices, 2 clarinets, and 2 horns
MS   A:Wn Sm 5803

Umstatt, Joseph (d. 1762)

MGG attributes to Umstatt 22 wind partitas, 'mostly for 2 clarinets and 2 horns,' (MS, D:BAs).

MUSIC WITH TWO CLARINETS, HORN, AND BASSOON

Eler, André-Fédéric (1764–1821)

(Three) *Quartets* for 2 clarinets, horn, and bassoon
EP   (Paris: Pleyel)
    F:Pn A.33.895

MUSIC WITH TWO CLARINETS, HORN, AND TROMBONE

Umlauff, Michael (1781–1842)

Graduale, for singer, 2 clarinets, horn, and bass trombone
MS   A:Wn Sm 5802

MUSIC WITH CLARINET, ENGLISH HORN, BASSET HORN, AND BASSOON

Triebensee, Josef (1772–1846)

Grand Quintet, for clarinet, English horn, basset horn, bassoon, and piano
EP   (Wien: Magasin de l'imprimiere)
     A:Wgm XI 10905

MUSIC WITH CLARINET, TWO HORNS, AND BASSOON

Fournier, Giuseppe

(Four) *Notturni,* for clarinet, 2 horns, and bassoon
MS   CH:Zz Ms. AMG XII 320 a-c

Pfeiffer, M.

Quartet, Nr. 1, for clarinet, 2 horns, and bassoon
MS   (Wien: Traeg's *Catalog,* 1799)

MUSIC FOR FOUR TRUMPETS

Buhl, David (b. 1781)

(Six) *Fanfares,* Op. 1 (1799), for 4 trumpets
MS   F:Pn L.9.635 (1-13)

(Two) *Marches* and (four) *pas-redoublés* (1812) for 4 cornets
MS   F:Pn L.9.634

[Untitled work] for 4 trumpets
MS   F:Pn L.9781

Cerclier, Jules-H. L.

(Thirty) *Marches* for 4 trumpets and timpani
EP   (Paris: Hartman, ca. 1891)
     F:Pn L.9.004

Martini, P. Giambattista

Ave maris stella, 1743, for SSAA, 4 trumpets, and violins
MS I:Bc

Mosel, M.

(Six) *kürze* & leichte *Aufzüge*, for 4 trumpets and timpani
MS A:Wn Sm 0348

Schicht, Johann Gottfried (1753–1823)

MGG attributes to Schicht *Am Grabe des Heilands* for cornett quartet in *200 Kornett-Quartette* (Leipzig: Zimmermann).

MUSIC WITH TWO TRUMPETS AND TWO HORNS

Quilici, Domenico (nineteenth century)

Sequenza a 4 voci Di S. Antonio di Padova (1815) for SATB, 2 trumpets, 2 horns, and bass
MS I:PAc

MUSIC WITH TRUMPET, TWO HORNS, AND TROMBONE

Pacini, Giovanni (1796–1867)

(Three) *Domini,* for 2 Bass, trumpet, 2 horns, trombone, and orchestra
MS I:Ls B. 116

MUSIC WITH FOUR HORNS

Abelshausser, J. G.

(Twelve) *Quartets* for 4 horns
MS BRD:F Mus.Hs. 745

Abt, Franz (1819–1885)

Waldesgruss, for male chorus and 4 horns
MS A:Wn Sm 20364 Sbd 2

Anonymous

(Two) *Quartets* for horns
MS A:Wn Sm 20471, 20472

Artot, ?

(Thirty-six) *Quartets* for horns
MS B:Bc Wotquenne 6346

Dauprat, Louis François (1781–1868)

MGG attributes to Dauprat, (Six) *Trios* and (Six) *Quartets*, Op. 8 (Paris: Zetter), for horns.

Eler, Andreas André-Frédéric (1764–1821)

(Three) *Quartets* for horns
MS F:Pn Mss.1929

Fuchs, Georg Friedrich (1752–1821)

(Three) *Quartets* for horns
EP (Paris: chez Boyer)
    F:Pn Con.A.34.041

Goldmark, Karl (1830–1915)

MGG attributes to Goldmark a *Frühlingsnetz,* Op. 15 (Leipzig) and a *Meeresstille und glückli-che Fahrt,* Op. 16 (Leipzig), both for male chorus and 4 horns.

Hummel, Johann Nepomuk (1778–1837)

Larghetto for 4 horns and klavier
MS A:Wn Sm 4713

Lachner, Franz (1803–1890)

Die Elementenweihe (1827) for chorus, and 4 horns
MS D:Mbs Mus.Ms. 6058

Oestreich, Carl (nineteenth century)

(Twelve) *Quartets* (1836) for 4 horns
MS BRD:F Mus.Hs. 789

Quartet for 4 horns
MS BRD:F Mus.Hs. 793

Richter, Anton (eighteenth century)

(Six) *Pieces* for 4 cors de chasse
MS A:Wgm VIII 38585

Rossini, Gioacchino (1792–1868)

Rendez-vous de Chasse for 4 horns and orchestra
MS I:Mc; F:Pn

Santner, Karl

Passionskantate (for Maximilian V) for male chorus and 4 horns
EP   (Wien: Gloggl, 1863)
   A:Llm III/32; A:Sca 43636

Walter, August (1821–1866)

MGG attributes to Walter *Lustige Musikanten,* Op. 18 (Leipzig: Rieter-Biedermann) for chorus and 4 horns.

Wunderer, Anton

Tänze und Marche (1885) for 4 horns
MS A:Wn Sm 9431

MUSIC WITH TWO HORNS AND TWO BASSOONS

Hertel, Johann Wilhelm (1727–1789)

Sonata, for 2 horns and 2 bassoons
MS B:Bc Wotquenne 6695

Hausler, Ernst (1760–1837)

MGG attributes to Hausler (Six) *Notturni* (Leipzig: Breitkopf & Härtel) for 2 horns and 2 bassoons.

MUSIC WITH TWO HORNS AND TWO TROMBONES

Hauptmann, Moritz (1792–1868)

MGG attributes to Hauptmann an *Ehre sei Gott* for male choir, 2 horns, and 2 trombones.

MUSIC WITH FOUR TROMBONES

Batka, Edvard (nineteenth century)

Libera, for SATB, 4 trombones
MS A:Wgm I 21619

Gagnebin, Henri (b. 1886)

MGG attributes to Gagnebin an unpublished *Choral* for 4 trombones.

Hanisch, Joseph (1812–1892)

MGG attributes to Hanisch the following works:
 Surrexit Dominus vere, Op. 27 (Regensburg: Seiling) for voices, 4 trombones, and organ
 Aurora coelum purpurat, Op. 31 (Regensburg: Seiling) for chorus, 4 trombones, and organ
 Hymnus Te Deum (Dûüsseldorf: Schwann) for chorus, 4 trombones, and organ

Hauptmann, Moritz (1792–1868)

MGG attributes to Hauptmann a *Cantata,* Op. 38, with 4 trombones and organ.

Krenn, Franz (1839–1890)

Tenebra factae sunt, for SATB, and 4 trombones
MS A:Wn Sm 13250

Lambel, Wenzel

(Five) *Equale* for 4 trombones
MS A:Llm

Pichler, Carl

Libera, for SATB, and 4 trombones
MS A:Wgm I 44075

Waelput, Hendrick (1845–1885)

MGG attributes to Waelput an *Andante cantabile* for 4 trombones.

MUSIC WITH THREE TROMBONES AND CORNETTO

Schneider, Franz

Messe, for SATB, 3 trombones, cornetto, organ
MS   A:Wn Sm 22671

PART 5

Music With Five
Wind Instruments

MUSIC WITH FIVE FLUTES

Boismortier, Joseph Bodin de (1691–1755)

MGG attributes to Boismortier 6 *Concerti,* Op. 15 (1727) for 5 flutes.

MUSIC WITH THREE FLUTES AND TWO OBOES

Rohde, Michael

Begrabnis Aria, for Soprano, 3 flutes, 2 oboes, and organ
MS S:L Wenster A, Nr. 25

MUSIC WITH THREE FLUTES, OBOE, AND BASSOON

Rohde, Michael

Aria Funebris, for Alto, 3 flutes, oboe, bassoon, and continuo
MS S:L Wenster F, Nr. 3

MUSIC WITH TWO FLUTES, TWO OBOES, AND BASSOON

Finger, Gottfried (ca. 1660–1723)

MGG attributes to Finger a set of *Sonatas* for 2 flutes, 2 oboes and bc (London, 1701), with a later edition by Roger in Amsterdam.

MUSIC WITH TWO FLUTES, OBOE, CLARINET, AND HORN

Mengal, Martin Joseph (1784–1851)

MGG attributes to Mengal a *Concertante* for 2 flutes, oboe, clarinet and horn.

MUSIC WITH FLUTE, TWO CLARINETS, AND TWO HORNS

Bassus, Jean M.

Sextet in E♭ Major for flute, 2 clarinets, 2 horns, and viola
MS   D:Mbs Mus.Ms. 5506

Weinberger, Joseph

Serenade (1803), for flute, 2 clarinets, 2 horns, 2 violas, and continuo
MS   A:Sca Hs. 396

MUSIC WITH FLUTE, TWO CLARINETS, HORN, AND BASSOON

Proch, Heinrich (1809–1878)

Lied, for singer, flute, 2 clarinets, horn, and bassoon
MS   A:Wn Sm 14618

MUSIC WITH FLUTE, TWO HORNS, AND TWO BASSOONS

Schiedermayer, Johann Baptist (1779–1840)

Aria, for Soprano, solo flute, 2 horns, and 2 bassoons
MS   A:Wn Sm 21659

MUSIC WITH FLUTE, CLARINET, TWO HORNS, AND BASSOON

Oestreich, Carl (nineteenth century)

Lied, for flute, clarinet, bassoon, and 2 horns
MS   BRD:F Mus.Hs. 774

MUSIC WITH FLUTE, OBOE, CLARINET, HORN, AND BASSOON

Anonymous

Andante con moto, for woodwind quintet
MS A:Wn Sm 13838

Ballay, Guillaumey (1889–1943)

L'Aurore sur le foret (1876), for solo horn, flute, oboe, clarinet, and bassoon
MS F:Pn K.1968

Bochsa, Charles Nicholas (1789–1856)

(Twelve) *Serenades*, for harp and woodwind quintet
EP (Paris: Bochsa, père)
    F:Pn K.3825

Brunetti-Pisano, August (early twentieth century)

Woodwind Quintet
MS A:Sca Hs. 1176

Farrenc, Jacques Hyppolite (1794–1865)

MGG attributes to Farrenc a *Sextet,* Op. 40, for piano and woodwind quintet.

Gebauer, Francois (1773–1844)

(Three) *Woodwind Quintets*
MS F:Pn L.2554 (1–6)

Kittl, Johann Friedrich (1806–1868)

MGG attributes to Kittl a *Grand Septuor* in E♭ Major, Op. 25 (Leipzig: Kistner) for piano, flute, oboe, clarinet, bassoon, horn and contrabass.

Krenn, Franz (1839–1890)

Sextet, for woodwind quintet with piano
MS A:Wn Sm 14152

Kretschmer, Edmund (1830–1908)

MGG attributes to Kretschmer a *Nonett* for woodwind quintet and 4 strings.

Lachner, Franz (1803–1890)

Quintet in E♭ Major, for woodwind quintet
MS D:Mbs Mus.Ms. 5783

Quintet in F Major, for woodwind quintet
MS D:Mbs Mus.Ms. 5797

Quintet in F Major, for woodwind quintet
MS D:Mbs Mus.Ms. 5796

Nonett, for woodwind quintet and string quartet
MS D:Mbs Mus.Ms. 5798

Lickl, Georgio

Quintet, for woodwind quintet
EP (Wien: Magasin)
     A:Wgm VIII 8076

Lindner, Fr.

Quintet, Op. 1, for woodwind quintet
EP (Leipzig: Hofmeister)
     A:Wgm VIII 5168

Lindpainter, Peter (1791–1856)

Sinfonia Concertante, for woodwind quintet and orchestra
EP (Mainz: Schott)
     A:Wgm XI 3473

Müller, P.

(Three) *Quintets,* for woodwind quintet
EP (Bremen: Praeger & Meier)
     A:Wgm VIII 25856

Onslow, Georg (1784–1853)

Quintet, for woodwind quintet
EP (Leipzig: Kistner)
     A:Wgm VIII 32602

Nonetto, Op. 77, for woodwind quintet and strings
EP (Leipzig: Kistner)
     I:Bc

Reicha, Anton (1770–1836)

(Six) *Quintets*, Op. 88
EP   (Paris: Boieldieu)
   A:Wgm VIII 5135

(Six) *Quintets*, Op. 91
EP   (Paris: Boieldieu)
   A:Wgm VIII 5137

(Six) *Quintets,* Op. 99
EP   (Bonn: Simrock)
   A:Wgm VIII 26335

(Six) *Quintets,* Op. 100
EP   (Mainz: Schott)
   A:Wgm VIII 5135 [here Nr. 2, 4, 5, and 6 only]

Quintet, for woodwind quintet
MS   *A:Wn* Sm 20467

Quintet, for woodwind quintet
MS   A:Wn Sm 20468

Rheinberger, Joseph (1839–1901)

MGG attributes to Rheinberger a *Nonett*, Op. 139, for woodwind quintet, violin, viola, cello, and string bass.

Rietz, Johann Christian (1767–1828)

MGG attributes to Rietz a *Concert-stuck*, Op. 41 (Leipzig: Seitz) for woodwind quintet and orchestra.

Rosenthal, Felix

Quintet, for woodwind quintet
MS   A:Wn Sm 23441

Quintet, for woodwind quintet
MS   A:Wn Sm 23442

Thuille, Ludwig (1861–1907)

MGG attributes to Thuille a *Sextet*, Op. 6 (Leipzig: Breitkopf & Härtel) for piano and woodwind quintet.

MUSIC WITH FLUTE, ENGLISH HORN, TWO HORNS, AND BASSOON

Knorr, Barone (eighteenth century)

Quintet, for flute, English horn, 2 horns, and bassoon
MS   A:Wgm VIII 1493

MUSIC WITH TWO OBOES, CLARINET, HORN, AND BASSOON

Roser, Johann Georg (1740–1797)

Tantum ergo for choir, 2 oboes, clarinet, horn, bassoon, and organ
MS   H:Bn Ms.Mus. 1187

MUSIC WITH TWO OBOES, TWO HORNS, AND BASSOON

Anonymous

Gloria, for TTB, 2 oboes, 2 horns, bassoon and organ
MS   I:Vcr Busta II N.25

(Twelve) *Partiti*, for 2 oboes, 2 horns, and bassoon
MS   I:Vmc Busta 1-8-N.1

Qui Tollis, for Baritone, 2 oboes, 2 horns, bassoon, and organ
MS   I:Vcr Busta III N.37

Bach, K. P. E. (1714–1788)

(Two) *Marche* for 2 oboes, 2 horns, and bassoon
MS   B:Bc Wotquenne 6370

Furlanetto, Bonaventura (1730–1817)

Tantum ergo, for TTB, 2 oboes, 2 horns, bassoon, and organ
MS   I:Vcr Busta VI N. 115

Gigl, Georg

Deutsche Messe in C Major, for 3 voices, 2 oboes, 2 horns, bassoon, and organ
MS D:TEG 151

MUSIC WITH TWO OBOES, TWO TRUMPETS, AND BASSOON

Eybler, Josef (1765–1846)

Ecce quomodo (1830) for SATB, 2 oboes, 2 trumpets, and bassoon
MS A:Wn Sm 13040

MUSIC WITH TWO OBOES, TRUMPET, AND TWO HORNS

Enders, Franz (nineteenth century)

Serenata, for 2 oboes, 2 horns, trumpet, bass, and timpani
MS D:Mbs Mus.Ms. 103467

MUSIC WITH TWO OBOES, OBOE D'AMORE, ENGLISH HORN, AND BASSOON

Flament, Edouard (b. 1880)

Divertimento, Nr. 2, for 2 oboes, oboe d'amore, English horn, and bassoon
MS F:Pn MS.9405

MUSIC WITH OBOE, TWO BASSET HORNS, AND TWO BASSOONS

Kospoth, Otto Karl (1753–1817)

MGG attributes to Kospoth a *Serenade*, Op. 19 (Offenbach: André, 1794) for cembalo, oboe, 2 bassoons, and 2 basset horns.

MUSIC WITH FIVE BASSOONS

Flament, Edouard (b. 1880)

Quintet for 5 bassoons
MS   F:Pn Ms.8656 (4) [F:Pn also has works for 6 and 7 bassoons by Flament.]

MUSIC WITH FIVE TRUMPETS

Gruber, Johann Georg (nineteenth century)

Deutscher, for 5 trumpets
MS   A:Wn Sm 5644

Wenusch, Stanislaus (nineteenth century)

(Eighteen) *Stücke*, for 5 trumpets and timpani
MS   A:Wn Sm 21798

MUSIC WITH TWO TRUMPETS AND THREE TROMBONES

Laube, Anton (1718–1784)

MGG attributes to Laube a *Te deum* for chorus, 2 clarini, trombones, timpani, and organ.

Rohde, Michael

Festo Trinitatis, for SATB, 2 trumpets, 3 trombones, and timpani
MS   S:L Wenster F, Nr. 23

MUSIC WITH CORNETTI AND TROMBONES

Donati, Ignazio

Salmi Boscarecci concertati, for 6 voices, cornetti, and trombones
EP   (Venetia: Vincenti, 1623)
    I:Bc

Polidori, Ortensio

> *Messe a cinque* (1639) for choir, cornetti, trombones, and organ
> EP   (Venetia: Vincenti, 1639)
>   I:Bc

MUSIC WITH FIVE HORNS

Anonymous

> *Quintet* for horns
> MS   A:Wn Sm 20470

Moser, Franz (d. 1930)

> (Two) *Stücke*, Op. 76a and 76b, for 5 horns
> MS   A:Wn Sm 21314

Richter, Anton (eighteenth century)

> (Six) *Quintets* (and Trios) for Waldhorner
> MS   A:Wgm VIII 38519

MUSIC WITH FOUR HORNS AND TROMBONE

Anonymous (arr.)

> *Bacchus Blessings* (from Handel's Alexander's Feast) for TTBB, 4 horns, and bass trombone
> MS   D:Mbs Mus.Ms. 9221

Index

Index of Names

A

B

C

Caffare, Giuseppe, Italian composer, 105

Cahusac, 18th and 19th century publisher in London, 4, 202

Cahusac, Thomas, 18th century English composer, 14

Cambini, Giovanni, 1746–1825, Italian composer, 14ff, 186

Campagnoli, Bartolomeo, 1751–1827, Italian composer, 15

Campbell, 18th century publisher in London, 97

Campini, Giuseppe, 1746–1825, Italian composer, 15

Campioni, Carlo, 1720–1793, Italian composer, 187

Canal, Giuseppe, 1703–1779, Italian composer, 15, 187

Candeille, Pierre, 1744–1827, French composer, 234, 282

Cannabich, Christian, 1731–1798, German composer, 15

Canobbio, Carlo, 1741–1822, Italian composer, 16

Canti, 19th century publisher in Milano, 272

Capanna, Alessandro, 1814–1892, 19th century Italian composer, 159

Caparelli, ?, 18th century Italian horn player and composer, 164, 256

Cappi, 19th century publisher in Vienna, 41, 48, 79

Carafa, Michele, 1787–1872, French band figure & composer, 130, 164, 257

Carcani, Gioseffo, 1703–1749, Italian composer, 188

Card, W., 18th century English flute professor in England in 1825, 16

Cardonne, Jean, 1730–1792, French composer, 105

Carr, John, 18th century English composer, 164

Carr, Robert, 17th century English composer, 16, 188, 267

Cartelieri, Antonio, 1772–1807, Bohemian composer, 16

Carulli, Benedetto, 1797–1877, Italian composer, 176

Caselli, Giuseppe, 18th century (?) Italian composer, 16

Castelbarco, conte Cesare, 19th century Italian composer, 16, 131

Castnis, Fran. de, 18th century (?) composer in Vienna, 235

Catel, Charles, 1773–1830, French composer, 131, 297, 299

Cauciello, Prospero, 18th century Italian composer, 188

Cavalari, Francesco, 18th century Italian composer, 16

Cazzati, Maurizio, 1620–1677, Italian composer, 160

Cecere, Carlo, 18th century Italian composer, 16, 188

Centroni, Professor B., dedication of a work by Raffaele Parma, 117

Cerclier, Jules, 19th century French composer, 307

Cervetto, Giacobbe, 18th century Italian composer, 17

Chapman, 18th century publisher in London, 11, 23, 104, 193, 215

Charles II of England, 190

Charles, ?, 18th century English composer, 188, 257

Chartrains, ?, 18th century composer, 188

Checci, Rene, 18th century Italian composer, 17

Chechi, ?, 18th century composer, 188

Chedeville, Espirit Philippe, 1696–1762, French composer, 17

Chedeville, Nicholas 18th century French composer, 17, 228, 273

Chemische Druckerei, 18th century publisher in Vienna, 31, 198

Cheron, André, 1695–1766, French composer, 17, 188

Chevardiere, 18th century publisher in Paris, 92, 187, 195

Chiapareli, ?, 18th century Italian composer, 17

Chiesa, Melchierre, 18th century Italian composer, 189

Chiesa, Natale, 19th century (?) Italian composer, 282

Chinzer, Giovanni, 18th century Italian composer in England, 189

Cimarosa, Domenico, 1749–1801, Italian composer, 17, 189

Cipriani, 19th century publisher in Firenze, 138

Cirri, Giovanni, 18th century Italian composer, 17

Ciurache, Giovanni, 18th century Italian composer, 18

Clementi, 19th century publisher in London, 47, 108, 245

Clementi, Muzio, 1752–1832, Italian composer, 18, 212 [unidentified music, arr. Neilson]

Cleton, 18th century publisher in Rome, 95

Cocchi, Gioacchino, 18th century Italian composer, 189

Coch, Johann, 18th century German composer, 189

Cochet, 19th century publisher in Paris, 129

Cooke, B., 18th century publisher in London, 5, 80, 190, 200, 236

Cooper, 18th century publisher in Edinburgh, 62

Cope, W., 18th century English composer, 189

Corelli, Arcangelo, 1653–1713, Italian composer, 18

Coreria, Cherubino, 18th century Italian composer, 190

Cormier, Carlo, 19th century (?) Italian composer, 271

Corrette, Michel, 1709–1795, French composer, 18, 190, 239, 257, 267

Corri, Dussek 18th century publisher in London & Edinburgh, 214, 216

Costallat, 19th century publisher in Paris, 50, 122, 170

Courteville, Raphael, 18th century French composer, 190

Cox, 18th century publisher in London, 81

Cramer, Johann, 1771–1858, English composer, 18ff

Cranz, 19th century publisher in Hamburg, 51, 73

Cranz, 19th century publisher in Leipzig, 50

Crémont, Pietro, 19th century German professor of clarinet in Vienna in 1825, 131

Croce, Giovanni, 17th century Italian composer, 219

Croft, William, 1678–1727, English composer, 18, 190

Cross, 18th century publisher in London, 31

Crusell, Bernard, 1775–1838, Swedish clarinetist, 131 [biographical note]

Culliford, Rolfe & Barrow, 18th century publisher in London, 210

Czapek, Leopold, 1792–1840 Bohemian composer, 19

Czerny, Gaspard, 18th century, 126 [biographical note]

D

Dale, 18th century publisher in London, 7, 89

Danvaux, Jean, 1742–1822, French composer, 273

Danzi, Franz, 1763–1826, German composer, 19, 105, 151, 232, 247

T

About the Author

Dr. David Whitwell is a graduate ('with distinction') of the University of Michigan and the Catholic University of America, Washington DC (PhD, Musicology, Distinguished Alumni Award, 2000) and has studied conducting with Eugene Ormandy and at the Akademie für Musik, Vienna. Prior to coming to Northridge, Dr. Whitwell participated in concerts throughout the United States and Asia as Associate First Horn in the USAF Band and Orchestra in Washington DC, and in recitals throughout South America in cooperation with the United States State Department.

At the California State University, Northridge, which is in Los Angeles, Dr. Whitwell developed the CSUN Wind Ensemble into an ensemble of international reputation, with international tours to Europe in 1981 and 1989 and to Japan in 1984. The CSUN Wind Ensemble has made professional studio recordings for BBC (London), the Köln Westdeutscher Rundfunk (Germany), NOS National Radio (The Netherlands), Zürich Radio (Switzerland), the Television Broadcasting System (Japan) as well as for the United States State Department for broadcast on its 'Voice of America' program. The CSUN Wind Ensemble's recording with the Mirecourt Trio in 1982 was named the 'Record of the Year' by The Village Voice. Composers who have guest conducted Whitwell's ensembles include Aaron Copland, Ernest Krenek, Alan Hovhaness, Morton Gould, Karel Husa, Frank Erickson and Vaclav Nelhybel.

Dr. Whitwell has been a guest professor in 100 different universities and conservatories throughout the United States and in 23 foreign countries (most recently in China, in an elite school housed in the Forbidden City). Guest conducting experiences have included the Philadelphia Orchestra, Seattle Symphony Orchestra, the Czech Radio Orchestras of Brno and Bratislava, The National Youth Orchestra of Israel, as well as resident wind ensembles in Russia, Israel, Austria, Switzerland, Germany, England, Wales, The Netherlands, Portugal, Peru, Korea, Japan, Taiwan, Canada and the United States.

He is a past president of the College Band Directors National Association, a member of the Prasidium of the International Society for the Promotion of Band Music, and was a member of the founding board of directors of the World Association for Symphonic Bands and Ensembles (WASBE). In 1964 he was made an honorary life member of Kappa Kappa Psi, a national professional music fraternity. In September, 2001, he was a delegate to the UNESCO Conference on Global Music in Tokyo. He has been knighted by sovereign organizations in France, Portugal and Scotland and has been awarded the gold medal of Kerkrade, The Netherlands, and the silver medal of Wangen, Germany, the highest honor given wind conductors in the United States, the medal of the Academy of Wind and Percussion Arts (National Band Association) and the highest honor given wind conductors in Austria, the gold medal of the Austrian Band Association. He is a member of the Hall of Fame of the California Music Educators Association.

Dr. Whitwell's publications include more than 127 articles on wind literature including publications in Music and Letters (London), the London Musical Times, the Mozart-Jahrbuch (Salzburg), and 39 books, among which is his 13-volume *History and Literature of the Wind Band and Wind Ensemble* and an 8-volume series on *Aesthetics in Music*. In addition to numerous modern editions of early wind band music his original compositions include 5 symphonies.

David Whitwell was named as one of six men who have determined the course of American bands during the second half of the 20th century, in the definitive history, *The Twentieth Century American Wind Band* (Meredith Music).

A doctoral dissertation by German Gonzales (2007, Arizona State University) is dedicated to the life and conducting career of David Whitwell through the year 1977. David Whitwell is one of nine men described by Paula A. Crider in *The Conductor's Legacy* (Chicago: GIA, 2010) as 'the legendary conductors' of the 20th century.

'I can't imagine the 2nd half of the 20th century—without David Whitwell and what he has given to all of the rest of us.' Frederick Fennell (1993)

9 781936 512522